CRITICAL ACCLAIM FOR

ORPHANS PREFERRED

"Vivid and lively . . . Any frontier buff would appreciate going along for this ride."

—*Kansas City Star*

"It's safe to say that probably no other book will ever need to be written on the subject."

—*Richmond Times-Dispatch*

"Christopher Corbett shows us that the line between the historical record and a colorful yarn is sometimes hard to distinguish when it comes to the Pony Express. He makes the point with sly good humor."

—*Los Angeles Times*

"Corbett keeps a healthy awe for the Pony, never selling short the accomplishment of traveling all those miles across so much unforgiving terrain, but also winnowing out the more fabulous accounts to reconstruct the workings of the business, as well as the world in which it operated . . . Throughout Corbett remains a witty guide, and one unafraid to get lost every once in a while in a subject whose established lore frequently contradicts itself."

—*The Onion*

"An absolutely fascinating study of the Pony as both legend and reality."

—*History*

"With a wink and a nod, deconstructs much of what 'we know' about the Pony Express from dime novels and early histories A fun book, particularly when you recognize that the author quickly adapted his research and

writing when he discovered that virtually everything understood to be true about the Pony Express was made up out of whole cloth."
—*Charlotte Observer*

"Not so much a history as it is an effort to peel away the layers of fabrication that obscure the real Pony Express."
—*Baltimore Sun*

"It makes for fun reading as Corbett handicaps which writer was a jolly liar, who was a conscientious chronicler, or what old timer's memories of days on horseback have a smidgen of believability. The book is great entertainment in and of itself, but buffs of the West will virtually gallop to the checkout line."
—*Booklist*

"Of the many books that promise to guide us along the Pony Express's trail between history and legend, there is none more meticulous or judicious than *Orphans Preferred,* and few display a better grasp of the reverence, skepticism, and good humor required for the journey."
—*Chicago Tribune*

Pony Express *by* N. C. *Wyeth*.

ORPHANS PREFERRED

The Twisted Truth
AND
Lasting Legend
OF THE
Pony Express

CHRISTOPHER CORBETT

BROADWAY BOOKS · NEW YORK

BROADWAY

A hardcover edition of this book was published in 2003
by Broadway Books.

PRINTED IN THE UNITED STATES OF AMERICA

BROADWAY BOOKS and its logo, a letter B bisected on the
diagonal, are trademarks of Random House, Inc.

Visit our website at www.broadwaybooks.com

First trade paperback edition published 2004

Book design by Caroline Cunningham
Map and spot illustration by Laura Hartman Maestro

The Library of Congress has cataloged the hardcover edition as follows:
Corbett, Christopher.
Orphans preferred : the twisted truth and lasting legend of the
Pony Express / Christopher Corbett.— 1st ed.
p. cm.
Includes bibliographical references.
1. Pony express. I. Title.
HE6375.P65C69 2003
383'.143'0973—dc21
2003041792

ISBN 0-7679-0693-4

1 3 5 7 9 10 8 6 4 2

FOR REBECCA AND MOLLY

Contents

The cautious old gentleman knit his brows tenfold closer after this explanation . . . At length, he observed, that all this was very well, but still he thought the story a little on the extravagant—there were one or two points on which he had his doubts.

"Faith, sir," replied the storyteller, "as to that matter, I don't believe one-half of it myself."

—WASHINGTON IRVING, *THE LEGEND OF SLEEPY HOLLOW*

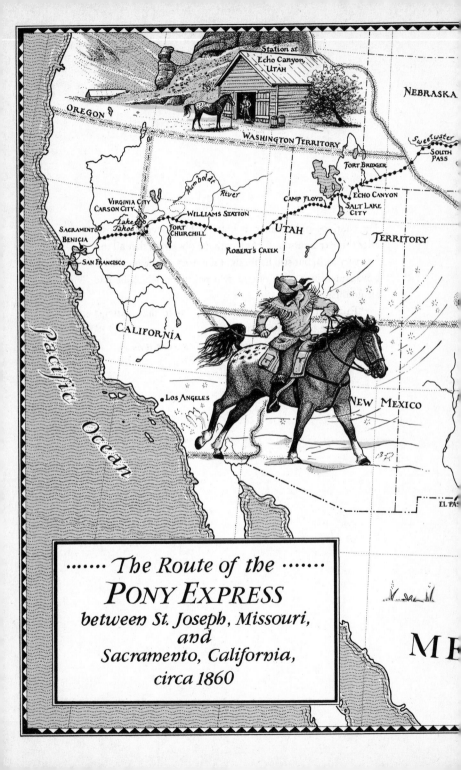

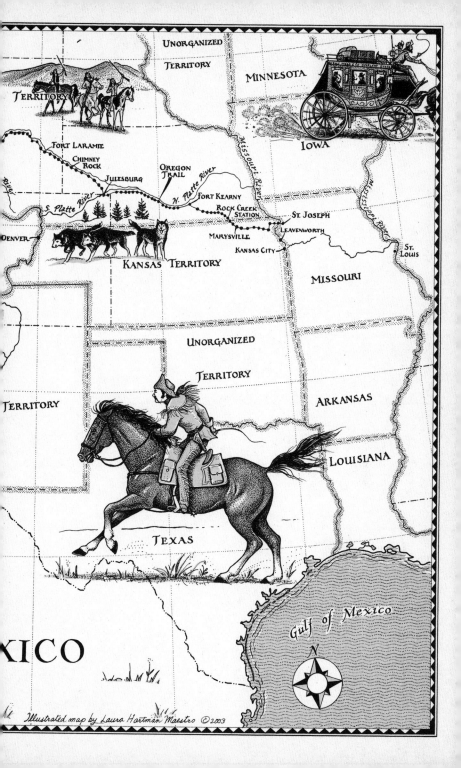

UNORGANIZED
TERRITORY

MINNESOTA

IOWA

TERRITORY

FORT LARAMIE
CHIMNEY ROCK
JULESBURG
OREGON TRAIL
N. Platte River
FORT KEARNY
ROCK CREEK STATION
ST. JOSEPH
LEAVENWORTH
DENVER
MARYSVILLE
KANSAS CITY
ST. LOUIS

S. Platte River
River
Missouri River
Mississippi River

KANSAS TERRITORY

MISSOURI

UNORGANIZED
TERRITORY

ARKANSAS

TERRITORY

LOUISIANA

TEXAS

XICO

Gulf of Mexico

N

Illustrated map by Laura Hartman Maestro ©2003

ORPHANS
PREFERRED

*Oldtimers on the porch waving to a Pony Express rider,
from a 1920 mural by Edward J. Holslag.*

HOW THE STORY GOES, OR
WHAT DO WE KNOW?

Where the years went I can't say
I just turned around and they're gone away . . .
— KATE WOLF, "ACROSS THE GREAT DIVIDE"

This is how the story goes.

About dusk on the evening of April 3, 1860, the Hannibal & St. Joseph Railroad train bringing the mail from back east was more than two hours late getting into St. Joseph, Missouri, through no fault of its engineer, Addison Clark. He was a good man and true at the throttle of the train, which consisted of merely a wood-burning engine, the *Missouri,* its tender, and a single car. Addison Clark would set what old railroad men later claimed was a speed record, which would stand for half a century. That trip was also believed to be the first time that mail was sorted on a moving railroad car. The few passengers on board this special train, dignitaries who arrived soot-flecked and frightened in St. Joe, swore later that they feared for their lives. Ad Clark brought the *Missouri* down from Hannibal to St. Joe—a distance of 206 miles—in four hours and fifty-one minutes.

Telegraphers reported that the train was going at the breathtaking speed of sixty-five miles an hour when it passed. Gangs of men standing along the line with firewood restocked the train's fuel supply in fifteen seconds. We know that much to be true.

About 7:15 that evening—depending on whose version of the story you prefer—Johnny Frey (perhaps it was spelled Freye or Fry or Frye) or Billy Richardson, sometimes confused with Johnson Richardson (he was said to be a sailor, but what a sailor was doing in the heart of the country is never explained), or Alex Carlyle jumped into the saddle or leaped into the saddle or perhaps he was already in the saddle and began to gallop westward across the continent.

Writing in the October 1898 issue of *Century* magazine, W. F. Bailey states flatly that Henry Wallace was the first rider. Poor Henry's name is never mentioned again in the chronicles. Mr. Bailey's story was written closer to the actual event than any other account, but what of it?

That historic gallop began down in front of the Patee House, the grandest hotel west of the Mississippi River in that day, a hotel that hosted Mark Twain, Horace Greeley, Oscar Wilde, Captain Sir Richard Burton, and William Seward, who was on his way to buy Alaska—or so the story goes. Or it happened down in front of the Pike's Peak Stables, about three blocks west. No, the stables weren't there, they were someplace else. Or it happened over on the other side of town at the telegraph office on the east side of Third Street—or was it Second Street?—between Felix and Edmond Streets. Or perhaps it was someplace else. Well, we know with complete certainty that it was in St. Joe. We know that much to be true.

The newspaper in St. Joseph is not much help in clearing up these matters, because the reporter—some say he became excited and ran back to the office without fully gathering the facts—neglected to mention who the first rider was. The style of newspapers then was very different from what it is today. But it does seem odd down these long years that a reporter sent to cover such an event would not have made mention of who was upon that horse. Long after the evening in question, a synod of St. Joseph worthies was mustered to ponder this matter, pray over it, and determine just who the first equestrian was on this momentous occasion. They advised, after lengthy deliberation and even the offering of a one-hundred-dollar reward, that they could come to no conclusion about the man aboard that first horse.

We know that the rider was wearing a bright red shirt and blue trousers and a yellow kerchief or that he was wearing a kind of military getup like a drum major's uniform or that he was clad in buckskin. We know that he was carrying two Colt revolvers and a Sharps rifle (it could have been a Spencer). Or he was unarmed. Or he was merely carrying two pistols. We know that he had a horn to blow to announce his arrival in stations down the line. Or maybe not. We know for certain that he had a Bible. Alexander Majors of the great freight-hauling firm of Russell, Majors & Waddell, which underwrote this venture, gave every employee a little calfskin-bound Bible, although the curious often wondered how a man riding a horse at a gallop from St. Joseph, Missouri, to Sacramento, California, would have had occasion for Bible study. But why quibble? We know that much is true.

Well, whoever was riding, or galloping, or cantering, or racing, or trotting, we are quite certain he was on a horse, although some of the riders rode mules. It was either a sorrel, a black, a bay, or . . . there is disagreement over the horse, too. Horse and rider somehow got themselves down to the banks of the Missouri River, where the steamboat *Ebenezer* ferried them across the water to Elwood, Kansas. But it is possible that it wasn't the *Ebenezer,* but the *Denver,* that made the crossing. Take your pick; there were two vessels to choose from to cross the Missouri.

We know there was music: Rosenblatt's five-piece German brass band had come down from Nebraska City on the riverboat. The musicians played "Skip-a to My Lou" and "What Was Your Name in the States." (Artists' renderings of the occasion always make the band much larger, a veritable symphony orchestra.) And we know that there were speeches, too. One of the speechmakers was the recent mayor of St. Joe, M. Jeff Thompson, an orator of considerable accomplishment who would soon distinguish himself in the Civil War, a local hero of the Confederacy.

We know that there was a big crowd on hand. And they plucked the poor horse's tail hairs for souvenirs. You could still buy those horsehairs woven into rings for a long, long time after that. Or so they say around St. Joe. Ask around St. Joe enough and you'll find someone who has one of those horsehair rings or used to have one until their uncle took it up to the veterans' hospital with him. True enthusiasts know the name of the horse: Sylph.

Or, if you choose to doubt these stories, consider that because the train was late and dusk was coming on, the crowd had dwindled to a handful. So we know that there was hardly anyone there to see the first rider off. Artists' renderings of the event (perhaps the most famous one was commissioned long years after by a now-defunct St. Joseph brewery) always show a jolly crowd on hand, a handsome rider in the saddle at full gallop, the sun shining. The sun set at 6:46 in that latitude on April 3, 1860, but it shines forever in the memory of illustrators—none of whom were present on the great day.

We know that about eight hours later, or maybe it was ten or perhaps twelve, with at least one change of rider and many fresh horses, the mail pouch, called a mochila reached Marysville, Kansas. We know that a girl in Marysville would live to be a very, very old lady and in the 1930s would tell a historian about witnessing the first rider come in. She always said it was Johnny Frey. She was there. She heard the horn blow, too.

We know with complete certainty that on that same day, actually a bit earlier that afternoon, another rider, Harry Roff, left Sacramento, California, racing east. Everyone seems to agree it was Harry Roff. Alexander Majors, who was at the other end of the line that day, in St. Joe, says it was Harry Roff. William Lightfoot Visscher, the first historian of the event, says it was Harry Roff. W. F. Bailey writing in *Century* magazine in 1898 goes along with Harry Roff, too. It's nice to have some agreement. Alas, there are now those who believe it was not Harry Roff, but William Fisher. Yep, Billy Fisher was the first rider out of Old Sac. But the horse was white. They all agree on that. The name of the horse is not mentioned.

We know that the riders east and west would change about every one hundred miles and the fresh rider would resume the race. The riders would change horses every ten to fifteen miles, and the mochila would be transferred to the back of each fresh horse. We know that the mail pouch going west from St. Joe that first day was carrying forty-nine letters and a few newspapers and telegrams. It cost five dollars to send a letter across the country. We also know that the riders passed one another—one heading east and one heading west—a few days later somewhere east of Salt Lake City. We do not know what these two riders said to one another or whether they stopped and chatted. We know that one eastbound rider later claimed that he rode so far and for so long without relief that he often slept in the saddle and passed the westbound rider without realizing it. We know that another rider, aboard a mule, fell asleep and the mule simply walked back to the station from which it had departed.

We also know that about eighteen months later—October 26,

1861, is widely accepted—the riders stopped galloping east and west. We do not know with utmost certainty who those last riders were, and we know that some mochilas were still arriving into November. Notices appeared in the California newspapers saying that the horses from the East and West would race no more.

We do know that Edward Creighton and his associates had by then completed the transcontinental telegraph; the east and west coasts of America were now linked by a new technology. The continent was spanned—"westward the course of empire" and all that. And we know that was the end of the Central Overland California & Pike's Peak Express Company, which we remember by its abbreviated name, a name that remains forever endearing and enduring: the Pony Express.

We know that the Pony Express went out of business in the fall of 1861 when the United States was in the throes of civil war. We know that the company that owned the Pony Express, a subsidiary of Russell, Majors & Waddell, fell upon hard times. We know the firm owed a fabulous amount of money; published reports range from $200,000 to $500,000 and even $700,000. We know that the records of the Pony Express, such as they might have been, were lost or stolen or destroyed intentionally or burned up in a bad fire, or they are hidden in the attic of a house in Lexington, Missouri. There were scandals, too. Two of the three principals involved in the venture, William H. Russell and William B. Waddell, died financially ruined. Russell nearly went to jail in connection with a bond fraud, a reckless attempt to bail out the foundering Pony Express.

The third partner, Alexander Majors, who looks in yellowed photographs like the paintings of the Old Testament prophet Daniel, come to judgment, lived a long, long time. Among the first to trade along the Santa Fe Trail, he was there, too, the day they drove the golden spike at Promontory Point in Utah, completing the transcontinental railroad. The old man got around. Majors lived to see the twentieth century, although he did not write his memoirs for more than thirty years after the last rider of the Pony Express galloped across the continent.

When Alexander Majors did finally settle down to chronicling the days of the Pony Express, his account was complicated by some creative assistance. Buffalo Bill was the de facto publisher; he paid Rand McNally to print the memoirs. And Buffalo Bill also obtained the services of Colonel Prentiss Ingraham, a public relations man and one of the most prolific dime novelists to ever take up the pen on behalf of Buffalo Bill and the American West.

Old Alexander Majors would say afterward with some alarm that Colonel Ingraham had taken liberties with the facts. There were embellishments. The colonel said Majors was too modest and he was just trying to tell a good story. And what a story it was: *Seventy Years on the Frontier: Alexander Majors' Memoirs of a Lifetime on the Border.* Whatever else it accomplished, Majors's book firmly established the vital role played in that "saga of the saddle" by William Frederick Cody, known better as Buffalo Bill.

But that was not the first effort made by Buffalo Bill to enshrine the legacy of the Pony Express. From 1883, when the first of Buffalo Bill's Wild West shows opened in Omaha, until the final season of 1916, when Cody was an old man, broke and sick, who no longer even owned the show and needed to be hoisted onto a horse so that he could briefly ride around the ring waving to his fans, wherever he went touring on the North American continent or in Europe, the sweet memory of the Pony Express went with him.

Buffalo Bill took the Pony Express with him to see Queen Victoria, and he took the Pony along to visit the pope in Vatican City. He took the Pony to Paris, Barcelona, and Berlin. No image was more romantic and more powerful as a symbol of the real Wild West than that of a galloping Pony Express rider. Buffalo Bill trouped his show from Pope Leo XIII in Rome to Queen Victoria in London to the kaiser in Berlin (Annie Oakley shot a cigarette out of the German monarch's mouth on a dare); from Baraboo, Wisconsin, to Lewiston, Maine; from Gloucester, Massachusetts, to Goshen, Indiana. Year after year, in rain or in shine, in sickness and in health, triumphant and broke, no one did more to permanently brand into the subconscious of the American and European spectator the glorious memory of the days of the Pony Express or the image of the brave horseman whom Mark Twain himself (and he had seen a Pony rider) had called "the swift phantom of the desert."

Buffalo Bill's Wild West show changed from year to year. New acts came and old acts left—a reenactment of Custer's Last Stand would be replaced by Teddy Roosevelt's Rough Riders charging up San Juan Hill—but the Pony rider was always on the "programme," generally right after Miss Annie Oakley offered a display of marks-

manship that never failed to stun a crowd and before the prairie emigrant train crossing the Great Plains had to be rescued by Buffalo Bill
from red savages. Just as the show always began with "The Star-
Spangled Banner," it included prominently the Pony Express. And no
one, from penniless orphans in Chicago and London, allowed in free
because Buffalo Bill had a good heart, to kings and kaisers and presidents, ever left Buffalo Bill's Wild West and Congress of Rough Riders of the World without seeing this one irreplaceable fixture of the
Old West. The Pony Express was as well known and revered as Buffalo Bill himself, or the legendary Deadwood stagecoach. For decades
the program note never varied; it read simply, "Pony Express. A former Pony Post-Rider will show how the letters and telegrams of
the Republic were distributed across the immense Continent previous
to the building of railways and telegraphs." It made a powerful impact on the American and European spectator. No one could ever forget it.

We know that nearly half a century passed before the first book-
length work chronicling the Pony Express was published. It was the
effort of Colonel William Lightfoot Visscher, an alcoholic and rambling newspaperman who had drifted across the American West. He
was no colonel, but that's another story. There is no index in the
colonel's masterwork on the Pony Express. There are no footnotes.
No bibliography. No indication whatsoever where he got his information. (Much of his research appears to have been done at the
Chicago Press Club's bar—his legal address for a number of years.)
No one had written much about the Pony Express when the colonel
sat down to do the fast-mail service justice. We know that he knew
Alexander Majors and Buffalo Bill Cody and Robert "Pony Bob"
Haslam, perhaps the most famous and bravest courier to actually ride
for the service. The colonel was a poet at heart—not a good poet, but
a published poet, and a prolific poet, too—and this is reflected in his
book, *A Thrilling and Truthful History of the Pony Express with
other sketches and incidents of those stirring times*. He put one of his
poems at the beginning of the book. It has nothing to do with the
Pony Express. But whatever else can be said about the colonel and his
book, he got the "thrilling" part down right.

No book ever published about the Pony Express since the colonel
took up his pen has not owed some debt to that first lively chronicle.
Serious historians and academics in general, unable to figure what the

Pony Express was all about, have ridden wide of the quicksand of the legendary cross-country mail service for more than a century.

Americans do not suffer failure gladly, but they forgive and they forget, too, and so the story of the Pony Express, lost in the hard years of the Civil War, became in time a recovered memory. First, America forgot the story of the Pony Express, then America remembered, and in memory, America remembered big.

In the retelling, the story of the Pony Express was not, as its critics charged, an eccentric publicity stunt aimed at securing lucrative government mail contracts that was doomed to fail and never make a dime, but a Pegasus for all time. Its rider was a true rider of the purple sage (and there was never a shortage of purple prose to back that up).

In memory, the Pony Express never failed. In memory, there were no squandered hundreds of thousands of dollars, bankruptcy, and shame. No unpaid employees. No congressional inquiry. In memory, the Pony Express became triumphant, victorious, its riders heroic.

A rogues' gallery of westerners, famous and infamous, helped turn the story into myth. Buffalo Bill Cody and Wild Bill Hickok (he was merely James Butler Hickok when Russell, Majors & Waddell hired him as a stock tender in Rock Creek Station, territory of Nebraska) were among the principals. The roving dime novelist Ned Buntline, who conspired in the invention of Buffalo Bill, and his successor, Colonel Prentiss Ingraham, who helped to patent the invention, played supporting roles. Eyewitnesses to "the great gamble" helped, too, including Mark Twain, who was merely Sam Clemens, a recent Confederate army deserter who had lit out for the territory ahead, when he watched a Pony rider flash by his rocking stagecoach. So, too, did the great British explorer Captain Sir Richard Burton, who was on his way to have a look at the Mormons when he crossed the Pony's path.

Down the years, the riders of the Pony Express galloped across the paintings of Frederic Remington and many a painter who wished to be Frederic Remington. They galloped, too, across the motion picture screen, from the films of John Ford and those who wished to be John Ford. Hollywood has been especially generous to the memory of the Pony Express. One of the best-known films, *The Pony Express,* made in 1953, starring Charlton Heston, had Buffalo Bill and Wild Bill

Hickok teaming up in "Old Californy" to start the Pony Express. There is not a splinter of fact in that tale.

Saved from failure and forgetting, the story of the Pony Express would become a great saga, a heroic episode in the opening of the American West. It would become a memory of the vanished West that Americans would be proud to recall. It would take its place alongside other American sagas, actual events that were much embellished, from Paul Revere's ride (a la Henry Wadsworth Longfellow's poem) to the defense of the Alamo to Custer's Last Stand. It would nearly become another sort of American story, the tall tale, in the tradition of Paul Bunyan, Johnny Appleseed, and John Henry.

But even if facts were never quite right, there is an essential truth about the Pony Express. It was a splendid moment of history, a rare event where the taming of the West took no victims. It remains forever fond and familiar because it is a recollection of the West unlike any other. This was not the West of the mindless slaughter of the buffalo, the decimation of the Indian, or the greedy exploitation of the land. This was not the West of gunfighters or cattle rustlers.

The story of the Pony Express was about a lone rider facing the elements, racing time and racing the transcontinental telegraph, too. It was the story of an audacious adventure and the bravura involved in crossing the country, night and day, in all kinds of weather, a man (or boy) alone on the back of a galloping horse. It was a story of chance and courage. It was the story of the West that might have been, the West that should have been. Americans love a race and they love a winner, and they loved that man on the horse.

We hear the fading distant hoofbeats of that horse across nearly a century and a half, faintly but still quite audibly. It is a sound that never fails to inspire. No memory of the vanished nineteenth-century West is more revered, and few are more beloved and cherished, than that of the long-ago riders of the Central Overland California & Pike's Peak Express Company. And some of those memories are even true.

Part I

IN THE DAYS OF
THE PONY

History, a fable agreed on, is not a science but a branch of literature, an artifact made by artificers and sometimes by artists. Like fiction, it has only persons, places, and events to work with, and like fiction it may present them in summary or in dramatic scene.

—WALLACE STEGNER

*The Patee House, headquarters for
the Pony Express, 1860–61.*

One

"CAPITAL FELLOWS"—RUSSELL, MAJORS & WADDELL

My design is to give a truthful and not an exaggerated and fanciful account of the occurrences of the journey, and of the scenery, capabilities, and general features of the countries through which we shall pass, with incidental sketches of the leading characteristics of the populations.

—EDWIN BRYANT, *WHAT I SAW IN CALIFORNIA*, 1848

In the spring of 1859 with carpetbag in hand, Horace Greeley, legendary editor of the *New York Tribune*, took the celebrated advice so often attributed to him and went west. He was no longer a young man that year—he was forty-eight—but he had the curiosity and energy of a young man.

"Want to learn what I can of that country with my own eyes," Greeley wrote, "and to study men in their cabins and at their work instead of reading about them in books."

Greeley, whom *Harper's Weekly* had called "the most perfect Yankee the country has ever produced," left New York City on May 9, traveled at first by rail and riverboat and then much of the way in a Concord coach, pitching and tossing across the continent. He would be on the road for five months. He traveled alone much of the time, too. "I then hoped, rather than confidently expected, that, on publicly announcing my intention, some friend might offer to bear me company on this journey; but my hope was not realized. One friend did propose to go; but his wife's veto overruled his not very stubborn resolve. I started alone . . ."

Horace Greeley was arguably the most influential and powerful opinion maker in the nation in those days. At the time of the Civil War, Abraham Lincoln compared Greeley's support to that of an army of 100,000 men in the field.

He was a flinty Yankee from poor New Hampshire who left his family farm and was apprenticed to a Vermont printer at fifteen, a printer's devil. When he was twenty, Greeley walked to New York City. He had ten dollars in his pocket. His first job was printing a tiny Bible.

He opposed slavery. He opposed the antiforeign, anti–Roman Catholic ravings of the Know-Nothings (he coined that term). He opposed tobacco (a bad experience with a cigar when he was five years old had turned him against smoking), he opposed alcohol (he took the pledge when he was but twelve), and he had reservations about the eating of meat. He rarely drank tea and had long forsworn coffee. He was a sometime vegetarian and a fairly strict disciple of the celebrated crank Dr. Sylvester Graham, whose cracker we remember a century and a half later. One biographer claimed that Greeley crossed the West eating graham crackers and drinking milk, but Greeley makes no mention of this diet in his travels. He met his wife at the Graham House, a New York City boardinghouse kept by Dr. Graham. She was an eccentric from New England, too.

A colleague described Greeley at the time as "careless and disheveled in dress as if he had put his clothes on in the dark, with the round and rosy face of a child and a cherubic expression of simplicity and gentleness . . . The power that he wielded was not equaled by any editor of his time—neither has it been equaled by any editor since."

He looked like an old baby from a very early age, with a soft, unlined pale face, a nearly bald head. He had poor eyesight made worse by his trade.

Greeley corresponded with Abraham Lincoln and Henry David Thoreau. Worshiped at a Unitarian Church in Manhattan with P. T. Barnum. Hired Karl Marx as a European correspondent. Published Charles Darwin for the first time in this country. Printed Edgar Allan Poe's "The Raven" in an American newspaper for the first time, too.

But he was first and foremost the founder and editor of the *New York Tribune,* the most influential newspaper in all of the United States in its heyday. Its weekly edition had 1 million readers. At the time of Greeley's western adventure, one of his reporters, Bayard Taylor, reported to him, "The *Tribune* comes next to the Bible all through the West."

Horace Greeley had been eager to turn his face westward, as he told his readers. The famous social reformer filed back to his newspaper a series of dispatches reporting on everything from his disapproval of shooting buffalo (he was quite certain that he had seen a million of them), to the plight of the abused Chinese miners in the West, to his prediction that the next great cities of the United States would be in Kansas: Atchison and Leavenworth.

He saw wild Indians (he thought little of them) and desperadoes (he disapproved) and drunkards (he disapproved) and gunplay (he disapproved). He survived a stampede of buffalo; they overturned his stagecoach, leaving him shaken but uninjured. He hit Denver when it was a remote mining town, six months old. The West was, indeed, wild. Greeley reported:

> There is a fighting class among the settlers in the Rocky Mountains. This class is not numerous, but it is more influential than it should be in giving tone to the society of which its members form a part. Prone to deep thinking, soured in temper, always armed, bristling at a word, ready with the rifle, revolver, or bowie knife, they give law and set fashions which, in a country where the regular administration of justice is yet a matter of prophecy, it seems difficult to overrule or disregard. I apprehend that there have been, during my two weeks' sojourn, more brawls, more fights, more pistols shot with criminal intent, in this log city of one hundred and fifty dwellings, not three fourths completed nor two thirds inhabited, nor one third fit to be, than in any community of no greater numbers on earth.

Greeley moved on to Salt Lake City, the Mormon Jerusalem, where he visited Brigham Young at a time when Mormons were regarded as variously dangerous and ridiculous. They discussed polygamy, the apostle Paul, slavery. Greeley crossed the Great Basin when Utah and Nevada were nearly uninhabited. He estimated that there were fewer than five thousand people living in all of Nevada. Carson City was a handful of shacks. Virginia City was a mining claim.

Wherever Horace Greeley went, he was grandly received. His opinion mattered and his impressions did, too. Greeley's was a whirl-wind trip; often he stopped only briefly to see the sights and then raced on in the next westbound stage. "Greeley has come and gone," reported the *Sacramento Union*. He had stopped in the California capital for a mere thirteen hours. He was out west in support of a transcontinental railroad.

Enormous crowds turned out to see Greeley when he alighted from the stagecoach. He wore "a very rusty and well-worn white coat, a still rustier and still more worn and faded blue-cotton um-brella . . ." A famous photograph of the time shows Greeley wearing a tall white hat. And his ever-present spectacles. His eyes were always poor. He squinted.

Writing about Greeley's western sojourn more than forty years later, George Tisdale Bromley, a celebrated Californian of that era, re-called its importance. "He was looked upon at that time as the great-est man who had ever visited California, and glorious results were anticipated on his return East, from his efforts in behalf of the great Atlantic and Pacific Railroad." The trip resulted in a book the next year: *An Overland Journey from New York to San Francisco in the Summer of 1859*.

During Horace Greeley's "celebrated journey across the Plains to California," he encountered the greatest force of progress on the frontier in the years before the telegraph and the railroad crossed the countryside. In eastern Kansas, on the edge of the wilderness, Gree-ley observed the mighty freight-hauling firm of Russell, Majors & Waddell, the major carrier of all freight in the United States west of the Mississippi River in the middle of the nineteenth century, an or-ganization that later narrators dubbed "an empire on wheels."

The firm made its headquarters at Leavenworth, Kansas—a river-front town fifty miles southwest of St. Joseph, Missouri. Horace Greeley found it an impressive operation:

> . . . Russell, Majors & Waddell's transportation establishment, be-tween the fort and the city, is the great feature of Leavenworth. Such acres of wagons! such pyramids of extra axletrees! such herds of oxen! such regiments of drivers and employees! No one who

does not see can realize how vast a business this is, nor how immense are its outlays as well as its income. I presume this great firm has at this hour two millions of dollars invested in stock, mainly oxen, mules, and wagons. (They last employed six thousand teamsters, and worked forty-five thousand oxen.)

The firm that bore the names of William Russell, Alexander Majors and William Waddell (Greeley described them as "capital fellows," though it's not clear whether he actually met them) was in its heyday the greatest force in shipping goods west in the country. Fueled by a virtual monopoly on providing freight service for a vast network of U.S. military outposts, the firm was prosperous and respected all along the frontier. Very little went west if it did not travel on an ox-drawn wagon owned by Russell, Majors & Waddell.

In the years before the Civil War, travelers into the West would have known well the names Russell, Majors & Waddell. They were the Mayflower Van Line of their time, the United Parcel Service of the prairie, the FedEx of the frontier. In the years before the railroads crossed the Great Plains, when there were still wolves in Kansas and Nebraska and wild Indians, no freight—either military or domestic—went west down the Santa Fe Trail or out to Fort McKay or to Fort Kearny or one of the handful of remote army posts that dotted the Great American Desert unless it did so on a miles-long train of Conestoga wagons pulled by plodding oxen teams. Most of those outfits were owned by Russell, Majors & Waddell.

John D. Young, a Chicagoan bound for the gold fields of Colorado in 1860, reported encountering immense government wagon trains on the plains of Kansas and Nebraska—owned and operated by Russell, Majors & Waddell. According to Young's journal, preserved at the Newberry Library in Chicago, twenty thousand people traveled with some of these trains, stretching out for many miles across the prairies.

In the spring of 1860, following Greeley's overland adventure, with the nation perched on the brink of civil war, Russell, Majors & Waddell established a subsidiary business, a privately financed gamble designed to prove that mail could be moved quickly—in ten days or less across nearly two thousand miles of still-wild North America. To do this, they would use a relay system of experienced riders and the best horses money could buy. No one today remembers the names

Russell, Majors & Waddell or the vast freighting empire they presided over in the good years before the Civil War. No one remembers their rolling armada of tens of thousands of oxen, vast fleets of wagons, or armies of bullwhackers—the greatest such venture of its kind ever assembled.

Their legacy would be the most obscure of footnotes in the history of the opening of the American West but for the little venture into which they poured their fates and fortunes. They spun the business off their stage line operations linking the Missouri with Denver and Salt Lake City, calling it the Central Overland California & Pike's Peak Express Company. The name was too long—even its initials, COC&PPEC, were too cumbersome—and so it was called simply the Pony Express.

Louisa P. Johnston, the great-granddaughter of Alexander Majors, recalled more than a century later: "A clerk of the firm wrote that all the company's wagon trains together would stretch forty miles. Russell, Majors and Waddell were freighting to Santa Fe and to all the U.S. Army posts in the West. They ran stage lines to Denver and Salt Lake City. So they were uniquely equipped to start a pony express."

The Pony Express was a daring and madcap and foolish idea. It was thought to be impossible (men wagered against it ever happening) to race a satchel, a saddlebag called a mochila, holding about twenty pounds of important mail written on the lightest tissue paper, across nearly two thousand miles of largely uninhabited and hostile country, country where there were no railroads, no telegraphs, and few towns. Two thousand miles. They would do this in ten days, less than half the time that it was then taking to move mail from "the Atlantic states" to "the far coast." They would do this eventually in even fewer days: the news of Abraham Lincoln's inaugural message crossed the country in a record seven days and seventeen hours.

Colonel Henry Inman, a great historian of nineteenth-century western travel, called the transcontinental feat "the quickest time for horseback riding, considering the distance made, ever accomplished in this or any other country."

Russell, Majors & Waddell would move a horse and rider across the continent, night and day, in all weather and in all seasons of the year. Their critics would say later that it was all a wild publicity stunt. What did it really prove? What did it matter? But on the frontier in

1860 when there was no railroad and no telegraph and "the states" were far, far away, when the known world ended at the Missouri River and mail could take months coming back and forth from east to west, men who had not had a letter from home for a year stood in the streets of California and cheered the coming and going of the Pony Express.

———

William Hepburn Russell, the senior partner in the then-famous firm, appears from the distance of nearly a century and a half a bit of a dude, an opportunist, a fancy dresser and self-made city slicker, an upwardly mobile general store clerk, a hustler, a talker, a man who liked the creature comforts. He spent little time in the West, preferring the easy life of New York and Washington. The newspapers called him variously the Brains of the Border and the Napoleon of the Plains. What did the newspapers know? He barely knew the border or the plains. He better knew the drawing room and the parlor car on the railroad. He liked a good hotel. He liked a good cigar. He liked to dress for dinner. He liked linen shirts and good suits. He was rich. Although he spent no time there, he was one of the founders of Denver. The halls of power in Washington and New York, where there were investors, deals, and government contracts, beckoned him, not the open spaces across the wide Missouri. His biographers have always stressed that he knew nothing about the frontier based on any firsthand experience. William Hepburn Russell was no plainsman.

Various writers recall that he was known, in the parlance of his day, as a plunger: a risk taker, a gambler, a speculator. An early observer of Russell's business ventures, some of which were not successful, called them Russell's Follies. He was deeply offended by criticism and angrily wrote once to his partner William Waddell, who fretted over Russell's antics, to chastise those who thought so of him: "I am not a reckless gambler and I will not be so posted."

His partners, Alexander Majors and William Bradford Waddell, were cautious middle-aged men who had come from nothing and knew the value of a dollar. A man could work all day in Kansas then, a long, twelve-hour day, for a dollar. Majors and Waddell knew, too, the terrible risks involved in doing business on the frontier.

Alexander Majors, who had walked to Santa Fe and back alongside a plodding oxen train, was a true pioneer on the frontier who had gotten his start in this immense freight-hauling venture peddling trinkets to the Potawatomi Indians in eastern Kansas. William Waddell had started life as a clerk in a grocery store in the Missouri River boomtown of Lexington. Like his partners, he had become fabulously successful, but he remained always something of the grocery store clerk back in Lexington anguishing over the ledgers. He was a worrier all his life, and given the course the firm was charting under Russell's prodding, Waddell had good reason to worry. Majors and Waddell were not dreamers, and they took risks in the most calculated and reasoned fashion. If it had been up to Russell's skeptical partners, there would have never been a Pony Express.

They were in many ways unlikely business partners, but they were well suited for the times and the tasks at hand, with complementary skills. Russell was a Vermont Yankee (born in Burlington on January 31, 1812) whose family went west to Missouri in the late 1820s. While he was still a teenager, Russell went to work for the dry goods merchants Ely & Curtis in the town of Liberty in northwestern Missouri, about a day's ride from St. Joe.

With little formal education, Russell studied wholesale and retail in the great school of life on what was then the frontier, married a preacher's daughter when he was twenty-three, and two years later went into the dry goods business for himself in Lexington. (His first business went bankrupt, a hint of what was to come.) But a decade later Russell was a prosperous landowner and businessman whose dry goods business branched out when he and some associates sent a wagon train of goods down the still-developing Santa Fe Trail. He moved from this into freighting military supplies.

He was a man of both business and social standing in Lexington, Missouri. He was a Baptist and he favored slavery, as did his partners. He lived in Lexington in a twenty-room brick mansion just down the block from his longtime business partner and friend William Bradford Waddell.

Waddell descended from Scots. His paternal grandfather had been apprenticed to a Virginia planter in Fauquier County when he was eleven. Born in Virginia on October 14, 1807, Waddell moved with his family to Mason County, Kentucky, in 1815. While a teenager, he moved to Galena, Illinois, worked briefly in the lead mines, and then moved to St. Louis, where he found a job in a dry goods store. Like his partner Russell, Waddell would be steeped in the dry goods business—first in Kentucky and then back in Lexington, Missouri. It was here that he met Russell; they both belonged to the same Baptist church and were instrumental in organizing the Lexington First Addition Company, an insurance company. From the mid-1830s, he was a fixture in Lexington, where his successful dry goods business expanded, like Russell's own ventures, into hauling military freight. By 1853 they were partners, Waddell & Russell, hauling military supplies into Kansas.

Raymond Settle, whose account of their business ventures, *Empire on Wheels,* was the first serious attempt to chronicle their lives, said that no two business partners could have been more dissimilar. "Russell was volatile, highly temperamental, and a bundle of supercharged nerves. Waddell was phlegmatic, stolid, and inclined to sulk when cross. They quarreled again and again, yet were always loyal to each other."

On January 1, 1855, Waddell and Russell took on another partner, Alexander Majors. Their businesses were conducted under different names, reflecting a variety of ventures and partners, but history knows the business best as Russell, Majors & Waddell.

Majors was a true son of the frontier, a pioneer, born on October 4, 1814, near Franklin, Kentucky, when that was still wilderness. When he was four, the family moved to Missouri, then in its "wild and uncultivated state," Majors would later recall. He grew up in a log cabin, splitting rails, clearing land, and farming. Majors reminisced years later that he only branched into the freight-hauling and trading business to support his daughters. One man could not provide for such a brood by farming. He started in 1846, trading with Potawatomi Indians on the Kaw River in eastern Kansas. This got him thinking about the Santa Fe Trail (linking Independence, Missouri, with the fabled Spanish outpost some eight hundred miles away), which had opened up to trade with the United States in the early 1820s.

"As I was brought up to handle animals, and had been employed more or less in the teaming business, after looking the situation all over, it occurred to me there was nothing I was so well adapted for by my past experience as the freighting business that was then being conducted between Independence, Mo., and Santa Fe, New Mexico . . . ," he wrote in his memoirs.

Majors started with one wagon and a dozen oxen. He made his

first trip down the Santa Fe Trail and back in the record time of ninety-two days. "I made that trip with remarkable success . . . The quickest on record . . . This fact gave me quite a reputation among the freighters and merchants . . ."

Majors is such a taciturn and serious witness that when he reports something that reflects well on himself, it pays to listen. Six years after his visit to trade with the Potawatomi Indians, he was traveling up and down the Santa Fe Trail and hauling military supplies with one hundred wagons, twelve hundred oxen, and 120 bullwhackers. A Calvinist, Majors was a deeply religious man, a fundamentalist who read the Bible daily and required his bullwhackers to sign a pledge that would become as famous as the business he ran: "While I am in the employ of A. Majors, I agree not to use profane language, not to get drunk, not to gamble, nor to treat the animals cruelly, and not to do anything incompatible with the conduct of a gentleman. I agree if I violate any of the above conditions to accept my discharge without any pay for my services."

Majors's outfits kept holy the Sabbath. And when Majors was along on a trip, as he often was, he would preach to his men of a Sunday. A seasoned bullwhacker and teamster, Majors knew the trails and oxen teams and bullwhackers firsthand. The men who worked for him knew that Majors understood their lives and work. He had their respect and trust. Majors recalled in his memoirs:

> With all the thousands of men I had in my employ it was never necessary to do more than give a manly rebuke, if any one committed any misdemeanor, to avoid a repetition of the offense.
>
> I do not remember a single instance of a man signing these "iron-clad rules," as they called them, being discharged without his pay. My employes seemed to understand at the beginning of their term of service that their good behavior was part of the recompense they gave me for the money I paid them . . . I will say to my readers, that, had I the experience of a thousand years, I could not have formulated a better code of rules of the government of my business than those adopted . . . The result proved to be worth more to me in a money point of view than that resulting from any other course I could have pursued, for with the enforcement of these rules, which I had little trouble to do, a few years gave me control of the

business of the plains, and, of course, a widespread reputation for conducting business on a humane plan.

In the business that became Russell, Majors & Waddell, Russell was the front man who represented the firm in the East. He did the talking. He was the rainmaker. He knew his way around in Washington, he knew whom to talk to, who made the decisions. Back in Kansas, Majors was a hands-on bullwhacker who could oversee the vast operations on the trails and understood the logistics of freighting. Waddell was an accountant who kept the books and worried.

Alexander Majors was the only one of the three partners to write an account of his life, and he was the partner who lived the longest, dying in 1900. It had been a memorable life. He had been one of the West's first millionaires, pioneered freighting on the Santa Fe Trail, known the fabled scout Kit Carson, known the legendary mountain man Jim Bridger, been a partner in the greatest freight-hauling business on the American frontier, and helped to start the Pony Express.

Neither William Hepburn Russell nor William Bradford Waddell wrote an autobiography. (Both died in 1872; Russell was sixty, Waddell was sixty-five.) Even their personal papers, journals, diaries, and correspondence are scant. So history has Majors's version of how the Pony Express got up and running. If the victors in war write its story, then the survivors of business ventures do so, too. From this memoir, written more than thirty years after the Pony Express went out of business, written when Majors was in his late seventies, written with the help of a dime novelist and Buffalo Bill, descend all other tales of the origins of the Pony Express. Its critics complained about how it was composed and about the accuracy of *Seventy Years on the Frontier: Alexander Majors' Memoirs of a Lifetime on the Border.*

According to the memoirs, the idea for the Pony Express originated in late 1859 as a result of conversations in Washington between William Russell and California senator William McKendree Gwin, a Democratic power broker in the West and a force in Congress at the time. Gwin, a patrician, Mississippi planter, and shrewd political operator, had gone west and made a success of himself as California's first senator in the Golden Land in the days after the gold rush. This Russell-Gwin connection appears in nearly all histories of the Pony Express, but none of Gwin's biographers mention anything to do with the Pony Express or William Hepburn Russell. Gwin's own public utterings on the matter were slight, although he did once tell a crowd of California voters—wildly enthusiastic about the newly implemented cross-country mail service—that it would have never happened if not for him.

Majors remembered more than thirty years later that Senator Gwin urged Russell to experiment with the so-called Central Route to prove its viability. The competition in those days was the Southern Route, or Butterfield Overland Mail Company Route, the Oxbow, which dipped from Missouri to California via El Paso, Texas, and the Southwest. It took twenty-one days—and that was good time—to move mail along this line. A central route—much shorter—would cross the West in a straighter path, linking the Missouri River with Salt Lake City and continuing to California.

Russell, Majors & Waddell was already operating a stage line between the Missouri River and Salt Lake City. Gwin wanted Russell to start an experimental fast-mail service, via horseback, over the same line, and from Salt Lake City on to Sacramento. Majors noted that Gwin and other proponents of this venture were curious about the practicability of crossing the Sierra Nevada and the Rocky Mountains in winter. The specifics of the Gwin-Russell discussion are not known, but what is recorded by Alexander Majors is that Russell came back from Washington in early 1860 and told his partners that he had given his word to Gwin that the freight-hauling firm would undertake this experiment. Majors recalled that both he and Waddell did not think such a venture would ever pay expenses.

"Russell . . . had committed himself to Senator Gwin before leaving Washington, assuring him he could get his partners to join him, and that he might rely on the project being carried through, and saying it would be very humiliating to his pride to return to Washington and be compelled to say the scheme had fallen through from lack of his partners' confidence."

Russell told Majors and Waddell that if the firm could demonstrate that the Central Route was practical and could be kept operating in the winter, Senator Gwin had vowed to use his influence to get a subsidy to pay the expenses of such a line. Russell had given his word, and in those days a man's word was still his bond (and the bond of his firm, too).

And so, on Russell's word (and Gwin's promise), Majors and

Waddell agreed to become involved in the venture that would become their legacy and their ruin.

"After listening to all Mr. Russell had to say upon the subject, we concluded to sustain him in the undertaking and immediately went to work to organize what has since been known as 'The Pony Express.' "

According to Majors's recollections, the firm used the existing line stations between the Missouri River and Salt Lake City and built additional facilities between Salt Lake City and Sacramento.

On January 27, 1860, William H. Russell sent his son and business associate, John W. Russell, a brief telegram:

HAVE DETERMINED TO ESTABLISH A PONY EXPRESS TO SACRAMENTO, CALIFORNIA, COMMENCING 3RD OF APRIL. TIME TEN DAYS.

Historians of the Pony Express usually invoke ancient Roman and Greek mail couriers or the mounted messengers of Genghis Khan in China in establishing the tradition and pedigree of the cross-country mail service, the practice of delivering mail using a fast relay system of riders.

But the custom of using a mounted courier in the American West was not inspired by such ancient tales. In colonial times, mail had been moved in such fashion in New England. Even the expression "pony express" was common long before Russell, Majors & Waddell launched its cross-country venture.

The nineteenth-century American writer and early Californian Joaquin Miller left this account of the days of the forty-niners and early mail delivery:

The Pony Express was a great feature in the gold mines of California long before anyone ever thought of putting it on the plains. Every creek, camp or "city" had its Pony Express which ran to and from the nearest office. At Yreka we had the Humbug Creek Express, the Deadwood Camp Express, the Greenhorn, and so on.

The rider was always a bold, right, young fellow, who owned the line, horses and all, and had his "office" in some responsible store. He crowded an immense deal of personality into his work;

would die in the saddle rather than delay ten minutes over the expected time. He was, of course, always a dashing rider, dressed gaily and blew a small bugle as he went up and down the creek at a plunging rate. "Three blasts, after the fashion of the London postman!" Whack and bang at the cabin door meant a letter for this or that "claim," as the rider dashed down the trail under the trees.

And then hats in the air! Hurrah, hurrah, hurrah! Whose is it—and which one of the half-dozen or dozen men at the long sluice-boxes is to hear from his wife, mother or waiting sweetheart? This one starts to get it—that one, then the other. They look at one another hastily, and then one of them—strangely enough nearly always the right one!—springs up the ladder. Away, over the boulders with a bound, with pay for the letter clutched in his fist! He grasps the letter, away bounds the spirited pony, another blast of the horn!

The inspiration for Russell, Majors & Waddell's daring risk of cross-country horsemanship was a feat that would have been familiar in the American West of the mid-nineteenth century. Horsemen knew it on the Plaza in Santa Fe and they knew it, too, on the edge of the Missouri frontier. It was a series of heroic one-man cross-country rides made in the early 1850s by Francis Xavier Aubery, a contemporary of Kit Carson's in Santa Fe. Aubery, described by Frank A. Root and William E. Connelley in *The Overland Stage to California* as "a man of pluck and indomitable energy and perseverance," was a near-mythic figure in the American West at the time. Root and Connelley's 1901 assessment of Aubery's horsemanship concluded that "not one man in 100,000 had the physical endurance to perform the seemingly important task."

Using a relay of horses, Aubery at first made the run from Santa Fe to Independence in two weeks. It was a trip that oxen hauling freight normally did in two to three months. Aubery, who was built like a jockey, then shaved that time to eight days. He arrived in Independence so exhausted that he could not dismount from his horse. But Aubery was not satisfied with this personal best. His next trip, which would set horsemen talking across the Great American Desert, was completed in only five days and thirteen hours.

The odd legacy of Aubery (he made his famous five-day ride for a thousand-dollar bet and was later stabbed to death in a bar fight in New Mexico) is sketchy, but Majors recalled in his autobiography the

French-Canadian trader's feats of horsemanship. Changing mounts every one hundred to two hundred miles, Aubery crossed the eight hundred dangerous miles that separated the old Spanish city from Independence in an unheard-of time. It nearly killed him, and he slept for twenty hours after making the run. But it made a powerful impression on Majors.

"This ride, in my opinion, in one respect was the most remarkable one ever made by any man. The entire distance was ridden without stopping to rest . . . At the time he made this ride, in much of the territory he passed through he was liable to meet hostile Indians, so that his adventure was daring in more ways than one. In the first place, the man who attempted to ride 800 miles in the time he did took his life in his hands. There is perhaps not one man in a million who could have lived to finish such a journey."

A dour Bible reader little given to hyperbole, Majors was not commenting on something that he had heard about secondhand while sitting around a buffalo chip fire on the trail drinking coffee with bullwhackers. Majors knew Aubery, and he witnessed some of the famous eight-hundred-mile ride. "I was well acquainted with and did considerable business with Aubery during his years of freighting. I met him when he was making his famous ride, at a point on the Santa Fe Road called Rabbit Ear. He passed my train at a full gallop without asking a single question as to the danger of Indians ahead of him."

Alexander Majors never thought William Russell's scheme of a cross-country mail relay was a sound one, and he never thought that it would make money. He told this to Russell and Waddell at the time. But in the back of the old bullwhacker's mind was galloping F. X. Aubery and the knowledge that it was indeed possible for a very good rider on a very good horse to cover a lot of ground.

Miner's shack in the Sierra Nevada, ca. 1860.

Two

"A WILD, UNINHABITED
EXPANSE"

Much has been written of the famous Pony Express, but most accounts have stressed the romantic and spectacular side, failing to show the motives which actuated its founders, or to portray its relationship to the other problems of overland communication and western expansion.

—LeRoy R. Hafen, *The Overland Mail*, 1926

In 1860, the year before the start of the Civil War, the West began at the Missouri River, the end of civilization then for "the states." During the previous two decades, homesteaders and mule- and oxen-pulled wagon trains heading west had plodded up the Oregon Trail or one of its tributaries from the Missouri frontier. Half a million pioneers had trekked the great path of western migration up through the Platte River Valley of Nebraska into Wyoming and across the Rocky Mountains at South Pass and on to Oregon or California.

Horace Greeley, who saw such wagon trains during his trip west, described them as "giving the trail the appearance of a river running through great meadows, with many ships sailing on its bosom." Travelers left in the spring to avoid winter in the mountains. Five months was considered excellent time in crossing the two thousand miles between Missouri and Oregon. One in ten died along the way, mostly from diseases such as cholera and diphtheria. While there were some notable incidents, Indians, at least along the eastern end of the route, did not pose a significant threat. The great Indian wars were yet to come, after the Civil War, when more and more pioneers poured into the West and threatened the Native American homeland.

In the year before the Civil War, none of the territories—Kansas, Nebraska, Colorado, Wyoming, Utah, or Nevada—were states yet. Only California, rocketed into statehood in 1850 following the discovery of gold, was formally part of the Union.

The permanent population of these territories was insignificant; there were few settlements. In the summer of 1859, Horace Greeley had found Denver, then six months old, a collection of one hundred cottonwood mining shacks. There was no railroad west of the Missouri River nor a telegraph line.

Greeley gives some idea about the remoteness of the West of that time by recording in his journal the gradual disappearance of creature comforts familiar to the easterner. "I believe I have now descended the ladder of artificial life nearly to its lowest rung," he told his readers.

In Chicago, on May 12, Greeley noted "chocolate and morning journals last seen on the hotel breakfast table." On May 23 in Leavenworth, Kansas (where he saw Russell, Majors & Waddell's operations), Greeley recorded that "room-bells and bath-tubs make their final appearance." The next day, in Topeka, Greeley added, "Beefsteaks and wash-bowls (other than tin) last visible. Barber ditto." One day later, in Manhattan in the Kansas Territory, he noted, "potatoes and eggs last recognized as blessings that brighten as they take their flight. Chairs ditto." Two days later, May 27, in Junction City: "Last visitation of a boot-black, with dissolving views of a board bedroom. Beds bid us goodbye." The following day, in Pipe Creek, Greeley noted, "Benches for seats at meals disappearing, giving place to bags and boxes."

The most important issue facing the American public in the inaugural year of the Pony Express was the imminent threat of civil war and the rancorous and often bloody conflict over slavery—most especially in border states like Missouri and the adjacent Kansas Territory—but that debate seemed far away for most westerners.

In the last year of Democrat James Buchanan's one term as president, about 31.4 million people, including slaves, lived in the United States, according to the census of 1860. But only about 2 percent of those people—620,000—lived in the sprawling and largely unsettled West and Southwest. California, with a population of 380,000 (up from about 18,000, not including Indians, before the gold rush), was home to two-thirds of those Americans.

For the vast majority of Americans, the West remained a distant and near-fabled place. Even on the eastern end of the Great Plains, fewer than 29,000 people lived in the territory of Nebraska. Wyoming did not have enough to count. The only two significant settlements were Fort Laramie in the east and Fort Bridger—established by mountain man Jim Bridger—in the southwest. The Colorado Territory, experiencing its own gold rush in the Rocky Mountains at the time, had a population of 34,277, but most of those pioneers were merely passing through, out west for a brief adventure.

Nevada had fewer than 7,000 residents, largely transient miners living along the California border near what today are Reno, Carson City, and Virginia City. About 40,000 people were living in Utah—mostly Mormons, members of the Church of Jesus Christ of Latter-day Saints, who had come to build the New Jerusalem.

Colonel Henry Inman, the author of *The Great Salt Lake Trail and the Old Santa Fe Trail,* believed gold was the inspiration for the Pony Express. Before the California gold rush, only a few thousand people lived on the Pacific slope and mail service was highly irregular and erratic, but no one cared. The year before John Wilson Marshall picked up some bits of gold from the tailrace at Sutter's Mill on the American River, one account precisely gauged the number of white men living at what is today Sacramento at 290. By 1860, with nearly 400,000 Americans living in the Far West, westerners would no longer tolerate mail delivery that could take months. They signed petitions—75,000 on one occasion—demanding better mail service. They were clamoring for a telegraph and a railroad, too.

"I cannot express the disappointment I have experienced in not as yet having received any letters," wrote William Swain, a farmer from near Niagara Falls, New York, in a letter to his family. Swain had left his wife and children and farm and traveled overland to California in the days of the forty-niners, hoping to strike it rich. A prolific letter writer and diarist, whose adventures are vividly chronicled in *The World Rushed In,* Swain wrote bitterly of the lack of mail. "I am as well satisfied that there is at least a dozen for me at Sacramento City as I am of my existence. I have sent after them by three express carriers, and failed to get any on account of the inability of the postmaster of that place to perform the duties of the office and no provision for clerks being made by the government."

William Swain was not alone; and where there was demand there would be supply. Independent mail contractors sprang up across the countryside. Many of these operations simply consisted of a man and a mule and a hundred-pound sack of mail. These entrepreneurs hauled mail to mining camps—places with names like Dutch Flat and Rough and Ready, You Bet and Shirtail Canyon (so poor they could only afford one "t")—mining camps that would figure in Bret Harte's *The Luck of Roaring Camp and Other Sketches* and Mark Twain's *Roughing It.*

The amateur mailman would wander from one digging to another attempting to find the recipients of the letters. Miners often paid as much as an ounce of gold dust—between $15 and $18—for a letter, the equivalent today of paying more than $300 for a piece of mail. Newspapers from New York, some five or six months old, sold for $8—$150 in today's money. One of the early entrepreneurs frequently mentioned by historians of the period, Alexander H. Todd, went up into the mining country delivering mail and reportedly returned carrying gold for the miners then valued at $250,000, or more than $4.5 million today.

The importance of mail, business aspects aside, was vital to life far from "the states." The pioneers who had trudged the Oregon Trail and the get-rich-quick dreamers of the gold rush wanted news of family and loved ones. To a man, they were homesick. Between them and home was a "wild, uninhabited expanse," as Alexander Majors called it in his memoirs.

William Swain, the New York farmer, wrote to his wife, Sabrina, and mother: "I find this voyaging life disagreeable, as it is here today and there tomorrow and prevents me from hearing from home regularly or writing regularly and gives me a disagreeable feeling about the folks at home."

Swain's brother, George, back on the farm, echoed these sentiments in his own letter to California, railing against the mail service:

Everybody is inquiring about you, and many have given you up and think we never shall hear from you. But I tell you, I have no such idea, and am quite sure we will receive letters by the mail now due from the Isthmus. The *Empire City* came into New York on the 7th with 290 passengers and $2,000,000 but brings no mail; that must come by the *Falcon,* which the Government, with admirable ingenuity, contrives to have always arriving behind private enterprise. There is a good deal of complaint about it. I wish I was mail agent on the Isthmus [Panama mail route]—I'd raise the devil with some of their ducks. Our big men in Washington don't know or care much about mail, if office and pay can be secured, apparently. But we have got to wait with patience to see what comes or don't come.

William S. McCollum, a physician who went west at the height of the gold rush, recorded this hunger for news and home vividly in 1850 in *California as I Saw It.* "The scene at the Post Office in San Francisco, on the arrival of the mail steamers, is one of intense anxiety and excitement. There will be not only the citizens, but those who have come down from the mines in scores; all expecting letters from friends at home; making in the aggregate such a jostling throng as is seen upon such an occasion in no other city in the world. As there are tens of thousands of letters expected, and usually come, so there are thousands of anxious waiters at the Post Office."

The scene Dr. McCollum described was near-bedlam. Men stood in line for days for mail. Men paid other men to stand in line for them. Miners offered substantial amounts of gold dust to buy a place in line from another miner. Opportunists stood in line even if they were not expecting mail merely to sell their position to someone who needed it. Men slept all night rolled in blankets in line just to wait another day for some news of home. The clerks were helpless. There were only a handful of them, and sorting mail under these circumstances was mayhem. McCollum realized his description might sound fanciful to readers back east. "This is seemingly an extravagant account of the matter, I am aware, but it falls short of giving the reader an adequate idea of the immense amount of letters that the steamers bring to San Francisco, and of the throng that rush after them in their intense anxiety to hear from home."

McCollum's account in part explains the reason—even a decade later—for the Pony Express and the wild enthusiasm the fast-mail courier immediately generated in California. Dr. McCollum understood something of the human heart, too. "And is it not an interesting moral spectacle? The heart, the affections, the kindlier feelings of our nature, are involved in it. These silent messengers that have found their way thousands of miles over the earth and ocean, bring tidings from HOME, and those that are cherished and loved there. It is a sad thing to be far, far away, from one's own hearth stone, and all the fond associations that cluster around it; but it is a moment of relief, of joy and gladness, when you can trace there a familiar hand, that assures you that wide seas have not sundered affections, or absence chilled them; that there are those that still hope for you and care for you; that ALL IS WELL, when you most hope that all should be well."

Another of the early California writers, the humorist Alonzo Delano, a veteran of the overland trek west, captured some sense of this longing for news in his *Pen-Knife Sketches 1853* in describing the arrival of the mail. "Every pick and shovel is dropped, every pan is laid aside, every rocker is stopped with its half-washed dirt, every claim is deserted, and they crowd around the store with eager enquiries, 'Have you got a letter for me?' With what joy it is seized, and they care little whether they pay two or five dollars for it, they've got a letter. Or perhaps, as is often the case, the answer is 'There's nothing for you' and with a 'Damn the luck' and a heavy heart, they go sullenly back to work, unfitted by disappointments for social intercourse the rest of the day."

———

In the years before the Pony Express, a series of bizarre and foolhardy mail delivery methods were tried. They all failed, some quite tragically.

In 1851, Major (it was an honorary title) George Chorpenning and Absolom Woodward contracted with the federal government to haul mail from Sacramento to Salt Lake City, about seven hundred miles of the most barren country in the United States (the state of Nevada today still calls part of the route, a grim stretch of two-lane blacktop, the loneliest road in America). Chorpenning and Woodward used mules—jackass mail, it was called. Their efforts were nightmarish.

Plagued by Indians, deep snow, and freezing temperatures, the jackass mail foundered. Woodward was killed by Indians. On one occasion, Chorpenning made the crossing between California and Salt Lake City alone when no one would go with him; the danger of Paiutes was simply too great for others. Chorpenning spent the rest of his life fighting Congress for compensation for his efforts; he died in poverty and is buried in an unmarked grave in Brooklyn, New York—far from the alkali flats of Nevada and Utah where he tried so hard to deliver mail. (In the summer of 2001, the Associated Press reported that Chorpenning's kin were still contemplating suing the federal government for money owed.)

The next step was camels. Reports vary on the venture, but as many as seventy-five dromedaries were bought after the American government studied the beasts at the London Zoo. The camels, obtained in Saudi Arabia for $30,000 and brought west, were considered a fine idea (Secretary of War Jefferson Davis proposed the venture in 1853). This was a stroke of genius, so the thinking went. Camels were ships of deserts, after all. They could walk tremendous distances without water. They were patient and strong. They were proven and reliable. (One account reports that the enthusiasm for camels was heaviest among Bible readers.) There were even military planners who wanted to mount light artillery on the camels' humps. But the rocky western terrain proved too hard on their hooves, accustomed to soft desert sand. The camels had to be outfitted with leather boots. The leather boots slowed them down, and the camels did not want to wear them anyway. And westerners were unfamiliar with camels. They did not know how to correctly pack loads on their backs. Camels terrified horses and mules, too. The mere smell of one camel could cause a stampede.

After one disastrous trip from Texas to California, the camels were retired from mail service and sold to circuses. Some were allowed to wander off into the brush to later terrify travelers not expecting to encounter such creatures in the American West.

The ships of the desert were merely the most exotic attempt to bring the news across the Great American Desert in the mid-nineteenth century. Other ventures were—however occasionally successful—equally odd.

Mail reached the remote Carson Valley in Nevada by coming over the Sierra Nevada—altitudes of six thousand to twelve thousand feet—carried by a Norwegian immigrant named John "Snowshoe" Thompson, who traveled alone on ten-foot-long cross-country skis.

Thompson, whose exploits are still commemorated in the Silver State, glided from Placerville to Carson City, nearly one hundred miles, in three days and made the return trip in two. Carrying mail weighing as much as a hundred pounds, Thompson crossed the mountains on his homemade skis, trudging through snow said to be thirty to fifty feet deep in some places. Lithographs from the period suggest that crude dogsleds were tried, too.

But the West remained impatient for mail. Most news coming from the East traveled along the meandering 2,700-mile Southern Route. Officially called the Butterfield Overland Mail Company Route, it crossed the Southwest from St. Louis, looping down to El Paso on the Mexican border, and then on to California and up to San Francisco, thus resulting in its nickname, the Oxbow Route. Sketched out on a crude map, the route resembled the bow of an ox's horns. Colonel Henry Inman called the route "outrageously circuitous." The British explorer Captain Sir Richard Burton, who delighted in pejoratives, described the Southern Route as "the vilest and most desolate portion of the West."

The other mail route from east to west involved government steamships from the Atlantic coast to Panama, fifty miles across the isthmus first by mule train and later by railroad, and then up the Pacific coast. Sailing trips around Cape Horn, the southern tip of South America, could take even longer, up to six months depending on weather.

Fast time in transporting mail from the Atlantic states to the West in 1860 was three to four weeks. The best time ever logged on the Southern Route at the time the Pony Express began was twenty-one days. Colonel Inman recalled the imperfections of this mail service in 1898. "The ocean route to the Pacific was tedious and circuitous, and the impetuosity of the mining population demanded quicker time for the delivery of its mails than was taken by the long sea-voyage. From the terminus of telegraphic communication in the East there intervened more than two thousand miles of a region uninhabited, except by hostile tribes of savages."

———

In 1860, St. Joseph, perched above the Missouri—the Big Muddy— was the jumping-off point for pioneers. Here ended the railroad and the telegraph, and here tens of thousands of immigrants began their travels up the Oregon Trail or elsewhere in the West in the 1840s and '50s. The observant traveler Horace Greeley on his fact-finding mission had found St. Joe a pleasant place, indeed:

> St. Joseph is a busy, growing town of some ten thousand inhabitants. It is beautifully situated on a bend of the Missouri, partly on its intervale (which the river is gouging out and carrying away), and partly on the southward slope of the bluff, which rises directly from the river bank, at the north end of the town. Other towns on the Missouri may have a grander future; I doubt that any has a finer location. The river bank must be piled or docked, or in some way fortified against the boiling current which sets against the town-site with fearful power and effect. I believe this is further west than any other point reached by a railroad connecting eastward with the Atlantic ports. At all events, the travel and part of the trade of the vast wilderness watered by the Upper Missouri and its tributaries seem to center here . . . I may never see St. Joseph again, but she will long be to me a pleasant recollection.

St. Joe was a boomtown when Horace Greeley passed through at the end of the decade following the California gold rush and on the heels of the Pike's Peak gold discoveries in Colorado. The town had begun life as a tiny trading post, the enterprise of one Joseph Robidoux, a canny and tireless French-Canadian entrepreneur who dominated the fur trade and had been on the river since the days of Lewis and Clark. Old Joe was still alive and well and doing business the day the Pony Express left the town that he had fathered.

Rudolph Friederich Kurz, a noted Swiss artist who kept a journal between 1846 and 1852, recalled Robidoux and his trading post at the foot of the Black Snake Hills. Kurz, sketching Native Americans and wildlife, spent three years wandering the western trading posts of the great fur companies on the Mississippi and upper Missouri Rivers. When he arrived in St. Joe—just before the California gold rush and during the early years of the Oregon Trail westward migration—it was still a wild town, the starting point for "a rough, lawless set of adventurers" heading for that "far country" that was the impenetrable West.

Most travelers arrived in St. Joe by riverboat. When Kurz traveled up the Missouri River from St. Louis to St. Joe aboard the steamboat

Tamerlane, it took thirteen days to travel five hundred miles because of the shifting sandbars in the powerful current of the winding river. Mark Twain, who as a licensed pilot knew a good deal about riverboating, complained of the same trip.

In *Roughing It,* Twain recalled the Missouri as "a confused jumble of savage-looking snags, which we deliberately walked over with one wheel or the other; and of reefs which we butted and butted, and then retired from and climbed over in some softer place, and of sandbars which we roosted on occasionally, and rested, and then got out our crutches and sparred over. In fact, the boat might almost have gone to St. Joe by land, for she was walking most of the time, anyhow."

According to Kurz, the development of St. Joe began in earnest after Robidoux bought the trading post in the Black Snake Hills in 1834 from the American Fur Company following a long business association with the firm.

Robidoux descended from Parisians who had migrated to Quebec in the 1600s and as part of the extensive fur trade eventually found themselves in St. Louis. A true voyageur, Old Joe, as he is still occasionally called by the citizens of the town he gave his name to, was born in St. Louis on August 10, 1783. When he was twenty, Robidoux and his father helped to outfit Lewis and Clark's Corps of Discovery. In 1809, Joe Robidoux settled on the banks of the Missouri River at what is today Council Bluffs, Iowa, and began trading with the Indians. The Missouri historian Sheridan Logan, author of *Old St. Jo, Gateway to the West,* recalled the trader. "He spoke French fluently, his English was broken, and he had learned a number of Indian dialects. He treated the Indians fairly and was successful in securing their business. After thirteen years of trading at the Bluffs, when he was thirty-nine years of age, the American Fur Company decided that his popularity with the Indians was a detriment to their business. So they proposed to buy his stock of goods at prices 50 percent above his costs, and to pay him $1,000 a year for a period of three years, on condition that he leave The Bluffs. Robidoux accepted the arrangement, returned to St. Louis with his family, and carried on the business of a baker and confectioner."

But city living was too docile for Old Joe, and so he persuaded the American Fur Company that he should open a trading post on the Missouri River at the foot of the Black Snake Hills. In 1826, he arrived there and began trading with the Fox, Oto, Kickapoo, Iowa, and

Potawatomi Indians. (He was well liked by the Indians and even better liked by Indian women, with whom he fathered an uncountable number of children.) At first Robidoux was an employee of the American Fur Company, but after a few years he bought them out and began to set up a far-flung fur-trading empire, according to Sheridan Logan. Two of his brothers, Louis and Isadore, went to Santa Fe and Taos, while another brother, Michel, established Robidoux Fort in Wyoming. Other brothers went to Colorado and Utah and to the Yellowstone region. The Robidoux brothers' business ventures covered parts of eight states. Old Joe also began operating a ferryboat across the Missouri River and built a gristmill. His town would follow.

Richard Hayes McDonald, who came out from Kentucky to see his uncle Dr. Silas McDonald, the first physician in the Platte Purchase, met Old Joe and left an account of the wily Frenchman in 1840. McDonald described him as "dressed in an old, red flannel shirt, his trousers strapped around his waist, on his head a slouched hat, and so tanned and weather-beaten that it was difficult to tell whether he was a white man, a mulatto, or an Indian." (The only known daguerreotype of Old Joe confirms this description. He looked like a troll.)

"His establishment consisted of three log cabins," McDonald wrote, "one or more of which were filled with furs of otter, beaver, buffalo, deer, bear, and other skins; in the other buildings were stored provisions, trinkets, and supplies for the Indians, the latter chiefly in whiskey, tobacco, and liquors. The old man [he was only fifty-three that year] seemed to be a very energetic, enterprising, shrewd business manager. He was familiar with several dialects of the Indian language, and was highly respected by all the natives who dealt with him."

Rudolph Friederich Kurz claimed that St. Joe's development from a trading post into a town of considerable substance in a few years was largely due to the enterprise of Joe Robidoux, who speculated in land and was the preeminent real estate developer in northwestern Missouri. When the town that took his patron saint's name was being laid out, Robidoux told the designers to make the streets narrow; he did not want wide streets, he wanted to sell land. (Even today the streets bear the names of his children: Jules, Felix, Edmond, Francis, Charles, Faraon, Messanie, Angelique, Sylvanie).

Kurz recalled Old Joe as a crafty businessman who often gave competitors the impression they were dealing with a simple French-

Canadian peasant. He once duped another fur trader by getting him to go down into a cellar under his trading post and then locking him up in there while Robidoux traded with the Pawnees. He was a famously hard bargainer who even tricked his son Joseph Jr. into signing away valuable property to his father while he was intoxicated.

Kurz also recalled Robidoux's great fondness for gambling and card playing and recalled an incident when the old man was returning by riverboat from a buying trip to St. Louis:

> The game usually played is one in which that player wins who risks the highest stake; whether he actually holds the highest cards in his hand is immaterial. The game is called poker. On one of the old man's trips up the Missouri he met with an experienced partner; they were strangers to each other. Robidoux, rather poorly dressed as was his habit, did not impress his opponent in the game as one to be feared, so, after they had been playing for quite a while, the latter, with the intention of springing a surprise, put up a considerable sum. Old Robidoux, however, instead of showing concern, called to the waiter: "Bring that old trunk of mine here! Here are one thousand dollars in cash; I bet 'em all!"

The stranger could not increase the amount; consequently, even though he had better cards, he lost the game and between seven hundred and eight hundred dollars.

Kurz noted, too, some oft-repeated details about Old Joe's life among the Native Americans and his tortured financial affairs. "He is now an immensely wealthy property holder, but his 60 papooses, his seven white children, and several brothers in rags and tatters continually consume his substance. Two years ago the city lots had advanced threefold in value."

That St. Joseph was a prime spot for development was apparent to travelers into the region. The artist John James Audubon, traveling up the Missouri River to the Yellowstone, recorded this observation in his journal: ". . . We reached the Blacksnake Hills settlement, which is a delightful site for a populous city. The hills are 200 feet above the level of the river, and slope gently down on the opposite side to the beautiful prairies that extend over thousands of acres of the richest land imaginable."

There were two hundred white men living on the site when

Audubon made that observation in 1843. Seventeen years later, when the Pony Express left St. Joe for California, there were 8,932 residents—more than the combined populations of Kansas City, Omaha, and Council Bluffs at the time. St. Joe had prospered.

At the time of the start of the gold rush to California, St. Joe was already developing a reputation for its sharp business practices. Great fortunes were grounded in outfitting pioneers heading west. "The prices of provisions, cattle, and goods became exorbitant. The farmer fixed no price for his products but advanced them higher and higher with each new band of adventurers," Kurz reported. A bushel of corn that had previously sold for fifteen cents now cost a dollar. Prices in general tripled and quadrupled as gold seekers hit town.

Riverboats were the principal means of travel to St. Joe until 1859, when the Hannibal & St. Joseph Railroad was pushed through straight across the top of the state of Missouri, linking St. Joe with the Mississippi River. The changes that had occurred in Joe Robidoux's lifetime were accelerating now. The railroad (and the telegraph) clinched St. Joe's position as a boomtown and natural starting place for travelers into the West.

Settled largely by Southerners who had migrated west, St. Joseph was a Southern city, a city with Confederate sympathies, just across the Missouri River from the Free State of Kansas. The river town was surrounded by miles of rich bottomland, fertile soil that produced corn, tobacco, and hemp.

Six months after the Pony started its cross-country gallop, William H. Seward stopped in St. Joe while stumping for Abraham Lincoln's presidential effort. Seward's secretary, George Ellis Baker, left this assessment of the city:

> We are most comfortably accommodated at the Patee House. It is very large, well arranged, and admirably conducted. Indeed, I know of no better hotel in the Western country. St. Jo, itself—so recently the outpost, as it were, of American settlement and civilization, is a handsome and busy town of 12,000 people. Nearly all travel for California, Utah, New Mexico, Pike's Peak, etc. passes through this point, and you daily meet, at the Patee House, acquaintances from all points of the Union. Thus, today, I encountered here a friend from Fond du Lac, one from Sheboygan, another from Chicago, and several friends from New York and Kansas.

Like other travelers, John D. Young of Chicago, headed for the Colorado goldfields, was impressed with the town that Old Joe Robidoux had begotten.

"One day's ride on the railroad brought us clear across the state of Missouri into the city of St. Joe, the furthest north western city of the United States," Young recorded in his diary. "It is situated on the banks of the river partly on the bottoms and partly on the bluffs. One would be surprised at finding such a large fine looking city away so far from civilization. It has a compact well built and substantial appearance. Many of its buildings would compare favorably with the finest of our own great city. The Paytee House is as large as the Fremont House. It is situated on the outskirts of the city on slightly elevated ground commanding a beautiful view of the Missouri river . . ."

First Rider Leaving St. Joe *by Charles Hargens.*

Three

"THE GREATEST ENTERPRISE OF MODERN TIMES!!"

> No enterprise of the kind in its day was ever celebrated on the Pacific coast with more enthusiasm than the arrival of the first pony express.
>
> —FRANK A. ROOT AND WILLIAM E. CONNELLEY,
> *THE OVERLAND STAGE TO CALIFORNIA*, 1901

Telegraphers along the 206-mile route between Hannibal on the Mississippi River and St. Joseph on the Missouri reported that the train carrying the first mail for the Pony Express passed at the astonishing speed of a mile a minute. The grueling trip that the intrepid Horace Greeley had made the previous summer, pitching and tossing for some twelve hours, was accomplished on that spring afternoon and early evening by the *Missouri* in four hours and fifty-one minutes, averaging a speed of forty miles an hour

An oft-quoted, if somewhat fabulous, account of the first train bringing mail for the Pony Express appeared later in the *New York Sun* (the newspaper best known for "Yes, Virginia, There Is a Santa Claus"). "The mail car used on the run of the Pony Express was the first car constructed for mail purposes in the United States. The engine, named the *Missouri*, was a wood burner. From an artistic standpoint it was a much handsomer machine than the big black Moguls of today. There was scrollwork about the headlight, bill and drivers, and all the steel and brass parts were polished till they resembled a looking-glass."

Fuel agents along the line were notified to be on hand with an adequate force to load the tender in seconds. The orders given to engineer Addison Clark were simple. He was to make the trip in record time.

The train pulled out of Hannibal amid the waving of hats and the cheering of a big crowd. All the way across the state at every station and crossroad it was greeted by enthusiasts, many of whom had journeyed miles to see it. Nothing in northern Missouri had ever excited greater interest.

Russell, Majors & Waddell's wild gamble began on April 3, 1860—as promised. Sixty-five days after Russell sent his son that brief telegram announcing plans for the Pony Express, the first couriers left St. Joseph and California at the same time.

The route from St. Joe to San Francisco was 1,950 miles, according to Majors. (The figure 1,966 appears in many of the popular histories of the Pony Express.) The path of the Pony Express crossed what is today eight states and virtually every terrain imaginable, from amber waves of grain to sand hills to high sierra to alkali desert—from Missouri into Kansas, Nebraska, Colorado, Wyoming, Utah, Nevada, and California.

On April 3, preparations had been made for the railroad line between Hannibal and St. Joe to be cleared for the train hauling the special mail for the Pony Express from the East. The *Missouri,* a single engine with tender, pulled one car that carried an assortment of unfortunate dignitaries who emerged at the end of the line in St. Joe covered with soot and terrified after a cross-country ride that old railroad hands would claim set a speed record that stood for half a century.

The *New York Sun*'s vivid account continues:

The first seventy miles of the journey were comparatively level and straight. Through Monroe and Shelby Counties the eager railway officials figured that the little train was making over sixty miles an hour. At Macon it began to strike the rough country, where hills and curves were numerous.

The *Missouri* stopped at Macon for wood. The fuel agent, L. S. Coleman, had erected a platform, just the height of the tender. On this spot he put every man that could find room, each bearing an armful of selected wood.

As the train slowed up, the men emptied their arms. The fuel agent, watch in hand, counted the seconds. Just fifteen seconds passed while the train was at a standstill. Then it was off again, like the wind. The spectators saw the occupants of the car clutching their seats as it rocked to and fro and threatened to toss them all in a heap on the floor.

It was like an avalanche. If there had been a tenderfoot on board, a more than reasonable doubt would have arisen in his mind as to whether all the wheels of the train were on the track or not. The furnace was drawing magnificently. A streak of fire shot out of the stack, and the wood sparks flew through the air like snowflakes.

Across the Chariton River came the New Cambria Hill, a still greater grade than that down from Macon. The momentum attained served to drive the train halfway up with scarcely any perceptible reduction in speed, but the exhausts became slower before the peak of the grade was approached. The fireman piled his dry cottonwood, and the safety valve sent a column of steam heavenward. The white-faced passengers breathed easier, but the relief did not last long. The summit of the hill was reached and the little engine snorted as something alive, took the bit in its teeth, and was soon rushing along at top speed.

Alas, somewhat anticlimactically, the train arrived in St. Joe about three hours late—through no fault of Addison Clark or the Hannibal & St. Joseph Railroad. Problems in the East had delayed the departure for St. Joe and the time could not be made up.

The first rider, Johnny Frey, left St. Joe at dusk on the evening of April 3, 1861—7:15 P.M. Most accounts agree that he was carrying forty-nine letters, some copies of eastern newspapers specially printed on tissue paper, five private telegrams, and numerous telegraphic dispatches for California newspapers (among the biggest promoters of this venture). The *St. Joseph Daily Gazette* also claimed in a front-page article on April 3 that a special edition of its newspaper would be carried by the Pony Express rider.

Meanwhile, on the other side of the continent, in San Francisco, the first rider heading east was preparing to depart from the Alta Telegraph Office on Montgomery Street. The *San Francisco Bulletin* noted: "From one o'clock until the hour of our going to press, a clean-limbed, hardy little nankeen-colored pony stood at the door of the

Alta Telegraph Company's office—the pioneer pony of the famous express which today begins its first trip across the continent . . ."

The departure from San Francisco was ceremonial, for the mail actually traveled from San Francisco to Sacramento on the steamer *New World*. It was from Sacramento that the cross-country run really began in earnest. The first rider out of Sacramento, William Hamilton, left at 2:45 A.M. on April 4. Four hours after leaving, Hamilton galloped through Placerville, already beginning the slow climb into the Sierra Nevada over a route where in some places the path was only ten feet wide and winter snows thirty feet deep in some mountain passes.

The first leg out of San Francisco for the East carried fifty-six letters and picked up an additional thirteen in Sacramento. Despite the hour of Hamilton's departure, the *Daily Bee* noted that "quite a crowd was in attendance who cheered lustily as Hamilton and his mettled steed dashed off at a rattling pace."

Back east in St. Joe, the inaugural was even grander, and the crowd—"all St. Joe, great and small"—that saw Johnny Frey off included William H. Russell, Alexander Majors, and former St. Joseph mayor M. Jeff Thompson, who would soon distinguish himself as a military tactician in the Confederacy. Thompson and Majors made speeches. Russell said nothing. A cannon was fired (to signal the ferryboat operator to be on the Missouri side of the river). Descriptions of the send-off vary wildly. Some report that most of the gawkers had gone home, tired of waiting for the train. There had been a band, but the musicians appear to have drifted off as time wore on and it began to grow dark. The sun set at 6:46 on April 3, and a half hour later it would have been dark. However, the *St. Joseph Gazette* of April 4, 1860, printed this account of the start of the Pony Express:

> At the hour of starting, an immense crowd had gathered around the Express office to witness the inaugurating of the novel and important enterprise—Mayor Thompson, in a few remarks to the spectators, briefly alluded to the significance of the Express from our city over the Central Route. Mr. Majors, being loudly called for, responded in a speech characterized by his usual practical manner of thought, in which he reviewed the rapid changes which have taken place in the condition and prospects of the West, predicting that the day is not far distant when other and powerful communities will

spring up in the shadow of the mountains, a region lately regarded as wild and sterile beyond the power or desire of reclamation. He spoke from personal experience of the changes which have taken place on the plains. But a dozen years ago the entire season was thought scarcely time enough to make the trip from Missouri to California, and companies of a less number than fifty, armed and organized, were deemed too weak to venture on the perilous route. Now a single man, aye, a defenseless woman, so far as Indians were concerned, need fear no evil.

The *Daily West*—under the headline "The Greatest Enterprise of Modern Times!!"—noted that the train bringing the mail down to St. Joe had set a modern record, and echoed the *Gazette*'s enthusiasms:

> Today inaugurates the greatest enterprise of modern times . . . And one that must benefit St. Joseph in a very marked and visible degree . . . That of running an express on the overland route between St. Joseph and San Francisco, in the extraordinary short space of ten days . . . The magnitude of this enterprise can scarcely be conceived . . . The transmission of messages over this route will be the most speedy known to modern times.

Thompson, a much livelier orator than Majors, who placed the mochila on the back of the first horse to be ridden west, called for a rousing send-off. "Hardly will the cloud of dust which envelops the rider die away before the puff of steam will be seen on the horizon. Citizens of St. Joseph, I bid you give three cheers for the Pony Express, three cheers for the first overland passage of the United States Mail!"

On this early spring day in 1860, the possibilities seemed limitless, which the poetical editor at the *St. Joseph Free Democrat* understood when he demonstrated his knowledge of the classics (and the Bible) and wrote these words:

> Take down your map and trace the footprints of our quadrupedantic animal: From St. Joseph, on the Missouri, to San Francisco, on the Golden Horn—two thousand miles—more than half the distance across our boundless continent; through Kansas, through Nebraska, by Fort Kearny, along the Platte, by Fort Laramie, past the

Buttes, over the Rocky Mountains, through the narrow passes and along the steep defiles, Utah, Fort Bridger, Salt Lake City, he witches Brigham with his swift ponyship—through the valleys, along the grassy slopes, into the snow, into sand, faster than Thor's Thialfi, away they go, rider and horse—did you see them?

They are in California, leaping over its golden sands, treading its busy streets. The courser has unrolled to us the great American panorama, allowed us to glance at the home of one million people, and has put a girdle around the earth in forty minutes. Verily the riding is like the riding of Jehu, the son of Nimshi, for he rideth furiously. Take out your watch. We are eight days from New York, eighteen from London. The race is to the swift.

***

There are many marvelous depictions of the departure of the first rider from St. Joe, crammed with vivid details that are hard to prove or disprove. Nearly all of them were written by scribes who were not present and based on things they had heard second- or thirdhand. Newspaper stories are not much help, either. No event associated with the Pony Express—including the dispute over the identity of the first rider—has been as much debated as the inaugural run out of St. Joe on the evening of April 3. But there was one firsthand witness to the departure of the Pony Express rider. He wrote an account in his journal.

John D. Young of Chicago, off to dig for gold in Colorado, left a detailed description of the start of the Pony Express in a diary he kept of his trip west. He did not strike it rich in the Rocky Mountains and went back to Chicago after a brief adventure. But he left a document of considerable value when it comes to chronicling Russell, Majors & Waddell's daring enterprise. It remains today at the Newberry Library in Chicago, apparently the only eyewitness account of the start of the transcontinental mail race.

Young was at the Patee House on April 3, 1860, preparing to cross the prairie and seek his fortune in the Rockies. He appears to have simply wandered up to the hotel on the evening of April 3. (The punctuation is Young's.)

". . . From this house the Pony Express starts for California I saw the arrival and departure of the first express that ever passed between St. Joseph and San Francisco and made a great display on starting the express. First the dispatches are all made up and laid on the counter then the horse is brought into the office and placed facing the officer of the letters are placed into the saddle-bags, the driver takes his seat the Telegraph operator makes up the last dispatches from New York and Washington and cannon at the doors thunders the warning to the ferry boat which is in readiness to convey the messenger across the river and now the last minute having expired the last dispatches are placed in the bag marked with the hour and minute of starting the cannon thunder out once more and before its smoke has cleared away the messenger is off swift as the best mettle of his horse can take him one mile at a headlong gallop through the city and then he gets on board the ferry boat in five minutes more he is in Kansas on the road for the Pacific this rider stays on his horse two hours and a half or while he is making twenty five miles, then there is another horse and rider waiting, the saddle bags are changed to the fresh horse the new rider jumps into his seat and off again once more and so on changing about the same distance until at last they reach San Francisco in seven or eight days. It was indeed a grand idea the interchange of news across the continent in such a short time almost equal to Rail Road speed the distance being about twenty hundred miles, over mountains and through deserts."

Young, alas, does not mention who that first rider was. But another traveler, George Ellis Baker, secretary to William Seward who was campaigning for Abraham Lincoln's presidential bid, concurred with Young's description of the Pony Express, writing on September 26, 1860:

"At eight O'clock this morning, the weekly 'Pony Express' started thence for San Francisco. The start was worth seeing. Just before the hour appointed for its departure, a horse and rider came galloping up, at full speed, to the office of the company here in the Patee House. The horse was ridden directly into the office; the saddle-bags, containing letters and telegraph dispatches, thrown across him; and the next minute, with a loud hurrah, horse and rider were tearing down the street, intent on making the first stage of five miles in four hours. The rider continues to the end of the stage; the horse is changed every fifteen miles; and the entire trip to San Francisco is accomplished in from nine to ten days."

Baker added this poignant and prescient note to his description of the Pony Express:

"The enterprise does not pay, in a pecuniary point of view, but is a great accommodation to the people on the Atlantic and Pacific coasts of the Republic. Ere long, the 'Pony Express' must give place to the telegraph, and not many years can elapse before the Pacific Railroad will supersede the overland express to California."

To put the fast-mail relay into business, Russell, Majors & Waddell had bought horses, recruited riders, and set up relay stations in slightly more than two months in the winter. The firm did this without a dime of government support (we may never know what Russell thought he had been promised in Washington) and in the face of considerable debt. It had lost nearly half a million dollars freighting supplies to the army in Utah attempting to discipline the Mormons, and there had also been significant weather-related freighting losses. Those losses were astronomical at the time—about $9.2 million today—losses that the firm would never recoup.

To put the Pony on its feet, Majors recalled more than thirty years later, the firm spent even more money, no precise record of which exists. (Russell, Majors & Waddell's records, such as they might have been, were lost or destroyed. There is no precise accounting of the firm's financial affairs.)

In the spring of 1860, the year after Horace Greeley made his celebrated visit to view the American West, and the year in which the California pioneer George Tisdale Bromley welcomed him to the Golden Land, William W. Finney, agent for the Central Overland Pony Express Company, began placing these notices in California newspapers:

PONY EXPRESS

NINE DAYS
FROM SAN FRANCISCO TO NEW YORK!

The Central Overland Pony Express Co.
Will start their LETTER EXPRESS from San Francisco
to New York, and intermediate points.
On Tuesday, the 3d of April next,
And upon EVERY TUESDAY at 4 o'clock P.M.

Letters will be received at PLACERVILLE until half past
7 o'clock A.M. on WEDNESDAY, 4th of April,
and every Wednesday thereafter
OFFICE—ALTA TELEGRAPH OFFICE
On the Plaza, opposite the Post Office
Telegraphic Dispatches will be received at Carson City
until 6 o'clock P.M., every Wednesday.
SCHEDULED TIMES FROM SAN FRANCISCO
TO NEW YORK
For Telegraphic Dispatches.........................Nine Days
For Letters.....................................Thirteen Days
Letters will be charged, between San Francisco
and Salt Lake City, $3 per half ounce and under,
and at that rate according to weight.
To all points beyond Salt Lake City, $5 per half ounce
and under, and at that rate according to weight.
Telegraphic Dispatches will be subject
to the same charges as letters.
All letters must be inclosed in stamped envelopes.
WM. W. FINNEY
Agent, C.O.P.E. Company

On the same day that this notice of overland express-mail service
via Pony Express appeared in the *Mountain Democrat* in Placerville,
California, March 20, 1860, another notice appeared in the *Sacramento Daily Union:*

OVERLAND EXPRESS—WE UNDERSTAND THAT ABOUT
TWO HUNDRED YOUNG MEN HAVE RESPONDED TO THE
ADVERTISEMENT OF THE AGENT MR. FINNEY FOR POST
RIDERS ON THE OVERLAND EXPRESS. THE REQUISITE
NUMBER HAVE BEEN ENGAGED.

Two days later the *Daily Union* reported that the first representatives
of the Central Overland Pony Express Company, twenty-five men
and one hundred horses and pack animals, started out from Sacramento to begin to stock the line eastward to Salt Lake City. The Pony
Express was scheduled to begin operation in less than two weeks.

On March 23, the *Daily Union* elaborated on the opening of the line, noting that Finney had purchased one hundred horses and twenty-nine mules. "They are California stock, and well adapted for riding and packing purposes." The *Daily Union* further noted that twenty-one men were going down to the line in anticipation of the opening of the fast-mail service. "The men and animals will be distributed between this city and Eagle Valley; the line to that point is to be stocked from Salt Lake." The distance of this route, Sacramento to Salt Lake City, was estimated to be seven hundred miles, a distance that could be covered in three and a half days at the rate of two hundred miles per day, according to the *Daily Union*.

The *Placer Herald* in Auburn, California, told readers during the same week something about the genesis of the service:

> This Express is a private enterprise, started by Messrs. Majors & Russell, of Leavenworth, Kansas, who have been heavy Government contractors. It does not receive assistance from Government, but depends upon the patronage of business men for maintenance . . . Day by Day the Atlantic and Pacific coasts are being brought closer and closer together. The opening of the Overland Mail route marked a new era in the page of California history—the establishment of the Overland express opens another leaf that points to the advancement and prosperity of the State. These lines are the avant couriers of the settlements of hardy and industrious people who, in good time will fill the waste plains of the great interior, and the heralds that announce the coming of the iron horse upon the great international highway, the Pacific Railroad.

While the California newspapers were eager for the Pony Express, they griped about the high price of news from the East. "We regret that the prices of telegraphic dispatches of news by this line has been placed at so high a figure as to preclude our publishing them . . . No paper without a fortune to back it, can afford the attending expense," complained the *Daily Appeal* in Marysville. Rates were four dollars per hundred words, according to the *Daily Appeal,* and the average cost of messages from the East would be about a hundred dollars. Small newspapers could not pay those fees.

Even so, editors were still enthusiastic about the fast mail. "This institution promises to be highly successful," predicted the *San Andreas Independent*.

All along the line, the news of progress was reported. California was always wildly enthusiastic about a fast-mail service linking it with the East. "A general desire seems to be prevalent for a more rapid and frequent communication between the citizens of the Atlantic and Pacific slopes of the glorious continent. The spirit and the necessities of the times appear to be pushing on this laudable and truly national object. Our eastern mail is now carried weekly from and to this city. And I suppose in a few weeks the 'Pony Express' will be inaugurated and in full blast, greatly decreasing the time, not the expense, of transmitting intelligence. This express is probably a prelude to a semi-weekly or daily central overland mail," observed the *San Francisco Herald* on Saturday morning, March 24, 1860.

Once the Pony Express left St. Joe or Sacramento, the rider vanished into the Great American Desert, a vast expanse separating East from West, where there were no means of rapid communication. Americans on either side of the continent did not know for days the fate of the man on the horse. Later, the eastbound and westbound riders reported that they had crossed paths just east of Salt Lake City but there is no record of them having spoken. It was only as the Pony pounded into the Sierra Nevada where telegraph lines had been extended that news of the horse and rider flashed into California. A series of joyful welcomings awaited the lone rider as he reached the Golden State.

The first glimpse of the Pony Express in action appeared on April 11, 1860, in the *Daily Alta California,* a San Francisco newspaper, two days before the first rider from the East reached Sacramento.

Adolph Sutro, a German-born mining engineer and entrepreneur who became fabulously wealthy in Nevada's Comstock Lode (and later mayor of San Francisco), was crossing the Sierra Nevada returning to California when he encountered a traveler. Sutro wrote in the newspaper that a week earlier, high in the mountains, in a blinding snowstorm, he had an unexpected encounter with a horseman in a hurry. "On the very summit we met a lonely rider dashing along at a tremendous rate. We wondered what could possibly induce him to go on through that gale, and thought it must be some very important business. It was the Pony Express." Sutro, who noted that two feet of fresh snow had fallen, had seen a rider headed east crossing the Sierra Nevada on the first run of the Pony Express.

The ferryboats linking Sacramento with San Francisco were detained to wait for the Pony Express if the courier reached Placerville in any reasonable time. The arrival of the first Pony Express in Sacramento was anticipated with giddy delight by the *Daily Bee*. "This is a fine impromptu demonstration on the part of our citizens, and it will be fun to see them ride, in John Gilpin or Tam O'Shanter style, helter-skelter, through the streets from the Fort in their endeavors to keep up with the renowned Pony. When you hear the guns firing and the bells ringing look out for it. We will hoist the American standard at the Bee office immediately on hearing the Plaza gun."

The first Pony Express from the East went through Placerville at two o'clock on the afternoon of April 13 ten days after leaving St. Joe. The main street was packed with people eager to welcome with the wildest cheers the rider from the East, according to the *Mountain Democrat*. Flags were displayed, ladies waved their handkerchiefs, Willson's Band, stationed on the balcony of the Cary House, "discoursed most eloquent music as the Pony Express shot like an arrow through the crowd, on its way to San Francisco." The rider stopped for seconds to change horses and was off as "the immense crowd that thronged the streets bade him a hearty God speed."

The evening after the first Pony Express arrived on the Pacific slope, the editors of the *Daily Bee* in Sacramento reflected on this momentous occasion:

The value to us of that mode of communication with the outer world, can hardly be estimated at present. It will prove—it has proved—the virtue of the Central route, and will advertise it to the world. We of Sacramento ought to do our part in sustaining this enterprise: but cheering will not do it. It must have something more substantial. The Pony could run very well the first time on the excitement of the moment—could strain his sinews to their greatest tension. Amid music and banners, and the shouts of the multitude: but he can't repeat and repeat on that pablum. He must have something more substantial—must be fed on oats and barley and hay, must be stabled and cared for kindly—and all that costs money. The Pony is not a bummer—no free luncher: he will not eat of your goods without offering to remunerate you. He is willing to earn his living in the seat of his skin, and will run your errands across the desert, quick as a zebra, if you will only say the word. He delights in honest industry, glories in being the connecting link between the lightnings on the great Atlantic and the growing Pacific, prides in conveying on his willing back, week by week, the world's current history, and feels his importance in the fact that people stand on tiptoe to look for and await his coming: but he is no chameleon—must live on something besides air—and to live he must eat, and to purchase him food he must have money.

The *Daily Bee* on that first running of the Pony Express implored its readers to back this venture. "Give him employment and he is your honored and very obliged humble and grateful servant . . . Send your letters by him . . . And he will become an institution in the land."

The *Daily Bee* quoted the *Red Bluff Beacon,* admonishing Californians to support the fast-mail service. The *Daily Bee* went so far as to encourage private citizens and businesses who could afford it to underwrite the Pony Express for a few months or a year. "One thing is patent—he ought to be sustained, and although he may not command success, he certainly deserves it."

The arrival of the first Pony Express rider in Sacramento was a cause for great public celebration. Impromptu, enormous crowds had assembled (with perhaps a little encouragement from the *Daily Union* and *Daily Bee)* to wave flags and cheer as the rider entered the California capital.

"The Pony Express achievement was the talk of the town," reported the *Daily Union* the day after its arrival.

The paper published an exclusive extra edition with news brought from the East by the Pony Express. The California Navigation Company, which operated the boats between Sacramento and San Francisco, announced that it would wait for the Pony Express.

A "cavalcade of citizens" went out to meet "the little traveler a short distance from the city and escort him into town," and fifteen Sacramento Hussars along with some eighty other horsemen lined the route into the city.

At 5:25 P.M. on April 13, a distant cloud of dust off toward the east could be observed from the center of Sacramento. Church towers and fire engine companies rang out "a merry peal of bells"—a feu de joie, the *Daily Bee* called it. The boys of Young America, No. 6, fired the cannon. Another artillery company answered with a volley of its own. The *Daily Union* could barely keep track of the ordnance salutes. "Amidst the firing and shooting, and wavings of hats and ladies' handkerchiefs, the pony—the veritable pony—was seen coming at a rattling pace down J street, surrounded by about thirty of the citizen deputation. The little fellow stretched his neck well into the race, and came at a rattling pace down the street, which was wild with excitement. A thick cloud of dust rolled over the heads of the party as it came dashing on in the most hopeless confusion."

The clerks in Dale & Co. placed their largest doll, replete with letters and papers in hand, on the back of a wooden pony and emblazoned it with the motto "Pony Express, Forever!" At Genella's Crockery Store, a sign was hung across the front of the business reading, "Hurrah for the Pony Express!—Hurrah for the Central Route!" The entire business district was a sea of American flags.

And by the time the Pony Express rider trotted up to the door of the telegraph office, the crowd was cheering, a scene of "confounded confusion, mingled fun and earnestness," reported the *Daily Union*.

The reporter at the *Daily Union* thought to interview the incoming rider, William Hamilton, who had been the first rider headed east out of Sacramento when the Pony Express began and had connected with the westbound rider in the town of Sportsman's Hall for the last leg of the trip. Hamilton, who was riding a roan that belonged to Rightmire's Stable over on K Street, told the *Daily Union* that the wild welcome he received had upset his horse. He said that he believed the Pony Express would make even better time when the roads dried up; they were muddy.

For all the celebration, there were only eight letters for Sacramento, two for the *Daily Union*, one for Governor John G. Downey. But that hardly mattered to the crowds in front of the telegraph office that spring afternoon.

A man on a horse—perishable flesh, as the editorial writers would call it—had just crossed two thousand miles of still-wild North America, traveling day and night in not ideal weather to bring in record time news linking the East and the West.

As William Lightfoot Visscher noted nearly half a century later, this was an event that rocked the nation.

The steamer *Antelope* took Hamilton and his cargo on to San

Francisco, where the first Pony Express to cross the continent arrived at 12:38 A.M. On April 14, the reception in San Francisco, even at that late hour, was jubilant.

The *San Francisco Bulletin* captured that mood. "It took seventy-five ponies to make the trip from Missouri to California in 10-1/2 days, but the last one—the little fellow who came down in the Sacramento boat this morning had the vicarious glory of them all. Upon him an enthusiastic crowd were disposed to shower all their compliments. He was the veritable Hippogriff who shoved a continent behind his hoofs so easily; who snuffed up sandy plains, sent lakes and mountains, prairies and forests, whizzing behind him, like one great river rushing westward . . ."

The *San Francisco Herald* described the citizens as "electrified" by the arrival of the Pony Express, which had brought twenty-five letters across the continent to recipients in the bay city. Announcements were made in public places, including theaters, that the Pony was coming. Some two thousand citizens turned out in the middle of the night to tend bonfires in the streets. Men shouted themselves hoarse, the newspapers reported. A lady took off her bonnet and tied its ribbons around the pony's neck. The fire companies paraded, and the California Band saluted the arrival of the Pony by playing "See, the Conquering Hero Comes."

The significance of the arrival of the first Pony Express in "the new El Dorado" was instantly grasped in California. In San Francisco, the *Daily Evening Bulletin* explained to its readers the importance of what had just taken place, calling the arrival of the Pony Express "an unparalleled feat." "California may be said to have been brought from ten to twelve days nearer to the rest of the civilized world."

To drive the point home with its readers, the *Daily Evening Bulletin* noted that the ocean mail from New York—which had departed on March 20—hadn't reached San Francisco until April 12. "This fact shows in bold relief the superiority of the land routes of the transmission of the mails; and we do not think the Government will long neglect, now that so convincing a demonstration has been made of this superiority, to establish a daily line of stages, and discontinue the contracts with the expensive ocean routes altogether. The money spent in carrying the mails by Panama, over foreign territory, would soon put the roads across the plains in excellent condition for stage traveling." In the streets of San Francisco and Sacramento and in the small towns, too, the talk was all of the pony.

Romance and enthusiasm aside, California understood even in the first weeks of the Pony Express that this was an experiment—desperately in need of public support. A week after the first Pony Express rider galloped into Sacramento, the *Daily Bee* was exhorting the citizens of the California capital to honor the messenger and appreciate what had been accomplished. On April 20, the next courier was to leave for the East, and the *Daily Bee* thought it appropriate to hail him on his way:

> This little fellow will leave to-night, again, on his long journey across the Great American Desert to carry tidings of weal and woe to other lands, but more especially to do little chores for us with our Atlantic brethren. To commence this Enterprise alone without consultation and on the spur of the moment—but then he goes on the spur, and his whole length, too—is proof of his spunk, and has been the means of commanding for him the esteem, nay, the admiration, of the whole people. Let us encourage him. Give him a chance to earn his bread—give him employment and keep him on the track—that he may soon lead the iron horse with heart of fire and breath of smoke in his wake. He will be here at midnight—for, like the Wandering Jew, he when once started on his course knows no rest by night or by day—and our citizens, after close of business this evening, who can find something to say to eastern correspondents or eastern friends, and can stand the press, should drop a line by the Pony and remunerate him for his labor.

The *Daily Bee* took the opportunity in hailing the Pony Express to scold Californians who failed to see the benefit of such a service and support it, adding:

> We know of some Sacramentans, and have heard of several, for whose correspondence the sloth of Uncle Sam is at present sufficient—at least they can get along with it without pecuniary loss—who have determined to send a letter a month at least by the Pony, just for the sake of giving him five dollars.

Let our citizens exhibit a little of this spirit for a while, or until the enterprise has been well started, and after that, it will doubtless be able to go on, on the strength of such communications as will pay to send by it. Of course it is an experiment, which will not be kept up many months at a loss, without a hope of remuneration in the not distant future; and if we would keep it going, we must do at least our share in its support. Let Sacramento to-night give the pony forty to fifty letters, and show its spirit.

On May 5, one month after the Pony Express began operations, the *Territorial Enterprise* in Virginia City, Nevada Territory, was bally-hooing the record time the courier was making. The *Enterprise* believed even after only a few weeks of service that the Pony Express had demonstrated the feasibility of the Central Route. "The rapid trans-continental communication now demonstrated beyond a doubt to be feasible, should induce Congress to grant to this company a mail contract between some point on the Missouri River and San Francisco."

But the success in the West of the Pony Express would soon be tempered, not by the failure of the mounted couriers, but by events far beyond the control of Russell, Majors & Waddell, events that reminded Pony Express enthusiasts that even if the route was proving successful, it was still crossing "a wild, uninhabited expanse." The *Territorial Enterprise* would have an even bigger news story to report less than a week after it trumpeted the triumph of the Pony Express. The Paiute Indians were about to go on the warpath.

"Persuit"—*Pony Express rider fleeing Indians, ca. 1860.*

Four

――――

PYRAMID LAKE

The accounts received at the time were greatly exaggerated,
if not in many essential particulars wholly unfounded.
—*San Francisco Daily Bulletin*, May 13, 1860

The Williams brothers were from Maine. We do not know much
about them except that they kept Williams Station about ten miles
east of the Pony Express stop known as Buckland's Station on a knoll
east of the Big Bend of the Carson River in Nevada. Historians dis-
agree on whether Williams Station was a Pony Express stop. But after
the first week of May in 1860, no one stopped there except to bury
the dead.

Some writers describe Williams Station as a ranch. Ranch could
mean almost anything in the mid-nineteenth century. Some writers
call it Millers Station. And some call it Williams Ranch at Millers
Station.

This is hard country, lonely even today, and we can only wonder
what illusions of wealth or a new beginning brought the three
Williams brothers from the green hills of the Pine Tree State to this
dusty outpost in the Great Basin. Two of them died here one cold
evening in early May.

James O. Williams was the only member of the trio to survive, so
we have filtered through the hearsay history of early Nevada only his
version of the events at Williams Station. James O. Williams was the
first on the scene. According to many historians, he had been away

from the station on business. One writer says he was camping out. Another writer says he was tending stock, while yet another says that James O. Williams was consorting with a certain Spanish woman on the evening in question.

We know that when James O. Williams returned to Williams Station early on May 8, he found his brothers, Daniel, twenty-two, and Oscar, thirty-three, both dead. (The *San Francisco Daily Bulletin* names one of the deceased Williams brothers Calvin.) They had company in death, too. Some versions say there were three bodies burned beyond recognition, others say five. In addition to the Williams brothers, Samuel Sullivan, who was twenty-five and from New York, James Fleming, twenty-five, also from New York, and a man identified only as Dutch Phil were also dead. Williams Station had been burned to the ground. The stock was gone, too. All accounts note that James was terrified.

Nevada historians agree that the events at Williams Station on May 7 were the trigger for the so-called Pyramid Lake Indian War, which is variously called the Paiute Indian War, the Pyramid Lake Uprising, or the Washoe Indian War. The early Nevada historian Myron T. Angel, writing in 1881, makes no explanation as to why the Indians would descend on Williams Station and slaughter its occupants. The next history of Nevada, published in 1904, makes no attempt, either. But subsequent versions of territorial history fill in the blanks.

James O. Williams did not tarry at Williams Station but rode his horse west as fast as he could ride the ten miles to Buckland's Station, also on the Carson River. In this grim and barren country, behind every high sagebush James O. Williams from Maine imagined Paiute Indians. He had good reason to be terrified. The dead at Williams Station had been terribly mutilated and tortured before they were killed, he reported. They may have been burned alive—a practice not uncommon among the Paiutes, who liked to take their time executing an enemy. The British explorer Captain Sir Richard Burton, who had an insatiable curiosity about such practices, reports in his account of crossing Nevada later that year that such cruelties were as horrible as anything he had seen in Africa. Live burials were another Paiute custom.

James O. Williams reached Buckland's Station in excellent time, stopped to sound the alarm, and galloped on west toward Virginia

City—then one of the largest concentrations of whites in what was soon to be the Nevada Territory. He stopped en route to warn the occupants of Dayton and Silver Spring that the Paiutes were on the warpath. One account of his ride notes that "his report caused the wildest excitement." The *San Francisco Bulletin* complicates this tale by claiming that a Pony Express rider brought the bad news from Buckland's Station to Carson City.

Dan DeQuille, the nom de plume of William Wright, one of the American West's most celebrated nineteenth-century journalists, agreed with the *Bulletin*. "A Pony rider—the mail was then being carried across the plains and over the Sierras to California by Pony Express—came in and reported that the Piute Indians, till then friendly toward the whites, had burned Williams' Station on the Carson River . . . And had murdered two or three men whom they found in charge," DeQuille wrote in his definitive account of the glory days of the Comstock Lode, *The Big Bonanza*.

Carson City responded to the news of the massacre immediately. "A large dinner-bell was rung violently by an excited individual, who, with great outcry, announced the same to the people, invoking them to meet and adopt measures for the speedy punishment of the Indians," the *Bulletin* noted.

Bad news traveled fast in the West via telegraph from Virginia City to California, where the *Sacramento Daily Union* of May 9 ran an account of the events at Williams Station. "Last night a most horrid massacre was perpetrated by the Indians below the Great Bend of the Carson. J. Williams arrived at Buckland's near the bend, and gave information of the murder of his two brothers and five other men, at the same hour, and the burning of the house after or during the perpetration of this shocking butchery." The *Union* quoted Williams as saying at least twelve or thirteen other whites in the area had apparently been murdered, too. "The Indians are about five hundred strong, and all mounted. They pursued him [J. Williams] to within six miles of Buckland's and gave up the chase."

The western historian Ferol Egan, whose *Sand in a Whirlwind: The Paiute Indian War of 1860* provides a detailed examination of these events, observed that the tales were much embellished. Most historians seem to agree that the party of Indians who attacked Williams Station numbered nine—somewhat fewer than the five hundred Paiutes whom James O. Williams claimed were chasing him as he rode west on May 8. Some historians later argued that the Indians were Bannocks, allies of the Paiutes. The *Bulletin*'s dubious correspondent reported that the number of Indians thought to be involved was increasing. By the morning after the news first reached Carson City, citizens believed at least one thousand savages were about to descend upon them.

In fact, no Indians were chasing James O. Williams when he rode hysterically across western Nevada that spring day. But the consequences of the attack on Williams Station and the subsequent events were real enough.

The *Bulletin*'s correspondent reported that attempts to reason with the mob planning revenge were hopeless. "Reason and remonstrance were alike unavailing." The *Bulletin* also noted that the Indians in the area did not have a history of violence and that whites who knew Indians thought the events at Williams Station needed to be thoroughly investigated before any action was taken. No one listened to these arguments.

LeRoy Hafen, author of *The Overland Mail,* believed the events that began at Williams Station could have finished off the Pony Express hardly before it was started. The fast-mail service—enjoying a flattering press in California newspapers and generating, if not much real income, a bonanza of publicity—had been up and running for less than five weeks when the Pyramid Lake Indian War broke out. The attack on Williams Station and its aftermath halted mail service, costing Russell, Majors & Waddell yet more money. The firm could not guarantee mail delivery but still had to maintain a vast chain of stations with supplies for horses and riders all across the West.

A precise chronology of the occurrences of early May 1860 is somewhat skeletal, but we know that the alarm was sounded across western Nevada. DeQuille, who spent four decades in the Comstock, recalled that the killings at Williams Station "paralyzed every industry and alike brought business and prospecting to a stand."

The killings and burning of Williams Station were the result of what DeQuille decorously describes as an incident when someone at Williams Station took several Indian women hostage and kept them in a cave for several days.

DeQuille, an associate of Mark Twain's on the *Territorial Enterprise,* was the source of much of this information about the Paiute Indian war. He was living in the territory at the time; his knowledge of early Nevada was encyclopedic.

An attempt by one of the Indian women's husbands to rescue them was unsuccessful. This Indian went for help, and his comrades killed the occupants of Williams Station and burned it down. The presumption here must be that the women were raped and the Paiutes—who had suffered a bad winter, were short on food, and were tiring of the increasing presence of whites in their country—had reached their limit. Later versions claim that the Indian women were mere girls who had been out gathering piñon nuts (a food staple for the Paiutes) when they were abducted and held in a root cellar under a barn at Williams Station.

Relations between Indians and whites had never been good in Nevada. The first recorded incident of the cruelty of whites venturing into Paiute country was in August 1832 on the Humboldt River when a mountain man named Joe Meek shot and killed a Shoshone Indian for no reason. When asked if the Indian had stolen anything, Meek supposedly replied, "No, but he looked as if he was going to." Shoot first, ask questions later was the standard practice for whites dealing with Indians in Nevada. The year after Joe Meek shot an Indian for looking like he might steal something, members of another expedition shot dozens of Indians (some writers claim as many as seventy-five) without provocation, also along the Humboldt River. Three decades of wanton violence against Indians in Nevada preceded the Pyramid Lake Indian War of 1860. In addition, white encroachment in Nevada was wiping out piñon nuts. Starvation was a real issue in the spring of 1860.

Major Frederick Dodge, Indian agent for the Paiutes, left no doubt in the matter, reporting to the government that "to intruders on the reserve and their gross outrages on Indian women lie one great cause of the present trouble."

The Indians who wiped out Williams Station (Paiutes or Bannocks) headed north to Pyramid Lake, where a large concentration of Paiutes was camped, according to most narrators, to discuss what the tribe was going to do about white encroachment. Myron T. Angel's early history of Nevada, while omitting the grim details and reasons for the Williams Station attack, notes that the Indians were not on the warpath but bent on specific revenge for something that had been done to them. Angel reports that the party of nine Indians passed at least one ranch without molesting the occupants and notes that years later Indians who participated in the attack were interviewed and indicated that they were not hostile to all whites. But the news that Williams Station had been destroyed—and the reason for that action—provoked all-out war between the settlers and Indians. The historian Raymond Settle claimed that at least nine other whites were killed in Nevada within a few days of the Williams Station incident, including station keepers for the Pony Express. DeQuille agreed with this death toll.

Perhaps one of the reasons for James O. Williams's terror and the alarm he aroused in his fellow settlers in western Nevada was the knowledge that the whites in the area were unprepared to fight an Indian war. There were few if any U.S. troops in Nevada and no fort (Fort Churchill, near Buckland's Station was built later that year as a result of the Paiute uprising). There was, however, Major William O. Ormsby, who decided that action must be taken. The major assembled an "expeditionary force" of volunteers which included a few real soldiers but mostly miners and ranchers, many recruited from the saloons of Carson City. Eyewitnesses later reported that many members of the column were drunk. DeQuille described the volunteers as "poorly armed, badly mounted and almost wholly unorganized." Reports of the expedition—there were four groups of volunteers—indicate it was regarded as a lark. Reports also claim that participants rode through the streets of Carson City shouting "an Indian for breakfast and a pony to ride." Even Snowshoe Thompson, the cross-country skiing Norwegian mailman, went along. They were headed up to Pyramid Lake to shoot a few Indians, rather like duck hunting. This turned out to be an enormous mistake. "The volunteers had more enthusiasm than discretion. They went out not as an organized company under discipline and with responsible leaders, but as a party might go out to hunt wolves," noted former governor James G. Scrugham in a 1935 history of Nevada.

DeQuille did not think much of the expeditionary force or its motives. "The majority of the men thought that there would not be much of a fight. They thought they should probably have a bit of a skirmish with the Indians, kill a few of them, capture a lot of ponies, and on the whole have a rather good time. Major Ormsby and a few of the leading men and old settlers doubtless knew the Indians better but most of the recent arrivals from California who volunteered for the occasion thought it would be a sort of pleasure excursion. They were woefully disappointed," DeQuille recalled in *The Big Bonanza.*

After first stopping at Williams Station on May 10 to bury the dead (where they could find only three bodies), the expeditionary force swung north to Pyramid Lake, a two-day ride. The party consisted of 105 men, most of whom had no experience fighting Indians and no military discipline. There was no leadership, and they appear not to have scouted their enemy. That might explain why late on the afternoon of May 12 they rode into a canyon a few miles south of Pyramid Lake (near the present town of Nixon). DeQuille reported that the Indians, who were sophisticated in military tactics (they fell back, drawing their enemy forward), were too much for the whites. The Paiutes easily picked them off, leaving, according to DeQuille and others, at least seventy-six dead (some say seventy-nine) and many of the remaining wounded. (According to Angel's first history of Nevada, three Indians were killed in the battle. However, a Paiute Indian, Johnny Calico, who was twelve years old at the time of the battle, told a historian in 1924 that no Paiutes died in the first battle at Pyramid Lake but three were wounded.)

There were heroes of the affray. The *San Francisco Herald* reported that Snowshoe Thompson, "the former indefatigable mountain expressman, fought like a tiger, and when he had lost his horse, was about to be tomahawked by the Indians, when a fine charger came galloping by, upon whose back he escaped unhurt."

Many histories of Indian wars in the West make scant reference to Pyramid Lake, although the disaster (83 percent dead) ranks near Custer's Last Stand in terms of casualties.

Indians interviewed two decades later for Nevada historian Angel's book reported that the whites who attacked the Paiutes (there were Bannocks and Shoshones there, too) scattered in panic when the Indian assault began. Indians who had been at the battle claimed that the whites threw down their guns and begged for mercy.

Dan DeQuille recalled that Paiutes chased some of the survivors up to fifteen and twenty miles. "The trail of retreating volunteers was strewn with dead bodies, saddles, guns, knives, pistols, and blankets, thrown away when the chase became desperate and every man was trying to save his own life."

The survivors of Pyramid Lake scattered, riding across the countryside in hysterical retreat. Some were found a day or two later at several locations. Major Ormsby, badly wounded, attempted to surrender to the Paiutes, who, not comprehending the civilities of warfare, killed him.

By the time this alarming news reached Virginia City and other points in the Nevada Territory, the terror that James O. Williams had triggered a few days earlier seemed mild. Angel wrote that news of the military disaster created "a panic of the most remarkable character." All accounts agree that pandemonium broke out in the Washoe region and whites barricaded themselves in the few fortified places they could find.

In Silver City, terrified citizens built a wooden cannon, but, a modern historian of Nevada noted, "fortunately for any potential operators it was never fired." DeQuille recalled that the cannon was filled with scrap metal and that "after the war was over, some parties one day concluded to fire this wooden gun off. They took it from the fort and carried it to a considerable distance back on the hill, rigged a slow match to it, and then got out of the way.

"When the explosion finally came, the air was filled in all directions, for many rods, with pieces of scrap iron, iron bands, and chunks of wood. Had it ever been fired in the fort it would have killed every man near it."

Settlers and miners fled the territory with, in the words of DeQuille, "many men suddenly remembering that they had business on the other side of the Sierra Nevada Mountains." Fear was so endemic in Nevada, according to Angel, that "many who remained in the Territory were so badly frightened that they would have been useless if the Indians had made further advance."

In Virginia City, a Dutch miner, hoping to escape the Indian attack, had himself lowered to a depth of fifty feet into a mine shaft where he could hide. But after he was down in the mine, the Dutchman's partner panicked and ran off, forgetting his comrade. "The poor Teuton roosted at the bottom of the shaft for three days and nights before he was discovered, and was almost dead when taken out," DeQuille reported.

The California newspapers of the period were full of what they admitted were "varied and discrepant rumors relating to the catastrophe at Pyramid Lake." Preposterous reports of Indian forces numbering as many as five thousand circulated. The citizens of Virginia City voted unanimously to suspend mining business for sixty days, effectively preventing claim jumping. This opened the floodgate, and a significant evacuation of the territory occurred.

While these events were going on, the most famous ride to take place in the history of the Pony Express began. The rider was Robert Haslam, a native of England, who had come to Utah as a teenager, part of the great Mormon migration. He was twenty that year.

Haslam, who was known as Pony Bob—a famous nickname on the frontier that would follow him around all of his life—was the regular rider for the Pony Express between Friday's Station (what is today Lake Tahoe) on the Nevada-California border and Buckland's Station, near Williams Station. Haslam did not know when he rode out of Friday's Station that he would become a legend in his own lifetime.

Reports on the Pyramid Lake Indian uprising seem to agree that Pony Bob left Friday's Station on May 9, riding east with the mail. He probably knew nothing of the killings and burning of Williams Station until he reached Carson City late on May 9 or early May 10. Major Ormsby's ill-conceived expeditionary force had already taken the field and had taken along, too, all the fresh horses in Carson City. So Pony Bob, being resourceful and independent, merely fed and watered his own mount and continued to ride east with the mail. He rode seventy-five miles to Buckland's Station without incident.

At Buckland's Station, W. C. Marley, the station keeper, whom some writers identify as an official with the Pony Express, and Johnson Richardson, the relief rider, were described as being "in something of a panic."

Richardson, in what is cited as the only incident of its kind in the history of the Pony Express, refused to ride. The expression often used is "dumped the blanket," a term for cowardice. Discretion was not regarded as the better part of valor in this country, and a rider was expected to ride his route. It was, however, permissible to quit after completing the run.

Marley reportedly offered Pony Bob fifty dollars to continue to ride. Many narrators include stirring dialogue between the two men. Some include dialogue between Pony Bob and his horse. Some question whether Marley would have been authorized to make such an offer and wonder where he would have gotten fifty dollars.

Haslam, we are told, felt he was duty-bound to continue to ride, and so off he went east across the alkali flats and desert to Sand Springs Station, where he changed horses and continued on to Cold Springs and then Smith or Smith's Creek, having ridden 190 miles without a rest—between two and three times the normal route of a Pony Express rider. This is the bleakest and most inhospitable country along the route, even if a rider is not expecting Paiute Indians.

Narrators of Pony Bob's famous ride tend to agree that he slept for eight hours at Smith's Creek Station and then took the westbound mochila, which had just arrived, back along the line (seeming to indicate that service had not stopped at this point).

At Cold Springs Station, Haslam found that the Paiutes had been there within the past day, the station keeper had been murdered, the station burned, and the stock run off. There were no fresh horses. There was good water at Cold Springs Station, so Haslam watered his horse and kept riding. This was pretty open country, too, and not quite as dangerous as some of the terrain Haslam would cross.

Back at Sand Springs Station, Haslam found the lone stock tender faithfully minding the store, blissfully unaware that the Paiute Indian War was fast closing in on him. Haslam told him what he had seen and persuaded the man (probably not much persuasion was required) to accompany him west. Most writers agree that this probably saved the stock tender's life.

When Pony Bob and the stock tender reached Carson Sink Station, they found fifteen terrified men barricaded in the station house. They were mostly survivors of the Pyramid Lake disaster. This would mean that Haslam arrived at Carson Sink on or after May 13.

Haslam left the stock tender with the fifteen men at Carson Sink and with a fresh horse rode on to Buckland's Station, where legend dictates he arrived only three and a half hours off schedule—this at the height of the Paiute uprising.

W. C. Marley—he of the fifty-dollar bonus—was astonished to see Pony Bob still alive and in the saddle two days later. The historian Raymond Settle claims Marley was "so overjoyed to see him back alive that he doubled the bonus promised him." Again, the question of where this money was coming from arises. Settle uses the word "promised"—an important word to consider in dealing with Russell, Majors & Waddell and matters involving money. No account indicates whether Pony Bob ever got a nickel for his efforts. But we do know that Haslam, whom one historian calls the Riding Fool, continued to ride west after resting for an hour and a half at Buckland's Station. Haslam rode on to Carson City and back to his point of origin at Friday's Station without incident. He had ridden—accounts agree—some 380 miles in thirty-six hours. No account actually mentions that he ever saw a Paiute Indian. Apparently, the Paiute Indians had been busy with Major Ormsby's amateur expeditionary force.

Newspapers at the time were busy, too, reporting the excitement of the Pyramid Lake Indian War and the fear of Paiutes, so there are no reports of Pony Bob's ride.

In late May, a combined expeditionary force made up of about 750 volunteers and regulars, many from California, seeking to avenge Pyramid Lake, took the field. They followed the Paiutes across Nevada, and in the course of several engagements as many as 160 Indians were reportedly killed and some fifty horses captured. The force disbanded in early June.

There were two immediate results of the Paiute Indian War: Fort Churchill, about one mile from Buckland's Station, was established that July to impose some military presence in the country, and the Pony Express, to make up for lost business, increased its cross-country rides from once to twice a week. James O. Williams from Maine is not heard from again.

Assessments of the impact of the Paiute Indian War on the Pony Express are contradictory. Historian Raymond Settle says the service was not regularly resumed until July 7 (depending on the writer, service was interrupted from anywhere from three weeks to two months), and there were frequent skirmishes with Paiutes for many months afterward. The *Mountain Democrat* in Placerville, California, told its readers in late June that the Pony would resume running, leaving the Sierra Nevada foothills town, on July 4. In passing, the *Mountain Democrat* exhorted its readers to support the Pony. "It is an expensive enterprise worthy of the most liberal patronage, and the people of Placerville, who are materially benefitted by it should not be backward in encouraging it."

Nearly two weeks later California newspapers were reporting that W. W. Finney was attempting to restock the line in Nevada and that a number of stations had been destroyed. On August 13, the *Sacra-*

mento Daily Union, quoting the *Territorial Enterprise,* said that the stations built by Finney to replace those destroyed by Indians were sixty feet square with stone or adobe walls "designed to serve as forts, if necessary . . ."

Asa Merrill Fairfield, an old California settler who wrote *Fairfield's Pioneer History of Lassen County California to 1870,* which chronicled the Pyramid Lake Indian War and its aftermath, noted that mail service "was not very regular during the Indian troubles of this year." The Paiute Indian uprising was widely reported to have cost the firm $75,000—more debt for Russell, Majors & Waddell. What is generally agreed upon is that the Pony Express and its way stations remained targets for Indian vengeance long after the military formalities were concluded.

To reestablish service and secure the line—and restock burned-out stations—Finney and Bolivar Roberts, the Pony Express supervisors in charge on the western end of the line, are reported to have appealed to the citizens of Sacramento for help. (This was common in the early days of California. The citizens of San Francisco and Sacramento had been asked to rescue the Donner party, too.) Donors raised $1,500 to pay for men and rifles. Roberts's party went east on June 9 and met Major Howard Egan's party from Salt Lake City on June 16 at Roberts Creek (near present-day Eureka), reestablishing the line.

The incidents surrounding the Paiute Indian uprising were not carefully chronicled at the time, and with the passage of years there was a lot of confusion. Even Pony Bob Haslam, who was there, a hero who saved the day, told Alexander Majors more than thirty years later that the uprising took place eight months after the Pony Express began operations. This would have placed the events in October/November of 1860. Pony Bob may have been simply confused, recalling these events from such a distance—or he may have been acknowledging that the Paiute Indian War lasted longer than is generally believed.

When the British adventurer Captain Sir Richard Burton came down the line in the early fall of 1860, he reported seeing the ravages of the Indian uprising, including the remains of burned-out stations and dead bodies, some partially eaten by wolves. Burton also reported that the Paiute Indian War was still the talk of Nevada. Always looking forward to some excitement, Burton wrote in his diary that one of his disappointments was not getting a chance to fight Indians, noting that the threat of Indian attack was often discussed by his companions. Pioneers along this lonely route traveled in groups. Burton found Egan's Station in eastern Nevada near the Utah border "reduced to a chimney stack and a few charred posts." This was five months after Williams Station was burned. News of Ormsby's military disaster had also reached Burton.

On September 30, 1860, Burton and members of his party were traveling in what is now western Utah between Fish Springs and Willow Creek, a particularly godforsaken stretch of countryside. (There are still no paved roads hereabouts.) Burton recorded in his diary for that date that about 11:00 A.M. "we met the party commanded by Lieut. Weed, two subaltern officers, ninety dragoons, and ten wagons; they had been in the field since May, and had done good service against the Gosh-Yutas [Indians]." The meeting proved a good opportunity for a drink.

"We halted and 'liquored up,' and, after American fashion, talked politics in the wilderness," reported the thirsty traveler, who says no more about encountering these American troops who had been crossing and recrossing Utah and Nevada to establish peace and maintain the overland stage and mail route in the spring and summer of 1860.

The troops Burton met had left Camp Floyd, then one of the most vital military installations in the West—about forty miles south of Salt Lake City—on May 26 "to look after the Indians on the California Mail Route who have been committing depredations," in the words of one narrator of the expedition.

The troops were under the command of Lieutenant Stephen Weed, an 1855 West Point graduate who had seen service in the West. Weed, later a brigadier general in the Union army, would be killed at Gettysburg during the Civil War.

A participant in the expedition was Private Charles A. Scott, who would celebrate his thirtieth birthday marching across the deserts of Nevada and Utah that summer. He had the self-discipline to keep a diary during the nearly five-month-long trek across the wilds of Nevada and Utah at the time of the Paiute Indian War. Scott seems unusually literate for a common soldier, making frequent allusions to the classics in his dispatches, *Don Quixote* being a favorite.

A native of Baltimore, Scott had led a colorful life. He had been in and out of the army, had prospected unsuccessfully for gold in California in the mid-1850s and had joined the military adventurer William Walker in his expedition to Nicaragua. Scott's wanderings led him back into the army in 1857 where he joined the Utah expedition.

Scott's diary—which covers the period from May 26, 1860, until early October of that year—is amusing and full of rich detail.

"No rest from the mosquitos," Scott reports one day. "Nearly tormented to death by mosquitos," he complained on another date.

Scott cheerfully reports that when he was given responsibility, placed in charge of the ambulance wagon, he broke open the company's liquor supply and got quite drunk with his men. He then wrote a lively, liquored-up account of his impressions of soldiering in the desert.

He regretted that he and his fellow soldiers could not join in Fourth of July revelry in Carson City because the commanding officer felt the troops were not dressed properly.

Scott describes Carson City as "a very lively little place and reminds one very much of the mining towns of California in the early days, there is the same degree of lawlessness, drinking, swearing, whooping and hallooing, the same Gamblers, Blacklegs and Sharpers, and it only needs the Fandango to complete the picture."

With military precision, Scott noted weather conditions and that the availability of grass, wood, and water was erratic along the route. Often the livestock went thirsty for long periods of time.

It is plain from Scott's diary that Indian troubles remained a constant threat into the fall of 1860 for all overland travelers, including the riders of the Pony Express. This differs from many histories of the Pony Express which suggest that Indian troubles only briefly interfered with the service.

Scott noted that the troops were nervous; they were expecting trouble. At Robert's Creek they charged a party of horsemen—a full-blown cavalry charge—whom they believed to be Indians only to find that they were white men from California. Every distant, hard-to-distinguish rider in the desert seemed to indicate trouble.

Scott wrote about numerous encounters with Pony Express riders who were moving back and forth across Nevada and Utah, providing a great deal of information about Indians for the troops. He also reported on several raids of Pony Express stations by Indians.

In early June, Scott wrote that a Pony Express rider at Willow Springs had been shot through the hand and his mule killed from under him by Indians who then cut off the mule's ears as a trophy. A day later, Scott noted that a Pony Express rider reported that the station at Antelope had been overrun by Indians. At Deep Creek Station, about a week later, the army took as prisoner an Indian nicknamed Leatherhead, who had been shot once in the thigh and three times in the head. Scott said the wounded Indian survived overnight and pulled a hatchet on his guard before he was shot once more and killed. Many stations across the countryside had been destroyed, usually burned, and the stock run off or stolen, Scott recounted.

On August 11, Scott wrote a detailed account of a skirmish between his company and some two hundred Indians in eastern Nevada. The troops were approaching remote Egan Station, located in a canyon, when they met a Pony Express rider galloping for help. The rider told the troops that the nearby station was surrounded by a large party of hostile Indians and that they had taken the station keepers prisoner. As the troops charged toward the station, a few unarmed Indians scattered, while the rest stood their ground.

"The action became general and quite a lively firing kept up for about an hour. The Indians retreating to the hills and rocks where four or five of them were killed at long distance . . . Two or three more must have been wounded as we saw them carrying off several bodies," Scott noted, adding that three of his comrades were wounded in the action. "All hands kept watch during the night, but nothing occurred to disturb us."

Although Dan DeQuille, with the support of his colleague at the *Territorial Enterprise,* Mark Twain, wrote a detailed and balanced account of the events of Pyramid Lake as early as 1876, no early historian of Nevada seems to have read it. The circumstances surrounding the killings and burning of Williams Station remained confusing.

But DeQuille was not the only narrator of the period whose observations were long overlooked. A correspondent from the *San Francisco Herald* who signed his dispatches "Tennessee"—thought to be William Doyle Malloy—raised some interesting questions. Writing in the *Herald* less than two weeks after the battle at Pyramid Lake,

Tennessee said the problems with the Paiutes had a lot to do with "grog shops" kept by unsavory opportunists at the end of the immigrant trail. Williams Station was such a place. He also wondered why, if the Paiutes wanted all-out war with the whites in Nevada, only Williams Station was attacked and burned. It was Tennessee's observation that the keepers of such stations were rascals and thieves whose dishonest business practices were most probably to blame for the Indian troubles.

Tennessee added further complications to the "Williams Station massacre" by reporting certain troubling facts about the scene of the slaughter. He claimed that only three men were slain, that they appeared to have been killed with an ax while asleep, and that the house was then set on fire. Nothing was taken except money. Guns were not taken and provisions in the nearby storehouse were not stolen. The stock had not been driven off, either. "No other place had been attacked, nor had any persons besides these been murdered," Tennessee told his readers.

"On observing these facts, several of the whites most conversant with the Indian wants and mode of warfare, satisfied that the killing was not their work, declined to prosecute the inquiry further . . . Perhaps others would have followed their example, had they not happened to find an Indian knife not far off, and been led to suspect these poor creatures were guilty from the fact that they saw none about in the neighborhood."

Tennessee believed that hysteria and inexperience with Indians held sway and that the Indians had nothing to do with the attack on Williams Station. He concluded that the attack at Williams Station was committed by whites. Newspaper stories also quoted Judge John Cradlebaugh, a prominent citizen in the territory who rode out to Williams Station with Ormsby's party. Cradlebaugh, noting that no suspicious Indians could be found in the area, blamed the killings on whites or Shoshones, Indians who had fled the area.

Tennessee reported in the *San Francisco Herald:* "The house was evidently set on fire to conceal, so far as might be, the manner of the killing. No perceptible trail or other Indian signs were to be found. None of the inhabitants either above or below Williams' had been troubled, nor had any attempts been made to run off their stock— facts strongly tending to show that the aborigines had nothing to do with this atrocious murder."

The questions of guilt, observed Tennessee, had not been conclusively established. But there were theories that the correspondent of the *Herald* noted. One rumor making the rounds, according to Tennessee, was that "a well-known but disreputable and worthless fellow named 'Yank,' with perhaps one or two of his equally worthless companions, went to Williams' and engaged in gambling—a pastime that seems to be much in vogue at that place. This fellow, it is related, lost all his money, and afterwards his animals, playing with those at the house."

Tennessee reported the rumor that Yank thought he had been cheated and committed the murders to recover his money, then set the fire to cover his tracks.

Tennessee also introduced the theory that James O. Williams was away on the evening in question consorting with "a certain Spanish woman" and thus escaped the fate of his brothers.

Tennessee's dispatches in the *San Francisco Herald* argued forcefully that the events leading up to the Pyramid Lake Indian War had little or nothing to do with Indians. It was really the work of grogshop rascals and the hysteria of mob rule. "How humiliating to look back over the work of the past five days, and see what disaster to business, what disgrace to our national character, what widespread prejudice to our interests and honor, if not danger to our citizens, are sure to ensue when timid, untruthful and inexperienced men get control of, and give direction to public affairs!"

The Comings and Goings of the Pony Express
by Frederic S. Remington.

Five

"ORPHANS PREFERRED" AND "THE WORST IMPS OF SATAN"

In those days I did not know what it was to be tired.
—Thomas Owen King

The riders of the Pony Express lived rough, ate beans and bacon and corn bread, and drank black coffee. They slept when they could in shelters often worse than those constructed to house their horses.

"Riding express had more hard work than fun in it," William Campbell, a rider, remembered. "We got exciting adventures at times to help keep things more interesting than prodding oxen along the dusty roads; but our work was more strenuous than freighting. It took sheer grit and endurance at times to carry the mail through."

Once the mochila left St. Joe or Sacramento it was to never stop. The instructions were quite clear on this point. Regardless of the weather, day or night, sandstorms or snowstorms, the mochila had to move. "When we started out we were not to turn back, no matter what happened, until we had delivered the mail at the next station," recalled Nick Wilson, another rider. "We must be ready to start back at half a minute's notice, day or night, rain or shine, Indians or no Indians."

A mere two minutes was allowed for changing horses at stations along the route, but most changes took thirty seconds or less. The relief horse was ready to go and saddled, and all that was necessary was to swing the mochila from the back of one horse to another.

The riders were instructed to avoid confrontation with road agents or Indians. They were riding the best horses in the American West, and their instructions were to outrun any interloper. Speed and endurance were their first defense. The Colt revolver was a last resort. They outran Indians and they outran wolves. They rode around or sometimes through vast herds of buffalo. They rode by moonlight and they rode when there was no moonlight to guide them. They swam swollen streams. If a horse was lost or killed (and this happened), the riders were instructed to carry the mochila on their backs to the next station.

"Once my horse, Ragged Jim, stepped in a buffalo wallow in the dark, and I went over his head, dragging the mail with me," Campbell recalled nearly seventy-five years after the Pony Express went bust. "I could not find the horse so set off with the mail on foot for the next station. Buffaloes were in thousands along the trail. If a rider ran into a herd of them he was lost.

"One night I came to a pack of large buffalo wolves finishing the carcass of some animal. They refused to move when I rode at them, and my horse shied at the smell of blood and the animals. I blew my horn but it had no effect. There was nothing to do but try to flank and outrun them. I gave the scared horse his head and the wolves finally fell back when the lights of the next station showed in the distance. The next day I poisoned a carcass and twelve dead wolves were around it when I came back."

Changing horses on average every twelve to fifteen miles, depending on the terrain, riders like Campbell covered between seventy-five and one hundred miles before they were relieved. Early accounts of the rigors of riding such a route, miles of pounding on the back of a horse, claim that some riders finished their routes bleeding from their noses and mouths. Few riders who started at the beginning of the fast-mail service were still in the saddle when it ended about a year and a half later. This was not work for the faint of heart or amateurs.

"The pony ride across the continent for a goodly portion of the way was as lonesome and weird as it was long and tiresome," Root and Connelley noted in *The Overland Stage to California*. "Much of the region traversed was a vast wilderness, and had hardly begun to be settled up. For hundreds of miles it seemed as if nothing in the way of vegetation would grow . . . For a considerable distance only the stations where a change of animals was made broke the monotony of the dreary ride."

———

Nothing on the scale of the Central Overland California & Pike's Peak Express Company's Pony Express had ever been attempted before. The sheer scope of what Russell, Majors & Waddell were undertaking was nearly inconceivable. Two-thirds of the continent would be crossed in ten days' time or less by using the finest horsemen available on the best mounts money could buy. Newspaper ads from the period are wildly contradictory about the exact time involved. This was a cross-country, fast-mail relay race involving dozens of way stations and hundreds of men, riders, and station keepers. The complex choreography of such a wild scheme stunned the country. "Think of that for perishable horse and human flesh and blood to do!" exclaimed eyewitness Mark Twain in recalling the days of the Pony Express.

The western transportation historians Frank A. Root and William E. Connelley, writing in 1901, give some idea of the secrecy and scope of the project. "The great enterprise was so quietly and systematically worked up that, in a little over four months after the subject was first whispered, the entire line was fully equipped and in successful operation."

Only sixty-seven days after William Russell sent his famous telegram to his son announcing his intentions of putting a Pony Express on the road, the first riders left from St. Joe and Sacramento. To put this risky venture in motion, Russell, Majors & Waddell divided the route into five sections and placed seasoned frontiersmen in charge of each division. The firm then began buying the best horses available, paying upwards of $200 a horse (nearly $4,000 by today's reckoning)—big money. The operation was highly secretive. Russell, Majors & Waddell was already in debt (although that was not widely known), and it would be even further in arrears after this operation was in working order. (Alexander Majors's son, Greene, who lived until the 1930s and was a municipal judge in California, wrote later that his father's business spent $100,000 in gold coin to outfit the line—the equivalent of $2 million today.)

In his memoirs, Alexander Majors recalled that "five hundred of the fleetest horses to be procured were immediately purchased and the services of over two hundred competent men were secured." They came from the ranks of Majors's veteran teamsters and frontiersmen and pioneers who knew the countryside and the dangers and difficulties involved. They were typical, too, of men and boys on the American frontier at that time—they had been born riding. "Among their number were skillful guides, scouts, and couriers, accustomed to adventures and hardships on the plains—men of strong wills and wonderful powers of endurance," Majors recalled.

Eighty riders were hired from St. Joe to Old Sac—tough, experienced lightweights, built like jockeys, weighing on average 100 to 120 pounds. They were riders who had to be able to stick in the saddle over brutal distances—with or without relief. "Not many riders could stand the long, fast riding at first, but after about two weeks they would get hardened to it," recalled Wilson, who had ridden in Nevada and Utah. Despite the lack of personnel records, historians of the Pony Express have estimated that nineteen years was the average age of riders, although the age of the riders is one of the most disputed subjects in Pony Express lore.

One of the most famous pieces of Pony Express arcana is a newspaper notice that Bolivar Roberts, superintendent of the western end of the line, is said to have placed in a San Francisco newspaper in March 1860 when the firm was first hiring riders.

WANTED

—young, skinny, wiry fellows, not over eighteen.
Must be expert riders, willing to risk death daily.
Orphans preferred. Wages $25 a week.
Apply, Central Overland Express,
Alta Bldg., Montgomery St.

The pedigree of the mounts used by the Pony Express was much disputed. Captain Levi Hensel of Pueblo, Colorado, told Root and Connelley in 1901 that the horses were not thoroughbreds by a long shot. Hensel was working as a farrier for the Pony Express in Seneca, Kansas—about seventy-five miles west of St. Joe—when the fast-mail service was running. He provides some lively information about the half-wild horses used by the firm which he called "the worst imps of Satan in the business."

"The only way I could master them was to throw them and get a rope around each foot and stake them out, and have a man on the head and another on the body while I trimmed the feet and nailed the shoes on, and then they would squeal and bite all the time I was working on them. It generally took half a day to shoe one of them."

Hensel insisted there was no question that these were the fleetest horses available for racing across the country. "They never seemed to get tired," recalled Hensel, who remembered that Johnny Frey, the legendary first rider out of St. Joe, rode one of the half-wild horses fifty miles without relief.

"The stock used by the pony-express riders was in every way far superior to anything possessed by the Indians," Root and Connelley wrote. "In a race for life on the plains, the pony riders, mounted on their fleet of animals, could soon leave the redskins far in the rear. It took the Indians only a short time to learn that they were not in it in such a race."

In 1932, Arthur Chapman noted in *The Pony Express* that veteran riders still living concurred with these stories. Chapman found William Campbell, then ninety-four, in Stockton, California. "The men who bought the horses knew their business," Campbell recalled. "Sometimes we used to say that the company had bought up every mean, bucking, kicking horse that could be found, but they were good stock and could outrun anything along the trail."

Writing in 1960, Frank C. Robertson, then president of the Western Writers of America, claimed that Russell, Majors & Waddell tried to introduce "fine Eastern horses that had blood lines" but that these proved inadequate to the grueling cross-country race. Robertson said "native" horses were preferred. "No horse has ever surpassed the native Cayuse or mustang in intelligence or hardihood. And the spirit of the devil was born in most of them . . . None were easy to ride," Robertson wrote in a special assessment of Pony Express horses prepared for Robert West Howard's *Hoofbeats of Destiny*.

Robertson claimed these half-wild horses weighed less than a thousand pounds and recalled that Pete Neece, keeper of Willow Creek Station, who broke horses for the Pony Express, considered a horse broken "when a rider could lead it out of the stable without getting his head kicked off." Nick Wilson, who worked for Pete

Neece, said horses ridden by the Pony Express in Nevada and Utah were only half broken. "Very likely they had been handled just enough to make them mean. I found it to be so with most of the horses they gave me to ride," Wilson recalled.

The horses of the Pony Express might have been wild, but the riders were held (at least officially) to another standard. All members of the firm were required to take a version of the oath that Alexander Majors had imposed upon his teamsters on the Santa Fe Trail and those hauling freight to army posts along the frontier. Riders were issued the small calf-bound Bibles, and when the Civil War began, they were also required to swear an oath of allegiance to the Union.

The employees of the firm were a merry mix of men. On the eastern end of the line, based in St. Joe at the Patee House, were riders like Johnny Frey, a Kansan who had grown up in the saddle on a ranch in the eastern part of the state and was famous around the countryside as a horse racer. Along the middle section of the route, in western Nebraska, the firm hired Joseph Slade to oversee operations. Slade, a notorious desperado whom Mark Twain vividly describes in *Roughing It,* was a famous badman on the frontier, later lynched by vigilantes in Montana. And elsewhere down the line, Russell, Majors & Waddell hired Mormon farm boys, born in the saddle and familiar with the rough country they would have to cross in the wilds of Nevada and Utah.

Nick Wilson was one of those Mormon boys. He was eighteen the year the Pony Express began. He was hired in eastern Nevada and based first at a home station called Ruby Valley.

Half a century after the days of the Pony, Wilson, who had lived long among the Shoshone Indians, recalled his days in the saddle. "When we were hired to ride the express, we had to go before a justice of the peace and swear we would be at our post at all times, and not go farther than one hundred yards from the station except when carrying the mail."

The height and weight of the riders, like jockeys, was important, too. "The lighter the man the better for the horse," Majors would remember, "as some portions of the route had to be traversed at a speed of twenty miles an hour." The route on average required a speed of eight to ten miles an hour—a relatively modest pace along much of the trail.

Majors recalled that the weight of the mail was never to exceed ten pounds and the cost of sending a letter across the country on the back of a Pony Express mount was not cheap—five dollars in gold (about a hundred dollars today) for a half ounce—paid in advance (the cost of sending a letter would gradually be reduced until it was only a dollar).

The riders wore their own clothing, perhaps a buckskin hunting shirt or one of red flannel, cloth trousers, high boots, a jockey cap or slouch hat. There were no uniforms. They carried only what they needed, only what was absolutely necessary. Armed at first with a Spencer or Sharps rifle and two Colt revolvers, the riders eventually carried only a single Colt, often with an additional cylinder of ammunition.

The letters and telegrams and newspapers (fresh news was highly valued) were written on the thinnest of tissue paper and carefully wrapped in oilcloth and enclosed in the locked saddle pouches of the mochila.

"There were no silly love missives among them nor frivolous correspondence of any kind; business letters only that demanded the most rapid transit possible and warranted the immense expense attending their journey, found their way by the Pony Express," Colonel Henry Inman recalled in 1898. The mochilas were made by Israel Landis, a celebrated saddlemaker in St. Joe known to generations of Americans headed west.

Nick Wilson described the mochila in his memoirs:

Two large pieces of leather about sixteen inches wide by twenty-four long were laced together with a strong leather string thrown over the saddle. Fastened to these were four pockets, two in front and two behind; these hung on each side of the saddle. The two hind ones were the largest. The one in front on the left side was called the "way pocket." When the express arrived at the home station, the keeper would unlock the "way pocket" and if there were any letters for the boys between the home stations, the rider would distribute them as he went along. There was also a card in the way pocket that the station keeper would take out and write on it the time the express arrived and left his station.

When the service began, riders were equipped with a horn to blow to announce their arrival in a relay station, but horns appear to have been discarded. Within weeks of the start of the Pony Express, the riders had been stripped down to the absolute essentials. Speed was everything, and unnecessary weight on the back of a fast horse was the enemy of speed.

These light horsemen were paid $120 to $125 per month, about $2,500 today, according to Majors. This included board and was good money (if and when the riders were paid). That may have been some of the allure for young men on the frontier where an unskilled laborer at Fort Atkinson or Fort Leavenworth might make a dollar for a ten-to-twelve-hour workday, and even a skilled carpenter would be lucky to earn two or three dollars. Riding for the Pony Express was an exciting thing to do—and the money, at least in theory, was good. Here a young man could earn two to four times what he might make elsewhere. The risks, however, were considerable, and the rigors of the ride brutal. As an old man, Nick Wilson remembered only the dangers of riding the fast mail and thought the wages were flinty.

"Our pay was too small for the hard work and the dangers we went through," he told Howard R. Driggs, a New York University professor who helped him write his life story, *The White Indian Boy*. Wilson also remembered that Russell, Majors & Waddell charged their riders for any equipment supplied. "At first the rider would be charged up with the saddle he was riding, and his first wages were kept back for it. If he had no revolver, and had to get one from the company, that would add another heavy expense to be deducted from his wages. Some of the boys were killed by the Indians before they had paid for these things."

William Campbell, who lived to be ninety-six, recalled his route in Nebraska between Valley Station, about eleven miles east of Fort Kearny, and Box Elder Station, three miles west of Fort McPherson. A bullwhacker who had been hauling supplies to Pony Express stations, Campbell, at six feet and 140 pounds, was too tall and too heavy for the Pony Express. But by December 1860—about eight months into business—the fast-mail service was having a hard time getting riders to stick with the job. And so Campbell got to ride.

"Driving slow oxen seemed pretty tame compared with jumping on spirited ponies and going full tilt along the old trail, past the emigrant trains and freight outfits, or even bands of Indians. I was just eighteen, and boylike, craved such excitement . . . ," Campbell told Howard Driggs at the end of his long life.

Campbell, like many of his old colleagues interviewed many years after the Pony Express folded, did not tell wild stories of Indians or desperadoes. His chief complaint, like that of so many others, was the weather and the physical rigors of riding.

"Once I spent twenty-four hours in the saddle carrying the mail 120 miles to Fairfield with snow two or three feet deep and the mercury around zero. I could tell where the trail lay only by watching the tall weeds on either side and often had to get off and lead my horse. There was no rider to go on at Fort Kearny, so I went on to Fairfield twenty miles away," Campbell told an interviewer from *Dots and Dashes* magazine in 1932.

In his interview with Driggs, Campbell elaborated about riding in hard weather. "The worst difficulty I ever had was with the storms. Sometimes the fierce wind and rain that came on that level country would slow us up a good deal. It was the blizzards, though, that gave us the toughest treatment."

On the flat, featureless plains of Nebraska, Campbell remembered battling all day to ride the mail through a blizzard with snow piled three feet high and drifts over his head in some places along the route. "It was hard work for my brave horses to wallow through some of them. At night I just had to trust to the instinct of the horses. We couldn't make more than five miles an hour on that run.

"When I finally did reach the home station where I was supposed to get relief, there was no rider to carry the mail on. The station keepers refused to do it. It meant another twenty miles for me through the bitter storm, but I'd given my word of honor to put the mail through; so I mounted a fresh horse and struggled on, until I finally reached the next station and turned it over to another rider I found there. It had been twenty four hours in the saddle for me. I tell you I was pretty stiff."

Richard Cleve, who had ridden in the same country traversed by Campbell, wrote down some of his memories late in life, too. Cleve's recollections of winter in Nebraska indicate that the weather was as dangerous as the threat of Indians and probably a greater concern.

Cleve, who rode from Midway Station to near Fort Kearny, about seventy-five miles, modestly told his interviewer that he had little of interest to report. "I don't know that I can write of anything that will interest you very much, but I will speak of one long hard ride I had."

Cleve then went on to recount riding in late January or early February 1861 during a raging blizzard that was so bad there had been no Pony Express or stages from the East for four or five days because of waist-deep snow.

Cleve left Midway Station one morning in a howling nor'easter, which he described as "one of the worst blizzards that I ever saw, and I have seen a good many of them for I was in western Nebraska for nine years." Cleve rode all day and got to his station near Fort Kearny about nine o'clock that night.

Cleve's relief rider, William Campbell, was sick, so Cleve rode on from east of Fort Kearny. He had already been riding all day—about seventy-five miles in a blizzard. It was thirty-two miles to the next station, called Thirty-Two Mile Creek Station. Cleve traveled only seven miles before the road became nearly impassable, the blizzard blinding.

"I . . . found it impossible to find the road. I would get off the horse and look for the road, find it and mount the horse, but in five yards I would lose it again. I tried it several times, but gave it up, so I dismounted and led the horse back and forth until day light." Cleve recalled that it was a long night and that the horse seemed to suffer more from the cold than he did. "I got to the station about nine o'clock, hungry as a wolf. It was forty below zero."

After breakfast, with still no relief in sight, Cleve got back on his horse and continued to ride through the whiteout. First leg, twenty-five miles to Liberty Farm. Still no relief. Next leg, twenty-eight miles to Kiowa. Still no relief and no letup in the weather, either.

"That twenty-eight miles tired me more than all the others. There was twenty or more deep gullys that were drifted full of snow. I had to dismount, lead the horse, and kick and tramp the snow to get the horse through. I got there about dark and no rider from the east yet."

Cleve then rode on to Big Sandy, about twenty-eight miles more. At this point, he was exhausted—he'd been out riding in a blizzard on the Nebraska plains for thirty-six hours in temperatures of between thirty-five and forty below zero. A stock tender offered to take his place at Big Sandy.

"He only went about a mile and met the Pony Rider and four or five coaches coming from the east. I went to the house as soon as the young man started with the mail. I saw a cot in the corner of the room and went for it. I believe I was asleep before I even got to it."

Cleve said that when the nearby coaches reached the station, travelers tried to wake him and put him in the coach. He recalled later that he was talking, but he had no recollection of what he said. "It showed plainly how near I was worn out. I don't consider 160 miles a long ride, but it was the terrible weather that used me up."

Winter was the enemy of the Pony Express. It often doubled the time to move the mochila across the country. William F. Fisher, who immigrated to Utah from the county of Kent in England as a fifteen-year-old boy, recalled riding the winter snows between Camp Floyd and Salt Lake City. "I was lost . . . in a blizzard for 20 hours . . . Pretty badly exhausted, as I was fighting the storm all the way."

Long-distance rides, while not necessarily through hostile Indian country, were pretty much the norm. During the Paiute Indian War, Fisher rode from Ruby Valley (in eastern Nevada) to Salt Lake City—three hundred miles in thirty hours, using eight horses and mules. He recalled the dangers of working as a station tender for the Pony Express during the war. He remembered that at least three station tenders were killed—John Ouldcott at Simpson's Park and Ralph Locier and John Applegate at Dry Creek. "Two of the boys, Lafayette Ball and Silas McCandless, made their escape at Dry Creek and were chased by the Indians for ten miles."

Fisher, who rode for the Pony Express from April 6, 1860, until July 1, 1861, recalled that several stations in Nevada had been burned and the stock stolen. "The Indians committed great atrocities, burning some of their victims on wood piles, scalping some and badly mutilating others. They had a good many bloody fights."

Fisher also recalled one of the most famous rides in the history of the Pony Express: the November 1860 delivery of the election results showing Abraham Lincoln's victory. At that time, Fisher rode seventy-five miles in three hours and forty-five minutes, using five horses.

Root and Connelley's early history of western communications and transports and the exploits of the Pony Express claimed that Jack Keetley, who rode on the eastern end of the line out of St. Joe, also logged a record amount of time in the saddle. On one occasion, Keetley rode from Rock Creek (in southern Nebraska) to St. Joe and back and then back to Seneca and then back to Rock Creek without relief—a distance of 340 miles in thirty-one hours. "The last five miles, from a small stream east of Ash Point, he fell asleep in the saddle, and in that condition rode to the end of his long 'run' into Seneca."

The dangers of riding a horse from St. Joseph, Missouri, to Sacramento, California, in the Wild West of 1860–61 seem obvious. But some of the greatest perils facing the Pony Express were those experienced by the station keepers and stock tenders hired to maintain relay posts along the route. A young and skilled rider on a fast horse might escape danger and outrun hostile Indians or bandits, but a station tender in places like Cold Springs, Jacob's Wells, or Alkali Lake was often alone and far from assistance.

When the Paiute Indian War broke out in the late spring of 1860, temporarily shutting down the Pony Express line in much of what is today Nevada, effectively stopping service east and west, the station tenders in the remote Nevada desert were most at risk, and several died defending these lonely outposts from Indian raiders. Stations were strung out across the countryside at points favorable to the route, located for the convenience of the horses and riders racing mail cross-country. The locations depended on the terrain, and were often located in places that were undesirable, simply because there had to be a relief station at this point along the route. Depending on the terrain and the availability of materials, stations ranged from quite comfortable if modest cabins (Hollenberg Station in eastern Kansas seems rustic chic) to dugouts and adobe shelters constructed of mud bricks made at the site. Captain Sir Richard Burton found Pony Expressmen living in a hole in the ground in eastern Nevada. Lean-tos, tents, and various other temporary quarters were thrown up as needed.

On his way west to Willow Creek from Salt Lake City, crossing the vast deserts of Utah and Nevada, Burton made these observations on the stations: "On this line there are two kinds of stations, the mail stations, where there is an agent in charge of five or six 'boys,' and the express station—every second—where there is only a master and an express rider . . . It is a hard life, setting aside the chance of death—no less than three murders have been committed by the Indians during this year—the work is severe; the diet is sometimes reduced to wolf-mutton, or a little boiled wheat and rye, and the drink to brackish water; a pound of tea comes occasionally, but the droughty souls are always 'out' of whiskey and tobacco."

The section of the Pony Express line upon which Burton was traveling between Salt Lake City and California was, in addition to the inhospitality of the terrain and extreme dangers, impossible to supply. Water often had to be hauled great distances. There was no wood, either. That, too, had to be cut elsewhere and hauled overland.

No crops could be grown here; the land was arid and barren with little annual rainfall. So virtually everything needed to operate these far-flung outposts along the line of the Pony Express from an ax to a sack of flour had to be hauled great distances at considerable expense. Russell, Majors & Waddell was spending yet more money on this fabulous gamble.

Frederic S. Remington's
The Old Stage-Coach of the Plains, *1901.*

Six

CAPTAIN SIR RICHARD BURTON

From St. Jo. to Great Salt Lake City, the mails might easily be landed during the fine weather, without inconvenience to man or beast, in ten days; indeed, the agents have offered to place them at Placerville in fifteen. Yet the schedule time being twenty-one days, passengers seldom reached their destinations before the nineteenth—the sole reason given was, that snow makes the road difficult in its season, and that if people were accustomed to fast travel and if letters were received under schedule time, they would look upon the boon as a right.

—RICHARD BURTON, *THE CITY OF THE SAINTS*, 1861

Like the doughty traveler Horace Greeley of the *New York Tribune*, Captain Sir Richard Francis Burton went into the West from the Patee House, high on a bluff overlooking bustling St. Joe. John Patee's magnificent hotel—"the Fifth Avenue Hotel of St. Jo," Burton would call it—offered the British adventurer his last bits of pleasure before he plunged into the Great American Desert, reaching San Francisco after slightly more than three months of traveling.

Explorer of Central and East Africa, Burton was one of the first westerners to enter the holy cities of Mecca and Medina (in disguise), would be credited with the discovery of the Hindu love treatise the *Kama-sutra*, introduced the tales of the Arabian Nights to the West, and fought Her Majesty's battles in Africa, the Middle East, and

India. Going west was a predictable excursion for a Victorian mandarin with Burton's adventurous pedigree. He was eager to have a look at the Mormons, then a curiosity in both England and the United States. He also appears to have wanted to get away from the woman he would eventually marry.

Burton's account of traveling in the American West is not full of encomiums. But he approved of Old St. Joe. One of his biographers reports that he enjoyed a "briskly chilled Veuve Clicquot" while he studied maps and reports about the American West from the hotel overlooking the Missouri River.

Four months after the Pony Express began operating, Burton traveled from St. Joe in a Concord coach operated by Russell, Majors & Waddell, which was not always comfortable, pulled by mules, tougher and more surefooted than horses when the going got rough. And the going was always rough. Travelers along the route of what was essentially the course of the Pony Express and all overland stage travel crossed the countryside at a plodding five miles an hour, on average, time aplenty to take notes and observe. No traveler was better at this than Burton, who left behind a detailed account of flora and fauna and Indian life.

Although thousands of pioneers had already made the trek up the Oregon Trail, that did not deter Burton from complaining about the horrors of the trip. He started grousing when he crossed the Missouri into Elwood, Kansas, and he would still be grousing three months later in the Sierra Nevada as he entered California, carping that he had been cheated by tradesmen in rough-and-tumble Carson City. Burton complains with considerable humor and a sense of irony that would have appealed to H. L. Mencken, but he complains nevertheless. He loathed stagecoach travel. He loathed most of the people he met along the way. He loathed Indians. He loathed the food. Burton can hardly be accused of romanticizing the Pony Express, either. How much of this is an affectation designed to please a sophisticated London reader is hard to gauge.

It was not all hyperbole, though; other witnesses describe rough passages. Long after the end of the Old West, in 1928, Major General Hugh Lenox Scott, an old cavalryman and veteran of the Indian wars, recalled the vagaries of stage travel on the Deadwood line in his autobiography, *Some Memories of a Soldier.* "One night on a stage is enough to play out a strong man, but they were seven days and nights on that stage on account of the condition of the gumbo soil, which rolls up on the wheels like glue when at all wet. I have known a stage on that line to be eight days going twenty miles."

Burton spent three weeks en route to Salt Lake City, stopped over in the Mormon capital for another three weeks, and then traveled on to San Francisco. A superb, if subjective, reporter who spared no one's feelings, Burton wrote voluminous descriptions of everything he saw. His adventures in the West would include the first published account of the Pony Express. He traveled along the route at the height of its operation, stopped at its way stations, interviewed its employees, and painstakingly jotted down every shard of information.

Burton's long and detailed narrative of his travails along the route of the Pony Express in the summer and fall of 1860 provides a wildly different view of the heroics of the Pony Express and its employees than that which has evolved in the nearly century and a half since the business operated. Burton's account, however, caustic though it is, is trustworthy and specific.

Details mattered to Burton, who was fascinated by everything from prairie dogs to Indian sign language. We know, for instance, the precise minute that his coach departed from the front of the Patee House (headquarters of the Pony Express) on August 7, 1860: 8:00 A.M.

This diary entry was made on his first day out of St. Joe, only a few miles from the Missouri River, and sets the tone for Burton's trip and the style of his report: "Passing through a few wretched shanties called Troy—last insult to the memory of hapless Pergamus—and Syracuse (here we are in the third, or classic stage, of U.S. Nomenclature) . . ."

Another traveler along the line in the same year, Dr. C. M. Clark, a physician bound for the goldfields of Colorado, was more generous in describing this typical way station. "Troy is a small town, located some nine miles west of Bellemont, comprising a blacksmith shop, several whisky shops, denominated groceries, etc. It is prettily located on the summit of a hill, is the county seat, and is surrounded by a well settled country. The Trojans receive their principal trade and support from the emigrants, as well as the other towns along the line of travel."

Burton's Concord coach stopped for a dinner break at Cold

Springs Station in Kansas to change mules and allow the passengers to stretch. Here Burton found the occupants filthy, poverty-stricken, and ill. "Squalor and misery were imprinted upon the wretched log-hut, which ignored the duster and the broom, and myriad of flies disputed with us a dinner consisting of doughnuts, green and poisonous with saleratus [baking soda], suspicious eggs in a massive greasy fritter, and rusty bacon, intolerably fat. It was our first sight of squatter life, and, except in two cases, it was our worst. We could not grudge 50 cents a head to these unhappies; at the same time we thought it a dear price to pay—the sequel disabused us—for flies and bad bread, worse eggs and bacon."

The British explorer did not have to travel far down the line of the Pony Express to see its first rider. Burton was not quite at Marysville, which claims to be the first home station on the line, about one hundred miles west of St. Joe, when he observed the first courier. "At Guittard's I saw, for the first time, the Pony Express rider arrive," he records.

"The riders are mostly youths, mounted upon active and lithe Indian nags. They ride 100 miles at a time—about eight per hour—with four changes of horses, and return to their stations the next day—of their hardships and perils we shall hear more anon. The letters are carried in leather bags, which are thrown about carelessly enough when the saddle is changed, and the average postage is $5 = one [British] pound per sheet."

Not long after spotting his first Pony Express rider, Burton and his party came to Marysville, then a point where several immigrant routes west converged. "Passing by Marysville, in old maps Palmetto City, a country-town which thrives by selling whiskey to ruffians of all descriptions . . ." As Burton and his fellow travelers moved into Nebraska, he noted that the driver of the coach was drunk, quite common along the line.

When the party reached Rock Creek in southern Nebraska later that night, Burton had a splendid opportunity to display his disgust and contempt for the trip and the people he met along the way. Rock Creek Station, both a Pony Express and an overland stage stop, was a great disappointment for this English gentleman. (It would become famous in the annals of the Pony Express and the American West the next summer when James Butler Hickok began to earn the name

Wild Bill by dispatching various members of the so-called McCanles gang in a legendary shoot-out. Hickok was not at the station the night Burton arrived.)

"A weary drive over a rough and dusty road, through chill night air and clouds of mosquitoes, which we were warned would accompany us to the Pacific slope of the Rocky Mountains, placed us about 10 P.M. at Rock, also called Turkey Creek—surely a misnomer, no turkey ever haunted so villainous a spot! Several passengers began to suffer from fever and nausea; in such travel the second night is usually the crisis, after which a man can endure for an indefinite time. The 'ranch' was a nice place for invalids, especially for those of the softer sex. Upon the bedded floor of the foul 'doggery' lay, in a seemingly promiscuous heap, men, women, children, lambs and puppies, all fast in the arms of Morpheus, and many under the influence of a much jollier god. The employes, when aroused pretty roughly, blinked their eyes in the atmosphere of smoke and mosquitoes and declared that it had been 'merry in the hall' that night—the effects of which merriment had not passed off. After half an hour's dispute about who should do the work, they produced cold scraps of mutton and a kind of bread which deserves a totally distinct generic name. The strongest stomachs of the party made tea, and found some milk which was not more than one quarter flies. This succulent meal was followed by the usual douceur. On this road, however mean or wretched the fare, the station-keeper, who is established by the proprietor of the line, never derogates by lowering his price."

After a Salt Lake City sojourn, Burton resumed his critique of the Pony Express and its operations on October 15 when the party arrived at Cold Springs Station in what is now Nevada (a site mentioned in connection with Pony Bob Haslam's famous long ride and the Paiute Indian uprising of 1860). "The station was a wretched place half built and wholly unroofed; the four boys, an exceedingly rough set, ate standing, and neither paper nor pencil was known amongst them. [Burton seems to be implying they were illiterate.] Our animals, however, found good water in a rivulent from the neighboring hills and the promise of plentiful feed on the morrow, whilst the humans, observing that a 'beef' had been freshly killed, supped up an excellent steak. The warm wind was a pleasant contrast to the usual frost, but as it came from the south, all the weather-wise predicted that rain would result. We slept, however, without such accident, under the haystack, and heard the loud howling of wolves, which are said to be larger on these hills than elsewhere.

"The station house was no unfit object in such a scene, roofless and chairless, filthy and squalid, with a smoky fire in one corner and a table in the center of an impure floor, the walls open to every wind, and the interior full of dust. Of the employees, all loitered and sauntered about as cretins with the exception of the cripple who lay dying on the ground." Cold Springs Station, curiously, remains one of the few largely extant outposts along the line.

There has never been an account of the Pony Express—from Alexander Majors's autobiography, to hundreds of newspaper articles across the two-thousand-mile hinterland of Pony Express country—that has not mentioned the inspiring oath sworn upon the Bible by the men and boys who were working for the Central Overland California & Pike's Peak Express Company.

Burton, whose droll observations on the Pony Express and its employees differ on virtually every point with the image of wholesomeness portrayed by Majors's oath, was highly amused by tales of the virtuous Pony riders.

"At Saint Joseph [Mo.], better known by the somewhat irreverend abbreviation of St. Jo., I was introduced to Mr. Alexander Majors, formerly one of the contractors for supplying the army in Utah—a veteran mountaineer, familiar with life on the prairies. His meritorious efforts to reform the morals of the land have not yet put forth even the bud of promise. He forbade his drivers and employes to drink, gamble, curse, and travel on Sundays; he desired them to peruse Bibles distributed to them gratis; and though he refrained from a lengthy proclamation commanding his lieges to be good boys and girls, he did not the less expect it of them. Results: I scarcely ever saw a sober driver; as for profanity—the Western equivalent of hard swearing—they would make the blush of shame crimson the cheek of the old Isis bargee; and, rare exceptions to the rule of the United States, they are not to be deterred from evil talking even by the dread presence of a 'lady.' The conductors and road-agents are of a class superior to the drivers; they do their harm by an inordinate ambition to distinguish themselves. I met one gentleman who owned to three murders, and another individual who lately attempted to ration the mules with wild sage. The company was by no means rich; already the papers had prognosticated a failure, in consequence of the Government withdrawing its supplies, and it seemed to have hit upon the happy expedient of badly entreating travellers that good may come to it of our evils. The hours and halting-places were equally vilely selected."

Burton observed uncountable instances of drinking along the route; being a traveler who enjoyed a dram himself, he commented frequently when the liquor supply was low. He does not appear to have passed up any opportunities to "liquor up," as he calls it. His account seems to indicate that Alexander Majors's famous admonition about sobriety was widely ignored, and modern research appears to confirm that.

Archaeological excavations conducted by Donald L. Hardesty of the University of Nevada–Reno in the late 1970s on Cold Springs and Sand Springs Stations in central Nevada uncovered hundreds of fragments of wine, champagne, gin, ale, brandy, beer, and whiskey bottles at both sites dating from the time of the Pony. Hardesty noted in a report prepared for the federal Bureau of Land Management in 1979 that there was ample evidence that dictums against taking strong drink were ignored. "The firm of Russell, Majors & Waddell was adamantly opposed to the use of alcohol beverages by its employees and required them to sign an oath saying that they would not indulge. But observations of drunken pony express riders falling off their horses [Hardesty cited Buffalo Bill Cody's memoirs as offering an example] suggests that the oath was not too effective. The archaeological record of Cold Springs and Sand Springs stations supports that conclusion."

Richard Burton not only noted countless instances of drinking but wryly reported that he had observed no indications of scriptural study, either. "There was no sign of Bible, Shakespeare, or Milton: a Holywell Street romance or two was the only attempt at literature," he observed.

Although he was not writing to entertain a London audience, as Burton was, Dr. Clark recorded ample critical observations about pioneers along the Pony Express route, too: "The emigrant, in traveling across the plains, acquires many debasing habits. I do not wish to be understood as saying that all do, but then all are more or less lax in their morals. Many who had never before indulged in the use of profane language, or in draughts of whisky, soon learned to intersperse his conversation with big oaths, and to smack his lips after a swig at 'Old Bourbon,' with a decided relish. Smoking and chewing tobacco, together with drinking a quarter or so of strong coffee at a meal, were other accomplishments—they were the necessities."

Dr. Clark also reported that the Sabbath was not widely observed:

> Sunday was by many entirely disregarded; the majority had seemingly left all their humanity and their morals at home, bringing along their brutality and all the evil propensities of human nature, and those most moral at home were generally the most abandoned abroad; they were under no restraints, far away from the benign influences of home and civilization, surrounded by all conditions of men and manners, and as man is an imitative being, it is not strange that he was insensibly coerced into practices that would have shamed him in the community he had left behind. They apparently lost all pride of character, as well as pride in personal appearance, not caring how they looked or acted; and it was generally remarked, "If you wish to develope a man's true character, bring him out on the plains." There was no masquerading there; crossing the plains was the furnace that tried him, the scales that weighed him, and if he was found wanting, it was soon known—no man's reputation could cover up his true character. If he was prone to be irritable, cross and peevish, it was soon evinced; if vicious, the propensity was sooner or later manifested.

Dr. Clark, who spent most of his professional life as a military physician and surgeon, saw action in the Civil War, and later practiced in Chicago, also observed the comings and goings of the Pony Express. He got the distance the fast-mail service traveled wrong and the time to cross the country, too, but he thought enough of this phenomenon to make note of such a wonder in his journal. "The Pony Express is a comparatively new institution, conveying letters and dispatches from St. Joseph to California, a distance of fifteen hundred miles, in less than seven days. We have frequently seen this express on the road, the pony on the full run and wet with perspiration."

While traversing the route of the Pony Express, Burton railed and ranted at America, Americans, Indians, and the horrors of overland stage travel. It is hard to believe that he was the seasoned traveler and famous adventurer that he was. He hated the food and he hated the fleas. All the men were drunkards or rascals, the women mostly slatterns, the Indians shiftless and dishonest ("neither gospel nor gunpowder can reform the race"), and the travel experience nightmarish. Each day for Burton was an added misery. He reserved a special contempt for the Irish, whom he seemed to encounter in some numbers. The drivers on the stage line were drunk or having alcoholic fits, the station tenders were thieves or idiots.

"At 1:15 P.M. we reached Plum Creek, after being obliged to leave behind one of the conductors, who had become delirious with the 'shakes.' "

Burton found the route, and the climate in particular, threatening to the health of the traveler, "a hotbed of febrile disease." It was often cold at night, near freezing even in the late summer. During the day, the temperature soared into the nineties.

Burton traveled with two revolvers and a bowie knife, which he delighted in referring to as "an Arkansas toothpick" (Burton loved American slang). He brought along for good measure (and in good measure, too) opium and quinine, and "the holy weed Nicotian"—a plentiful number of cigars (the coach driver helped himself to Burton's smokes) and two pipes. He hoped to have a chance to kill a few Indians, but the occasion never arose. He was curious about the mechanics of scalping, going so far as to try to persuade a wary Sioux he met in Nebraska to demonstrate the bloody technique (the Indian declined). He brought along what seems today a rather odd assortment of accessories, including a top hat, a frock coat, and a silk umbrella, which he donned while visiting Brigham Young in Salt Lake City. Burton was a high-Victorian gentleman. One of his many biographers, noting the adversities Burton had experienced in his adventurous life, offers the explanation that complaining about the absence of small creature comforts is merely an affectation for such a man.

Only at Forts Kearny, Laramie, and Bridger was Burton able to properly refresh himself; otherwise, the stopping points along the stage line, which closely paralleled the Pony Express route, consisted of halting briefly at some "wretched ranch, apparently for the sole purpose of putting a few dollars into the station master's pockets.

The travel was unjustifiably slow, even in this land, where progress is mostly on paper."

Opportunities to be cheated and mistreated abounded. With a few exceptions, Burton denounces the station masters from Kansas to the Comstock Lode. In central Nebraska, a few days out of St. Joe, the party arrived at Midway Station about eight o'clock one evening. The welcome mat was not out.

"Here, whilst changing mules, we attempted with sweet speech and smiles to persuade the landlady, who showed symptoms of approaching maternity, into giving us supper. This she sturdily refused to do, for the reason that she had not received due warning. We had, however, the satisfaction of seeing the employees of the line making themselves thoroughly comfortable with bread and buttermilk. Into the horrid wagon again and 'a rolling': lazily enough the cold and hungry night passed on."

Nights on the road were rough, but so, too, were the overnight stops along the way. Nearly all occasions to dine filled this traveler with disgust. Burton enthusiastically describes the horrors of breakfast in western Nebraska (and notes that an aperitif was called for, too). "The flies chasing away the mosquitoes—even as Aurora routs the lingering shades of night—having sounded our reveille at Cotton Wood Station, we proceeded by means of an 'eye-opener,' which even the abstemious judge could not decline, and the use of the 'skillet,' to prepare for a breakfast composed of various abominations, especially cakes of flour and grease, molasses and dirt, disposed in the pretty equal parts. After paying the usual $0.50, we started in the high wind and dust, with a heavy storm brewing in the north, along the desert valley of the dark, silent Platte."

The unsavory fare along the route whetted Burton's appetite for complaint. "After satisfying hunger with vile bread and viler coffee,—how far from the little forty-berry cup of Egypt!—for which we paid 0.75 . . . We dined at Plum Creek on buffalo, probably bull beef, the worst and driest meat, save elk, that I have ever tasted, indeed, without the assistance of pork fat, we found it hard to swallow."

Burton dismissed the reports of western travelers about the delights of eating buffalo steaks. "The voyageurs and travellers who cry up the buffalo as delicious, have been living for weeks on rusty bacon and lean antelope," he added.

At Lodge-Pole Creek, the travelers attempted to eat antelope meat, which caused dyspepsia. Near Chimney Rock in western Nebraska, a welcomed landmark for travelers crossing the prairies, the Burton party made do with "a frugal dinner of biscuit and cheese."

Breakfast never failed to disappoint Burton, making him particularly bilious. In the endless reaches of western Nebraska, he had yet another bad breakfast upon landing at a station kept by Germans who aggravated the British explorer. "We sat down, stared at the fire, and awaited the vile food. For a breakfast cooked in the usual manner, coffee boiled down to tannin (ever the first operation), meat subjected to half sod, half stew, and lastly, bread, raised with sour milk corrected with soda, and so baked that the taste of the flour is ever prominent, we paid these German rascals $0.75."

This was not Burton's last, or even worst, experience dining along the line. Later he recalled stopping at a station near Fort Laramie kept by a French half-breed:

Our breakfast was prepared in the usual prairie style. First the coffee—three parts burnt beans—which had been duly ground to a fine powder and exposed to the air, lest the aroma should prove too strong for us, was placed on the stove to simmer till every noxious principle was duly extracted from it. Then the rusty bacon, cut into thick slices, was thrown into the fry-pan; here the gridiron is unknown, and if known, would be little appreciated, because it wastes the "drippings," which form with the staff of life a luxurious sop. Thirdly, antelope steak, cut off a corpse suspended for the benefit of the flies outside, was placed to stew within influence of the bacon's aroma. Lastly came the bread, which of course should have been "cooked" first. The meal is kneaded with water and a pinch of salt; the raising is done by means of a little sour milk, or more generally by the deleterious yeast-powders of the trade. The carbonic acid gas evolved by the addition of water must be corrected and the dough must be expanded by saleratus or prepared carbonate of soda or alkali, and other vile stuff, which communicates to the food the green-yellow tinge, and suggests many of the properties of poison. A hundredfold better, the unpretending chapati, flapjack scone, or as the Mexicans prettily called it, "tortilla"! The dough after being sufficiently manipulated up a long, narrow smooth board is divided into "biscuits" and "doughnuts," and finally it is placed to be half cooked under the immediate influence of the rusty bacon and graveolent antelope. "Uncle Sam's stove," be it said with every reverence for the honoured name it bears, is a triumph of convenience, cheapness, unwholesomeness and nastiness—excuse the word, nice reader. This travellers' bane has exterminated the spit and gridiron, and makes everything taste like its neighbor by virtue of it, mutton borrows the flavor of salmon-trout, tomatoes resolve themselves into greens—I shall lose my temper if the subject is not dropped.

For Burton, the stations were as bad as the food, perhaps worse, filthy and full of fleas. At Hams Fork in southwestern Wyoming, he described the stopover, which afforded him with an opportunity to salute still more "exiles from Erin," as he was wont to call them:

The station was kept by an Irishman and a Scotchman . . . It was a disgrace; the squalor and filth were worse almost than the two—Cold Springs and Rock Creek—which we called our horrors, and which had always seemed to be the *ne plus ultra* of western discomfit. The shanty was made of dry-stone piled up against a dwarf cliff to save backwall, and ignored doors and windows. The flies—unequivocal sign of unclean living!—darked the table and covered everything put upon it; the furniture, which mainly consisted of the different parts of wagons, was broken, and all in disorder; the walls were impure, the floor filthy. The reason was at once apparent. Two Irishwomen, sisters, were married (to the station agent, a Mormon and polygamist) and the house was full of "childer," the noisiest and most rampageous of their kind. I could hardly look upon the scene without disgust. The fair ones had the porcine Irish face—I need hardly tell the reader that there are three orders of physiognomy in that branch of the Keltic family, viz. Porcine, equine, and simian: the pig-faced, the horse-faced, and the monkey-faced.

Traveling among the Mormons, Burton had the good fortune to stop at another station kept by an exile from Ireland. "The station-keeper was an Irishman, one of the few met amongst the Saints. Nothing could be fouler than the log hut, the flies soon drove us out of doors; hospitality, however, was not wanting, and we sat down to salt beef and bacon, for which we were not allowed to pay . . . As the hut contained but one room we slept outside."

At Deep Creek, the Burton party reached yet another pigsty. "The station was dirty to the last degree: the flies suggested the Egyptian plague, they could be brushed from the walls in thousands, but though sage makes good brooms no one cares to sweep clean."

Many of the stations along the route of the Pony Express, particularly those between St. Joe and Salt Lake City, had been operating before Russell, Majors & Waddell began the fast-mail service. Originally designed to trade with Indians, offer travelers some services, and support overland stage lines, they became stops to provide fresh mounts for the riders of the Pony Express. Burton, despite his detailed record keeping, did not stop at every station. Near Cottonwood Station in western Nebraska, which Burton pronounced "a foul tenement" and where he complained about paying fifty cents for a greasy breakfast, was the Gilman ranch. Established in 1859 by John Kendall Gilman and his younger brother, Jeremiah Chandler Gilman, this stopover became a landmark for travelers in western Nebraska.

The Gilman brothers had left the family homestead in Bartlett, New Hampshire, in 1854 and drifted west, stopping first in Iowa and then moving on to Nebraska. In the early summer of 1859, at the height of the Pike's Peak gold rush, they were hauling merchandise to sell to the miners in the Rocky Mountains: drugs, goods, clothing, whiskey, ammunition, iron pipes, wheelbarrows, tools, and one luxury item—"a fine red, iron pump . . . A sign of affluence on the frontier where a windlass and bucket were the usual means of getting water from the well."

About eighty miles west of Fort Kearny, nearly to the Colorado border, the Gilman brothers had the good fortune to break a wagon axle. They were about seventeen miles east of Cottonwood Springs, a well-established stop for travelers along the Oregon Trail (it would become the site of Fort McPherson). Unable to go forward to Colorado or retreat back to Nebraska City, John and Jeremiah Gilman settled where the wagon gave out. Within days they were trading their goods with nearby Sioux and Cheyenne Indians for buffalo robes. Emigrants headed west in wagon trains soon stopped, too. The Gilman brothers decided to grow where fate had planted them. The first sign of their permanence was that they dug a well, lined it with cedar posts, and installed the red iron pump, a landmark for travelers into the West that would become beloved in Nebraska folklore.

The Gilman brothers hung a tin cup from the pump so that passersby could enjoy the cold, clean water. Within weeks, they had built two sod houses. The Gilmans had themselves a "road ranche," as these way stations were called in the years before the Civil War— a vital part of the expansion across the West.

The Gilman ranch, on the south bank of the Platte River, near Fort McPherson (established in 1863 and disbanded in 1891) became a celebrated landmark on the route west, variously an Indian trading post, a stage stopover, and a Pony Express station. The Gilman brothers eventually sold telegraph poles to Edward Creighton, when he was stringing the first transcontinental telegraph in 1861, and railroad ties a few years later to the gandy dancers on the Union Pacific railroad.

Strictly speaking, the Gilman ranch was not a ranch, but more a stopover on the route west, a trading post, the Oregon Trail equivalent of a service plaza on an interstate where travelers could buy fuel (wood), replenish their water supply, make wagon repairs, buy or trade livestock, such as oxen, horses, or mules, and purchase supplies (often exorbitantly priced). Sharp practices were not unknown among the operators of such hostelries. Reviews of such operations were decidedly mixed, but life was hard on the plains.

Not all the travelers along the line were as critical as Captain Burton. Dr. Clark, who also traveled west in 1860, commented on road ranches in his book *A Trip to Pike's Peak and Notes Along the Way.* Clark described Smith's ranch, ten miles east of the Gilman ranch:

Smith's ranch is a small building constructed of logs where liquor, preserved fruits, etc. are to be had. Why these buildings, or stations, are called ranches, is more than I can say. The proprietors do not cultivate the soil, nor do they raise stock, they merely squatted along this line of travel, for the purpose best known to themselves. These miscalled ranches throughout the Platte Valley are essentially, one and the same thing; sometimes differing in size and style of construction—some are of the adobe species, while others are constructed of rough logs and poles, and sometimes we meet with one built of squared cedar posts that look very neat. The proprietors are generally rude specimens of humanity, in every sense of the word, and many of them dress in garments made from elk and deer skins, ornamented with long fringes of the same materials up and down the seams; their hair and beard, in many cases, had been suffered to grow, giving them a ferocious look and in fact, they are as primitive as the country they inhabit. In order to insure the respect and confidence of the Indians, many of them have squaw wives, who inhabit a lodge nearby.

The Nebraska writer Musetta Gilman, who married a descendant of the Gilman brothers, also quotes an unidentified English traveler along the Oregon Trail in 1863 describing a typical ranch:

It must not be supposed that these ranches imply farming on any scale whatever; they are simply business stations to meet the wants of the emigrants and travelers westward, and therefore each mainly consists of one room, which serves for store, grog-shop, and bedroom by night. In the smaller ones, and they are by far the most numerous, the stock in hand may be set down as consisting of much pork, ham, and a few pounds of coffee, salt, pepper, vinegar, pear ash, soda, flour, butter, eggs, corn, dried apples, peaches in tins, and oysters also, with a Falstaffian proportion of a vile compound of whiskey and I know not what, which is popularly known as "bust head" or "forty rod" because the unfortunate imbiber is seriously effected in either brain or legs, or even both, before he had gone the distance . . . But one of their great sources of wealth lay in "trading" oxen. For this purpose they begin with a few of their own, and when a man passes with a foot-sore ox which can go no further, they sell the traveler a fresh one at their own rate, while a dollar or two is considered the rule of the road for the faded ox . . . It will not be surprising that these ranchers make a pile quickly.

When Russell, Majors & Waddell put the Pony Express into operation in the late winter/early spring of 1860, the Gilman brothers' ranch was up and running. It would become a "swing station."

Musetta Gilman provides a glimpse at the sentiment in the West for Russell, Majors & Waddell and a sense of the time, too. "The mood of the country accepted speculation. No one knew how deeply in debt the company was. So again using their reputation as collateral, their leadership in attracting competent men, and their own abilities to organize, they began."

Musetta Gilman compiled a family chronicle of the ranch—*Pump on the Prairie*—more than a century after its heyday. She also recorded that by the time news of the express-mail venture appeared in the rare newspaper reaching the ranchers along the Overland Trail in Nebraska, the Pony Express was nearly up and running.

Shortly before the inauguration of the venture, probably in March 1860, although Musetta Gilman gives no date, a small news item in the *Nebraska City News* reported: "Colonel Russell completed arrangements for a pony express from St. Joseph to the eastern terminus of Col. Bee's telegraph, and the first express leaves each end of the line on the third of April next to make the distance in ten days. The government has nothing to do with the enterprise. It is entirely private energy and capital. There will be eighty stations, twenty-five miles apart. Horses and riders are now being placed."

She also explained the significance of the "swing station." "Here relief horses would be cared for, saddled, and made ready for the quick exchange of rider and mochila as the mail moved swiftly along the Trail. Cottonwood Station was designated a home station." (Here riders would exchange the mail with a fresh rider and rest up for a few days for the return ride.)

No violence was reported at the Gilman ranch, but life along the route of the Pony Express, for riders and station tenders, was both spartan and dangerous. En route from Salt Lake City to Carson City, Burton had a conversation with a young Pony Express rider, which gives a further idea of the nature of this risky occupation.

"Here I rode forwards with 'Jim,' a young express rider from the last station, who volunteered much information upon the subject of Indians. He carried two Colt's revolvers, of the dragoon or largest size, considering all others too small. I asked him what he would do if a Gosh-Yuta appeared. He replied, that if the fellow were civil he might shake hands with him, if surly he would shoot him; and at all events, when riding away, that he would keep a 'stirrup eye' upon him; that he was in the habit of looking round corners to see if any one was taking aim, in which case he would throw himself from the saddle, or rush on, so as to spoil the shooting—the Indians, when charged, becoming excited, fire without effect."

Burton would not be the only traveler to note such dangers. Dr. Clark found the way west scattered with thieves who took advantage of travelers, too. Clark found his overland route in Kansas and Nebraska "inhabited by as scurvy a set of bipeds as ever demoralized any community, and I refer now principally to the many who have squatted along the line of travel for the purpose of genteel robbery . . . The emigrant has generally many little wants to gratify while traversing the troublesome way, and he expects to pay for them; but when he is called upon to pay five and twenty per cent more than residents, it is an imposition." Clark also noted that travelers along the line were distrusted, too. "The majority of emigrants were considered as a low thieving set, too poor to be honest . . ."

Clark's letters chronicling his adventures crossing the West also stressed the dangers of western Nebraska. "This country is infested with bands of thieves and robbers, whose sole business is to stampede and secure the emigrant's stock. Along some portions of the route, constant vigilance has to be exercised." Again: "Suspicious looking characters have often been seen lurking around the camp at night, in the endeavor to secure the horses or mules lariated out; and when so seen, they are often fired upon, as the emigrant has no mercy on these villains."

At a grim Pony Express station in the wasteland of eastern Nevada appropriately named Robber's Roost, Richard Burton logged yet another example of all that horrified him:

> It is about as civilized as the Galway shanty, or the normal dwelling-place in Central Equatorial Africa. A cabin fronting east and west, long walls thirty feet, with portholes for windows, short ditto fifteen; material, sandstone with big ironstone slabs compacted with mud, the whole roofed with split cedar trunks, reposing on horizontals which rested on perpendiculars. Behind the house a corral of rails planted in the ground; the enclosed space a mass of earth, and a mere shed in one corner the only shelter. Outside the door—the hingeless and lockless backboard of a wagon, bearing the wounds of bullets—and resting on lintels and staples, which also had formed parts of locomotives, a slab acting stepping-

stone over a mass of soppy black soil strewed with ashes, bos of
meat offals, and other delicacies. On the right hand a lot of wood;
on the left a tank formed by damming a dirty pool which had
flowed through a corral behind the "Roost."

. . . The inside reflected the outside. The length was divided by
two perpendiculars, the southernmost of which, assisted by a half-
way canvass partition, cut the hut into unequal parts. Behind it
were two bunks for four men; standing bedsteads of poles planted
in the ground . . . and covered with ragged blankets. Beneath the
framework were heaps of rubbish, saddles, cloths, harness, and
straps, sacks of wheat, oats, meal, and potatoes, defended from the
ground by underlying logs, and dogs nestled where they found
room. The floor, which also frequently represented bedstead, was
rough . . . A redeeming point was the fire-place, which occupied
half of the northern short wall: it might have belonged to Guy of
Warwick's great hall.

The furniture in this station was exceedingly primitive by Burton's
standard. No one washed anything. The inmates, as Burton called the
station's occupants, chewed tobacco and lived in filth.

The Burton party was entertained with a Pony Express rider's account of an Indian attack near Egan's Station the previous August (it
was early October at this point in his trip). "The fellows [Indians]
had tied up the master and the boy, and were preparing with civilized
provisions a good dinner for themselves, to be followed by a little
treat in the form of burning down the house and roasting their cap-
tives." The Pony Express rider brought a detachment of soldiers, who
rescued the station's occupants and drove off the Indians. This is apparently the incident referred to by the wandering Private Scott in his
diary of trekking across Nevada during the summer after the Paiute
Indian War.

In a letter to his friend Norton Shaw, secretary of the Royal Geo-
graphical Society, written from Salt Lake City, Burton jokes about
"living in the odour of sanctity" among the Mormons. He was eager
to get back to civilization. He had had enough of the West.

Anticipating the last leg of his trip, the dangerous stretch across
Utah and Nevada from Salt Lake City, Burton wrote, "The road is
full of Indians and other scoundrels, but I've had my hair cropped so
short that my scalp is not worth having."

As it turned out, Burton survived the Mormons and survived the Sierra Nevada, too. He enjoyed San Francisco immensely and produced a seven-hundred-page book based on a mere one hundred days in the United States. It contains some of the most detailed information that history has about the Pony Express and is the first printed account of the fast-mail service. An actual book-length work on the Pony was nearly a half century away—but another eyewitness of the fabulous overland mail gamble was just down the trail.

The overland Pony Express (rider waving to telegraph linesmen), ca. 1876.

Seven

THE TELEGRAPH:
"OUR LITTLE FRIEND THE PONY
IS TO RUN NO MORE"

In its day [the Pony Express] was a blessing to the country;
but after it was fairly in operation, annihilating space
between the Missouri river and the Golden Gate, beating the
fastest time that had ever been made across the continent, it
was not long until it was distanced itself by the magnetic
telegraph.

—FRANK A. ROOT AND WILLIAM E. CONNELLEY,
THE OVERLAND STAGE TO CALIFORNIA, 1901

Two days before Independence Day in the summer of 1861, Edward
Creighton and Charles Brown dug the first post hole in Julesburg,
Colorado. A few days later Creighton and Brown got into a Concord
buggy pulled by two mules named Mary and Jane, forded the Platte
River, and began rolling west toward Mud Springs in the Nebraska
panhandle. Racing across the plains of Nebraska and Wyoming, racing against the coming winter, racing at the ferocious pace of up to
twelve miles a day, the crews they supervised finished up 113 days
later. The transcontinental telegraph linking the Atlantic and Pacific
was complete, the continent was spanned.

"No telegraph line on earth was ever rushed through so rapidly," pronounced the historians Frank Root and William Connelley, noting: "While it was believed to be an impossibility to finish the great enterprise by the time specified by Congress, yet so rapid was the work of construction pushed, that in less than four and a half months from its inception the entire line was completed, and dispatches for the first time could be sent from ocean to ocean."

Among a number of congratulatory telegrams sent on completion of the telegraph line was one sent at 7:40 P.M. on October 24, 1861, by Horace W. Carpentier, president of the Overland Telegraph Company. It was a two-sentence message across the wire from San Francisco to Abraham Lincoln in Washington, D.C.:

I ANNOUNCE TO YOU THAT THE TELEGRAPH TO
CALIFORNIA HAS THIS DAY BEEN COMPLETED. MAY IT BE
A BOND OF PERPETUITY BETWEEN THE STATES OF THE
ATLANTIC AND THOSE OF THE PACIFIC.

Two days after that telegram was sent, the Pony Express went quietly out of business. The notices in the California newspapers—California was always most passionate for the Pony—said that *our little friend the Pony is to run no more."*

With time out for the Paiute Indian War in the spring and early summer of 1860, the Pony Express had been in operation for a mere seventy-eight weeks. In the end, it was bested by technology. "While the pony line was very useful in its day, the period of its life was comparatively brief. It could not stand the race with electricity, and when the telegraph line was finished, its usefulness was ended; the enterprise was wiped out almost instantly," Root and Connelley observed at the turn of the century.

The final summer of the Pony Express, the summer of 1861, was the summer that Mark Twain crossed the country on the adventure that would lead to *Roughing It;* and the summer that James Butler Hickok shot it out with the "McCanles gang" (his spelling) at Rock Creek Station, launching his career as "Wild Bill." In the summer of 1861, Abraham Lincoln was in the White House and the United States was in civil war. And Big Ed Creighton, the barrel-chested son of poor Irish immigrants, was spanning the North American continent with a telegraph wire—changing forever the American West.

When the veteran Pony Express rider William Campbell was a

very old man, remembering his days in the saddle on the plains of Nebraska, he told an interviewer in the 1930s that of all the things that he had lived to see in his long, long life, the telegraph was the greatest. Campbell had seen the Civil War, he had lived long enough to see men fly, and he had seen the crews of linemen, furiously working like busy ants, in relays, stringing the singing wire across the plains.

"Greatest of all inventions to me, because it affected me directly, is the telegraph. In the two minutes we used to be allowed to change horses at a station, Western Union now sends a message to New York or even London. The telegraph today does in a second what it took eighty young men and hundreds of horses eight days to do when I was a rider in the Pony Express," observed Campbell, who was ninety-four at the time.

Edward Creighton had all of the virtues that Alexander Majors admired. It is a pity that they were not partners. He was industrious, honest, humble, and not afraid to get his hands dirty. He was also religious, a Roman Catholic, whose parents had escaped Ireland in the early nineteenth century. Creighton was forty-one the year he supervised construction of the transcontinental telegraph line. Born on a farm in rural Ohio when the Midwest was still frontier, Creighton was a self-made man who had little formal education and had gone to work as a cart boy on the National Road at fourteen. Like Alexander Majors, he worked side by side with his men. They called him by his first name, and in the evening, when the work was done, he would play cards with them and joke (Majors might have drawn the line at cards). But Major's affection and respect for the man who would essentially put the Pony Express out of business was genuine.

"No man has an unkind word to say of Edward Creighton, and his memory is revered to this day as an upright, just, and kind man, who, out of his own sterling qualities, had wrought a successful and honorable career," Majors wrote in his memoirs long after Creighton's untimely death at fifty-four.

An experienced telegraph line supervisor, Creighton had strung the first wire from St. Joe to Omaha. In the year before the transcontinental telegraph crews began to run the wire across the West, Creighton personally surveyed every inch of the route. "It was a terrible journey, but the man who made it was of stout heart, and he braved the rigors of the mountains and accomplished his mission . . . ," recalled Majors, who knew firsthand what a terrible journey involved.

After enlisting the help of Brigham Young, Creighton rode from Salt Lake City to Carson City alone on a mule in January along the route followed by the Pony Express. It was a six-hundred-mile trip (there were still hostile Paiute Indians in this country), but it took him only twelve days. When he arrived in what would become the Nevada capital, Creighton was barely able to sit on the back of his mule. His face was burned raw from the wind and sun.

"Three times the skin peeled from Mr. Creighton's face; and when he arrived in Carson City, more dead than alive, he was snow-blind. The marvel is that he did not perish. But his constitution was healthy, his frame rugged and robust; above all, his iron will was strong in its purpose," wrote P. A. Mullens, a Jesuit priest at Creighton University in Omaha (founded as a legacy to the telegraph builder) in 1901.

Creighton rested briefly and pushed on to California and returned east by ship to New York and then back to Omaha, a city he would play a key role in developing. The following summer, with the blessing of Western Union, he began construction of the telegraph line. He had earlier determined that a transcontinental telegraph line following the Butterfield (Southern or Oxbow) Route was impractical and too long (2,700 miles).

In anticipation of the tasks ahead, Creighton hired twenty-seven-year-old Charles A. Brown, a Williams College graduate who had come west to seek his fortune, to serve as his secretary. Brown, who was paid fifty dollars a month, had been reading law in an Omaha attorney's office. Crossing the wilderness must have seemed alluring.

Western Nebraska was not the Berkshires, and everything fascinated young Brown, who kept a journal now housed at the Smithsonian Institution in Washington, D.C. Brown's journal is a record of hard work and hard men. They crossed a countryside where there was virtually no drinkable water. There was virtually no vegetation, either. Trees to be used as telegraph poles had to be cut and hauled tremendous distances. Everything they needed had to be brought in from outside. And when the line was strung, buffalo, still numbering in the tens of thousands, would knock the poles down by rubbing against them. Indians were less of a problem, but they were curious.

Once, Creighton convinced a group of curious Cheyenne Indians not to interfere with the telegraph line that was crossing their country by having them grasp a live wire. Brown's journal makes note of the occasion. "Creighton . . . told them [the Cheyennes] what we were employed at, that lightning ran along the wires, and talked and made them in a hazy way understand how dangerous it would be to interfere with our work. Creighton then, practically, to illustrate what he was saying, proposed to give them a shock from the battery. This being arranged . . . There was prancing then and there among the Indians. They did some talking and looked upon Mr. Creighton as a 'big medicine man.' "

On July 5, Brown wrote in his journal about the hard landscape they were traversing. "Not a drop of water is to be had on this route during the entire distance. We reached Mud Springs about seven P.M. [sixty-four miles west of Julesburg] and as expected found Jim Dimmock in camp here. His report on finding poles was very discouraging."

The poles were inferior, but the men continued to string the line. "We allowed from twenty-two to twenty-five poles per mile," Brown recorded. Working in various crews, men dug post holes, set poles, or scavenged for material for poles, as the line stretched westward.

"Mr. Creighton estimates that we must average at least eight miles of the constructed line every day in the week and every day in the month. Counting the days we cannot work, to realize his estimate we must build each working day ten to twelve miles of the line. This I believe we will be able to do." Failure meant the possibility of facing a winter in Wyoming, unthinkable in Creighton's mind.

Less than two weeks after leaving Julesburg, on July 16, Creighton's men were at Chimney Rock in western Nebraska, a natural monument familiar to thousands of pioneers who traveled the Oregon Trail. Less than three weeks later, on August 5, they were three miles west of Fort Laramie in eastern Wyoming. The riders of the Pony Express were used as messengers along the line of construction, relaying information from one crew to another. One of the most famous lithographs of the time—a picture worth the proverbial thousand words—shows a Pony Express courier waving furiously to a crew of telegraph linemen stringing the wire from pole to pole.

"Ed is a steam engine of energy and has wonderful powers of endurance, and the enterprise he now has in hand virtually compels him to be ubiquitous," Brown noted in his journal.

Creighton's reward for completing this technological miracle in a matter of months (critics had claimed it would take two years minimum) came in the form of stock options, which would make him a millionaire.

The impetus for the transcontinental telegraph line, eagerly awaited in both the East and California, was the Pacific Telegraph Act of June 16, 1860 (passed two and a half months after the Pony Express began running and at the height of the Paiute Indian troubles). The Telegraph Act in essence granted a $40,000 subsidy for ten years to the successful builder of a cross-country telegraph line. The hitch was that the subsidy was not payable until the line was built. Under the terms of the telegraph line construction, Creighton, starting in western Nebraska, was responsible for 1,100 miles of the line, while his competitors coming from the West had 450 miles to cover (the terrain was much tougher). Racing Creighton's crew was James Gamble, who was stringing telegraph line across the deserts of Nevada and Utah.

Crews were spread out along the entire route of the telegraph, stringing wire simultaneously in several places. The wires were finally joined at Fort Bridger in what was then Utah on October 24, 1861. The telegraph line was considered fully operational on November 15.

On October 17, 1861, with success in sight, Creighton sent his wife, Mary, a telegram from Fort Bridger:

IN A FEW DAYS TWO OCEANS WILL BE UNITED.

The linking of the East and West would be bittersweet. Lamenting that the telegraph would kill the Pony Express, Alvin F. Harlow, a melancholic postal historian, wrote: "The blighting hand of progress sounded the first tap of the death knell of the romance of the old West."

On October 26, 1861, an editorial notice appeared in the *Sacramento Bee* signaling the end of the Pony Express and capturing some of the sentiment and romance associated with the brief venture:

Our little friend, the Pony, is to run no more. "Stop it" is the order that has been issued by those in authority. Farewell and forever, thou staunch, wilderness-overcoming, swift-footed messenger! For the good thou hast done we praise thee; and, having run the race, and accomplished all that was hoped for and expected, we can part with thy services without regret, because, and only because, in the progress of the age, in the advance of science and by the enterprise of capital, thou hast been superseded by a more subtle, active, but not more faithful public servant. Thou wert the pioneer of a continent in the rapid transmission of intelligence between its peoples, and have dragged in your train the lightning itself, which, in good time, will be followed by steam communication by rail. Rest upon your honors; be satisfied with them: your destiny has been fulfilled—a new and higher power has superseded you. Nothing that has blood and sinews was able to overcome your energy and ardor; but a senseless, soulless thing that eats not, sleeps not, tires not—a thing that cannot distinguish space—that knows not the difference of the globe itself, has encompassed, overthrown and routed you. This is no disgrace, for flesh and blood cannot always war against the elements. Rest then, in peace, for thou hast run thy race, thou has followed thy course, thou hast done the work that was given thee to do.

The newspapers in California competed in praise of the Pony Express, a reflection of the genuine significance the overland mail relay had on the far coast. Californians had always been the strongest and most romantic supporters of the Pony. They had every reason to express some sentimental loss when the long riders ceased to run.

"A fast and faithful friend has the Pony been to our far-off state," eulogized the *California Pacific*. "Summer and winter, storm and shine, day and night, he has traveled like a weaver's shuttle back and forth til now his work is done. Goodbye, Pony! No proud and star-caparisoned charger in the war field has ever done so great, so true and so good a work as thine. No pampered and world-famed racer of the turf will ever win from you the proud fame of the fleet courser of the continent. You came to us with tidings that made your feet beautiful on the tops of the mountains . . . We have looked for you as those who wait for the morning, and how seldom did you fail us! When days were months and hours weeks, how you thrilled us out of our pain and suspense, to know the best or know the worst. You have served us well!"

Years after Russell, Majors & Waddell's fabulous folly, a historian subtitled his story of the Pony Express "the record of a romantic adventure in business." Musing on the failure, Arthur Chapman wrote, "Russell and his partners had put on the first Wild West show, and the public had cheered the performance but neglected to pay at the gate." In the end, Russell, Majors & Waddell's rash and risky venture was swamped with debt and making little money. Wags in the West claimed that the initials of the Central Overland California and Pike's Peak Express Company—COC&PP—stood for Clean Out of Cash and Poor Pay. The Pony Express—doomed to fail from its start, plagued by creditors, stalked by competition, and racing hopelessly against a new technology—was vanquished.

Raymond Settle, who wrote the first serious attempt to sort out the financial affairs of the firm nearly a century after it went out of business, believed that Russell, Majors & Waddell had been bankrupt since 1857–58. Massive losses linked to unsuccessful attempts to ship military freight during the Mormon War in the late 1850s had put the firm in a position of virtual insolvency. Russell, Majors & Waddell was in all probability dead broke before the first Pony Express rider left St. Joe. The firm had been largely trading off its reputation as a famous business and the personal appeal of its partners. If anyone required proof that William Hepburn Russell was "a plunger," they would need to look no further.

In addition, Russell became embroiled in a complex and dodgy scheme involving bonds belonging to the Indian Trust Fund. Godard Bailey, a clerk in the Department of the Interior, and custodian of the bonds, for reasons that are not entirely clear, loaned them to Russell to be used as collateral in securing short-term loans. This was done with the approval of War Secretary John B. Floyd (who bolted for the Confederacy about the time the bond scandal was being made public). But Russell's attempt to salvage his foundering financial empire unraveled when the bonds he borrowed against were sold. Russell had no right to have used them in the first place. The bond scandal exploded, and Russell wound up spending Christmas 1860 in a Washington jail. His bail was at first set at $500,000—a sum the flat-broke Russell could not possibly hope to raise. Under the threat of criminal prosecution, he was eventually dragged before a congressional committee investigating the affair. Russell, Bailey, and Floyd were indicted in connection with the scandal, but they were never tried on the charges. The federal government eventually reimbursed the trust fund to the tune of more than $700,000. Russell escaped prosecution on a technicality. But such a close call was hardly good for business. The freighting empire that had made Russell, Majors & Waddell famous never recovered from this scandal. There were no more military contracts. There would be no government support for a cross-country fast-mail service. And before the year 1861 had ended, the telegraph had crossed the West. The financial affairs of the Pony Express, such as they are possible to document, do not make easy or pleasant reading.

There are no records of receipts, but the simple math involved in the proposition tells the tale. A Pony Express rider could rarely carry more than twenty pounds of mail. Even if a courier had one hundred letters at five dollars apiece, five hundred dollars was hardly sufficient revenue to justify this expensive cross-country escapade, and rates dropped during the short duration of the service. (Root and Connelley even claim that on one run the rider carried only eight letters.) When it was all over, various critics and chroniclers of the Pony Express would estimate (educated guessing at best) that it had cost the firm sixteen dollars to move a single letter across the country, yet the rates had never been higher than five dollars a letter. This had never been a paying proposition. Even the most charitable historians of the Pony Express have acknowledged that the firm was hemorrhaging money from the evening that Johnny Frey met the *Missouri* bringing the first mail from back east.

Raymond Settle claimed that the Pony Express made 308 runs each way—a distance of 616,000 miles (twenty-four circumnavigations of the globe, he liked to point out). (Root and Connelley believed the Pony Express covered 650,000 miles—about 330 cross-country trips.) Settle also claimed that 34,753 pieces of mail were carried (18,456 originated in San Francisco and 4,900 in Sacramento). But even the redoubtable Settle, who spent decades studying the Pony Express, could only guess as to the amount of money the firm lost. Settle believed it was "at least $500,000."

"The absence of company records makes a break-down of items actually chargeable to it impossible, and the few random statements concerning it throw little light upon it. The complex activities of the company, which was also engaged in the stagecoach, express, and mail business, presents additional difficulties," Settle added.

"It so transpired that the firm of Russell, Majors & Waddell had to pay the fiddler," Alexander Majors recalled without providing further information except to say in his memoirs that the loss was "several hundred thousand dollars."

Settle, sympathetic to the legacy of the firm, concluded optimistically that "the Pony Express failed in only one respect; it made no money."

———

With the end of the Pony came the end of Russell, Majors & Waddell. Their fates and fortunes were intertwined. They would never shake off the shame of the bond scandal or recover from their enormous financial losses. In the last months of the Pony, the firm's assets—the remains of the once mighty "empire on wheels"—had already been seized by creditors Wells, Fargo & Co. and the stagecoach king Ben Holladay.

For the three partners, there would be no second chances. The world in which they built their empire no longer existed. The nation was torn by civil war, and the great migration westward stalled. The telegraph eliminated the need to carry carefully wrapped messages on the back of a galloping horse. The transcontinental railroad would follow at the end of the decade, so the rocking stagecoaches that carried Horace Greeley and Mark Twain through the dust would be gone, too. The West would soon have no need for mile-long ox-drawn wagon trains hauling freight to remote outposts.

William Waddell, shrewd grocery clerk that he was at heart, retreated to Lexington, Missouri, sold his house to his son for a dollar, and continued to live there. He never worked again, and hardly communicated with his former partners. His last years were hard; creditors stalked him, old friends turned against him, his land was sold for taxes, his house was raided again and again in the war. He died at age sixty-five on April 1, 1872.

Russell's fall was especially hard. At forty-eight, he had hoped to reinvent himself as a stockbroker in New York, but he was dogged by the bond scandal and tainted by his reputation as a Confederate sympathizer. "Bankers and financiers who once fawned upon him were now too busy to even grant him an interview, and his name, once a symbol for financial wizardry, was forgotten," wrote historian Raymond Settle. Russell maintained an office in lower Manhattan, but eventually lived in a succession of shabby boardinghouses. He wrote letters to his former partners, pleading for money. Toward the end of his cruel descent, he sold Tic Sano, a patent medicine that claimed to cure neuralgia. Finally, the family he had largely abandoned years before in Missouri brought him back home to die at age sixty. His grave was long unmarked. But all across America from tiny towns in Kansas to the deserts of Nevada, travelers can see his face and those of Waddell and Majors in bas relief markers commemorating the sweet and sad episode that was the Pony Express.

Alexander Majors outlived the others, living to see a new century before he died in Kansas City in 1900. The frontiersman of the three partners, Majors had eked out a living by doing what he knew best—hard labor—after the Pony folded. He ran small freighting operations, graded the roadbed for the Union Pacific Railroad, tried his hand at prospecting. He moved across the West, living variously in Nebraska, Utah, Montana, and Missouri. He eventually lived in a little mining shack outside of Denver, where he would be rediscovered by Buffalo Bill and enjoy a last act as a grand old man of the Old West. He would write his memoirs and remember when he and his partners risked everything, when they put a lithe lad on the back of a horse named Sylph to cross the wide Missouri and streak west.

Not everyone, however, had forgotten the Pony Express, and at the turn of the twentieth century there were still a few Americans alive who had actually seen the couriers race. One of these, an old California gentleman who remembered the days of the Central Overland California & Pike's Peak Express Company, was George Tisdale Bromley, who composed his memoirs of a life in the West in the days of '49.

"I wonder how many there are who remember the 'Pony Express'?" the then-eighty-seven-year-old Bromley wondered in his droll memoirs of a life that had taken him from years before the mast to the goldfields of California.

Bromley was writing in 1904, more than forty years after the last Pony Express rider turned in his mochila. No book-length work had been written on the subject. No history compiled. Russell and Waddell were dead. Majors was, too. Buffalo Bill was still alive, but he would be gone in 1917.

Bromley, like the wandering Horace Greeley, was a displaced New Englander who had washed up on the California coast in the very early days. A Connecticut Yankee, Bromley was born in Norwich, Connecticut, in 1817 and sailed out of the whaling port of New London at the age of fourteen on a little seventy-five-ton schooner, *Spark,* bound for the southwest coast of Africa on a sealing voyage. Bromley later sailed on packet ships plying the New York–London line and then shipped aboard a steamboat bound for Vera Cruz, arriving in time for the declaration of war between Mexico and France, with the port blockaded by a French squadron. He spent nearly twenty years at sea and came ashore in San Francisco as an official in the Custom House in 1850 as the gold rush was getting under way. A charter member of the Bohemian Club, Bromley would live long enough to see the twentieth century and the great earthquake that nearly destroyed San Francisco in 1906. Bromley came out to California, as many did in those days, on a ship via Panama. A great deal of the mail headed for California did, too. It took many weeks to make this passage. The old man vividly remembered the Pony Express and how it changed communication with the East in his autobiography, *The Long Ago and the Later On.*

Here was an eyewitness of a nearly forgotten chapter of western history. The old man's recollections of the fast-mail service were accurate and detailed. Bromley referred to the Pony Express by the name that it was always known by in the West—a name even common in the twenty-first century.

"The 'Pony' was a small, one-horse concern carrying a mail never exceeding twenty-five or thirty pounds. The regular overland mail, in 1861, carried letters and papers at the usual rates, and ranged from fifteen hundred to forty-five hundred pounds. The Pony Express was a great institution. It grew out of a desire to obtain as speedy communication with the East as was possible, a desire which was strengthened by the obvious need for the Federal authorities to be in touch with the Union men of the Coast in case that the already impending war cloud did not pass harmlessly overhead. It was Senator William M. Gwin, who afterwards joined the Confederates, who was the first to see the feasibility of a fast overland mail, as well as to point out the danger to both the Panama steamer route and the Southern Overland stage route, should secession become anything more than a threat."

Bromley unknowingly cleared up a confusion and the source of bitter argument over which city in California laid claim to the Pony

Express—San Francisco or Sacramento. "The mail was carried from San Francisco to Sacramento by boat, and it was from the latter city that the real start was made. The first express went through on time, and elaborate preparations were made to welcome the rider with the Eastern mail."

Bromley's memories of the arrival of the first Pony Express rider in Sacramento are vivid and specific—it is probable that he was in Sacramento the day the rider reached the California capital with his precious cargo from the East. Old Mr. Bromley was one of the first to reflect on the legend of the long-vanished Pony Express, but he would not be the last. He died in 1906, and the following year William Lightfoot Visscher stirred himself from the bar at the Chicago Press Club and began to write the first history of the Pony Express.

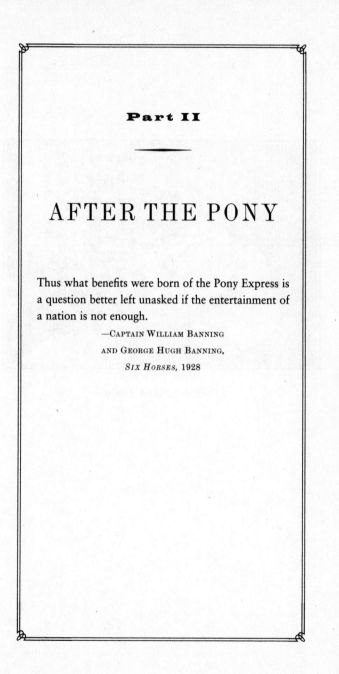

Part II

AFTER THE PONY

Thus what benefits were born of the Pony Express is a question better left unasked if the entertainment of a nation is not enough.

—Captain William Banning
and George Hugh Banning,
Six Horses, 1928

Portrait of Mark Twain.

Eight

MARK TWAIN . . . "TO THE
TERRITORY AHEAD"

I have scarcely exaggerated a detail of this curious and absurd
adventure. It occurred almost exactly as I have stated it.
—MARK TWAIN, *ROUGHING IT*

In the summer of 1861, the first summer of the Civil War, as Richard
Burton completed his hastily written account of his travels into the
American West at home in St. James in London (an appointment
from Queen Victoria as consul at Fernando Pó in the Bight of Biafra
meant that he wrote only one draft), another traveler was following
the same route westward. Burton was a famous and seasoned explorer whose observations, *The City of the Saints and Across the
Rockies to California,* would soon be published in London. The second pilgrim was an unknown. He had recently deserted from the
Confederate army. He was a former printer's devil. He had been a
Mississippi riverboat pilot whose career on the river was cut short by
the Civil War. He was not writing a book and would not compose an
account of his travels in the West for more than a decade. Samuel
Langhorne Clemens was twenty-five the summer that he crossed the
Missouri with his older brother, Orion, a lawyer who had just been
appointed Nevada's territorial secretary. Nevada had gained territorial status in the first year of the Pony Express, and a Pony Express
rider had brought the news overland to Carson City, the capital.

After what his first biographer, Albert Bigelow Paine, would call "a brief and altogether ludicrous experience as a soldier," Samuel Clemens had deserted the Confederate army (or more precisely a locally formed home guard called the Marion Rangers which saw no action). His personal account of this lark, *The Private History of a Campaign That Failed,* gives a fairly good idea of Clemens's bemusement with military life. The writer explained that his abandonment of a military career happened because he had been "incapacitated by fatigue through persistent retreating." Sam Clemens (he would not be Mark Twain just yet) then embarked on what he would later characterize as "several years of variegated vagabondizing," a western sojourn which included stints at mining and newspapering in Nevada and California as well as prolonged loafing.

Sam Clemens recalled his older brother's appointment in the Nevada Territory as "an office of such majesty that it concentrated in itself the duties and dignities of treasurer, comptroller, secretary of state, and acting governor in the governor's absence. A salary of eighteen hundred dollars a year and the title of 'Mr. Secretary' gave to the great position an air of wild and imposing grandeur. I was young and ignorant, and I envied my brother. I coveted his distinction and his financial splendor, but particularly and especially the long, strange journey he was going to make, and the curious new world he was going to explore. He was going to travel! I never had been away from home, and that word 'travel' had a seductive charm for me. Pretty soon he would be hundreds and hundreds of miles away on the great plains and deserts, and among the mountains of the Far West, and would see buffaloes and Indians, and prairie dogs, and antelopes, and have all kinds of adventures, and maybe get hanged or scalped and have ever such a fine time, and write home and tell us all about it, and be a hero. And he would see the gold mines and the silver mines, and maybe go about of an afternoon when his work was done, and pick up two or three pailfuls of shining slugs, and nuggets of gold and silver on the hillside. And by and by he would become very rich . . ." It was too much for Sam Clemens (who had in fact been away from home before, as a riverboat pilot on the Mississippi and itinerant printer). He went west, too.

Like Richard Burton, the Clemens brothers left St. Joe (probably from the Patee House) in a Concord coach, rocking their way across the countryside along the Central Route taken by overland stages and followed, as well, by the riders of the Pony Express. Unlike the industrious and observant Burton, who was fixed on recording every bit of flora and fauna he witnessed with a military precision, Sam Clemens made no notes of the trip. He did, however, bankroll the expedition into the West, paying for his and older brother Orion's one-way tickets to Carson City (as existing receipts of the overland stage tickets indicate). A decade later he would depend on his memory and Orion's personal journal to produce his second book, *Roughing It*.

But Sam Clemens was an observant traveler. He was also having the time of his life. Everything was marvelous on the road west, as Twain would write later, fondly recalling "ham and eggs and scenery." Stagecoaching on the great overland was a world of coyotes, wolves, buffalo, prairie dog villages, antelopes and alkali water, jackass rabbits and Indians, of whom the normally tolerant and sympathetic Twain was contemptuous.

The gradual construction of the myth of the Pony Express could not have gotten off to a much livelier start than in the hands of the young man who became Mark Twain. Unlike Richard Burton, who had hated the filth and flies and fleas of overland travel, Twain was enchanted. His enthusiasm and his penchant for storytelling showed. *Roughing It* turned out to be one of the most entertaining and most enduring personal narratives of life in the American West of the mid-nineteenth century. In Nevada, an old saw has it, Twain's travelogue remains second only to the Bible in popularity.

Written as an entertainment, part travel book, part personal memoir (critics have exhausted themselves noting its embellishments and fabrications), it provides readers nearly a century and a half later with a wealth of information about the world of the American West and the Pony Express in impressive and passionate detail. To young Sam Clemens, the Pony Express was a wonder to behold, its daring riders and half-wild horses heroic figures.

The travelers on Twain's coach had been hoping to see a Pony Express rider, and duly one appeared. "In a little while all interest was taken up in stretching our necks and watching for the 'pony rider'— the fleet messenger who sped across the continent from St. Joe to Sacramento, carrying letters nineteen hundred miles in eight days! Think of that for perishable horse and human flesh and blood to do!"

The Clemens brothers had left St. Joe on July 26, 1861 (exactly ninety days before the Pony Express ceased operations), after paying $150 each for seats on an overland stage. There was one other passenger in the stagecoach, a Mr. George Bemis, and 2,700 pounds of mail. They were allowed to bring along only twenty-five pounds of luggage, necessitating a last-minute repacking (long-tailed coats, white kid gloves, and patent-leather boots were shipped back home). They also hauled along a massive dictionary, which resulted in additional tariff because of its weight. The trip was rough going, pitching and tossing along in a Concord coach pulled by six horses for nearly three weeks from St. Joe to Carson City. (They arrived in Carson City on August 14—twenty days on the overland stage.)

"We changed horses every ten miles, all day long, and fairly flew over the hard, level road. We jumped out and stretched our legs every time the coach stopped, and so the night found us still vivacious and unfatigued."

Although Twain makes no mention of it, one of Musetta Gilman's fondest family recollections from the days of the Gilman brothers' road ranch in western Nebraska concerned the most famous traveler who ever visited. It was a story handed down over a century.

"One of the travelers who stopped was Samuel Clements [*sic*], a young newspaperman," she reported in *Pump on the Prairie*. And John Gilman's son wrote in 1932: "Among the noted men that stopped at our ranch was Mark Twain when he crossed the plains to get material for his book *Roughing It*. For a long time my mother kept the chair he sat in at the table, but finally when they left there, in moving it was lost or broken."

Clemens was not a newspaperman when he followed the central overland route in 1861, although it is indeed possible—probable, in fact—that he stopped at the ranch, perhaps only long enough to stretch his legs and have a smoke while fresh horses were harnessed. He was not writing *Roughing It* and would not do so for nearly a decade later in Hartford, Connecticut, far from the West that had become part of his imagination. But Twain would have certainly delighted in the Gilman family recollection if it was true—and even more so if it was not. He would have understood the latter perfectly.

What is certain is that the division superintendent for the Pony Express who stopped to enlist the Gilman brothers in the cross-country mail relay was a name that Mark Twain knew well.

In writing about Joseph (Jack) Slade in *Roughing It,* Twain recalled a famous and notorious published description of the bad man: "From Fort Kearny, west, he was feared a great deal more than the Almighty."

Joseph Slade was not a figment of Mark Twain's imagination. Nor was he a tall tale. Slade is perhaps the most solid example that everyone in the employ of Russell, Majors & Waddell was not enjoying a glass of sarsaparilla and the Psalms in the evening. The Central Overland California & Pike's Peak Express Company hired men who could get the job done, and some of those men were plainly outlaws. Joseph Slade was the most stunning example.

Young Sam Clemens first heard of Slade while crossing Nebraska, and he recalled a decade later in *Roughing It* that the bad man's name was on the lips of everyone he met. "There was such magic in that name, SLADE! Day or night, now, I stood always ready to drop any subject in hand, to listen to something new about Slade and his ghastly exploits," Twain recalled, adding, "From the hour we had left Overland City we had heard drivers and conductors talk about only three things—'Californy,' the Nevada silver mines, and this desperado Slade."

Twain remembered that "Slade was a man whose heart and hands and soul were steeped in the blood of offenders against his dignity; a man who awfully avenged all injuries, affronts, insults or slights, of whatever kind—on the spot, if he could, years afterward if lack of earlier opportunity compelled it."

Twain prepares the reader for the eventual encounter with Slade— "the most bloody, the most dangerous, and the most valuable citizen that inhabited the savage fastness of the mountains"—with a preposterous buildup.

According to Twain's version, Slade was a native of Illinois who had left "the states" and headed west after killing a man in a quarrel. Twain said that Slade had joined a wagon train headed for California at St. Joe. The first story that made up his legend took place on the trip when Slade killed another traveler. Twain and other writers about Slade report that he eventually wound up in Julesburg, Colorado—a celebrated junction on the way west where travelers either forked south toward Denver or continued on to California or Oregon. Julesburg was lawless at that time, and the stories of Slade claim that he was hired to restore order to the overland stage division centered hereabouts—a place plagued by horse thieves and outlaws. (Indians were not a serious problem here.) Slade was eventually credited with establishing law in this territory, or at least his version of it. But this happened only after a celebrated encounter with the founding father of Julesburg, one Jules Rene (his name is often spelled Reni, Bene, or Beni), a French Canadian who had turned this station into a kind of "robber's roost." After a long period of warring, Slade killed Jules after cruelly torturing him. Twain repeated a graphic account of the long-running feud between Slade and Jules, attributing it to stories he heard on the overland and read in California newspapers. Eventually Twain and his brother, Orion, arrived at a stage station and sat down to breakfast "with a half-savage, half-civilized company of armed and bearded mountaineers, ranchmen, and station employees. The most gentlemanly-appearing, quiet, and affable officer we had yet found along the road in the Overland Company's service was the person who sat at the head of the table, at my elbow. Never youth stared and shivered as I did when I heard them call him SLADE!"

The killer, Twain reports, turns out to be a friendly and gentle-spoken soul who does not seem at all dangerous. "It was hardly possible to realize that this pleasant person was the pitiless scourge of the outlaws, the raw-head-and-bloody-bones the nursing mothers of the mountains terrified their children with. And to this day I can remember nothing remarkable about Slade . . ."

Twain ends his story of meeting the fabled badman by having Slade offer him the last cup of coffee in the pot. "I politely declined. I was afraid he had not killed anybody that morning, and might be needing diversion."

Twain ends his account of meeting Slade by wondering if and when he will hear of him again and then reports in the next chapter how Slade was later lynched (although he begged for his life) by vigilantes in Virginia City, Idaho Territory (later Montana), who had suffered enough of his drunken and violent behavior. Among the six hundred miners and frontiersmen who assembled to watch Slade being hanged by the neck until dead that day was, or so the story goes, Pony Bob Haslam, hero of the Paiute Indian War—still in the saddle as an express-mail rider in Montana.

From the very earliest accounts of the Pony Express, such as Colonel Henry Inman's *The Great Salt Lake Trail,* historians noted that the employees of the Central Overland California & Pike's Peak Express Company were unlike most men on the frontier. "The employees of the Pony Express were different in character from the ordinary plainsmen of those days. The latter as a class were usually boisterous, indulged in profanity, and were fond of whiskey. Russell, Majors & Waddell were God-fearing temperate gentlemen themselves, and tried to engage no man who did not come up to their own standard of morality," Colonel Inman recorded in 1898.

But even Inman admitted that "there was one notable exception in the person of Jack Slade, the station-agent at Fort Kearny, who was a desperado in the strictest definition of the term; that is, he was a coward at heart, as all of his class are, and brave only when every advantage was in his favor."

According to Inman, Slade had murdered at least twenty men. The colonel then relates a sanitized version of the most famous of Slade's outrages.

"One of his most damnable acts was the killing of an old French-Canadian trapper, whose name was Jules Bernard, who lived on a ranch on the eastern border of Colorado." (Other versions of this story paint old Jules as a highwayman who supervised crime in western Nebraska and ran the station at Julesburg as a kind of criminal fiefdom.) Inman quotes one Mrs. Elton Beckstead, who claims to have been married to Jules at the time he ran afoul of Slade. "I was thirteen years old when Jules married me and took me to his ranch at Cottonwood Springs. He had three log buildings side by side; one contained our private apartments, one was the store, and the other the kitchen and quarters for the man and his wife who ran the ranch for us."

Old Jules's thirteen-year-old child bride remembered Slade as being from Kentucky, "a very quiet man when sober, but terribly ugly when drinking." Her version of the encounter between her husband and Slade attributes the violence to Slade's drinking. He is clearly the aggressor in this tale. The short version of this yarn is that Jules got the drop on Slade, wounded him badly with a shotgun blast in the stomach, took pity on the injured man, and hauled him to Denver for medical treatment, which Jules paid for. The former Mrs. Jules recalled that Slade agreed to shake hands with Jules and the matter was thus settled. But when Slade recovered, he swore that he would kill the French Canadian on sight.

Some time passed and Jules was ambushed by Slade and twenty-five other men, according to the wife's story told by Inman.

"They carried Jules to the ranch, and tied him up to a dry-goods box. Slade shot at him for a while, aiming as near as he could without hitting him, finally shooting off one of his ears; and then he ordered his twenty-five men to empty the contents of their revolvers into him. They then threw his body into a hole . . ."

Slade and his band also stole the contents of Jules's trading post and some $3,000, according to the Inman account. Inman also repeated the story that Slade nailed one of Jules's ears to the door of the Pony Express station and wore the other as a watch charm. (The only book-length version of Slade's wicked life is entitled, appropriately, *An Ear in His Pocket*.)

The important thing to keep in mind about this is not merely that Jack Slade was a bad employee of the Pony Express; he was the *supervisor* along a substantial portion of the route. He was "the law west of Kearny." No chronicle from Mark Twain to Colonel Inman to dozens of other accounts in newspapers and magazines and dime novels for more than a century fails to paint him as anything but "a desperado in the strictest definition of the term," to use Colonel Inman's description.

Like the story of the Pony Express, the life of Jack Slade is one of many contradictions and confusions. He appears to have been born Joseph Alfred Slade in Carlyle (Clinton County), Illinois, probably on January 22, 1831. According to several accounts, he served in the 1846–48 war with Mexico (he would have been young to do this). He had earned a reputation as a tough customer on the frontier long before Russell, Majors & Waddell hired him to oversee the Sweet-water Division from roughly western Nebraska and northeastern-most Colorado to central Wyoming, an area of about five hundred miles that contained some fifty stations.

Differing rather sharply from Colonel Inman's account, based on the child bride's recollections, are other versions of the life of Jules Bernard. (Richard Burton noted encounters with several of these French traders who had "gone native.") One account described Jules as "a sullen bear-like French-Canadian also reputed to be the leader of a band of cutthroats." The version of the fight between Jules and Slade features Benjamin Ficklin, general superintendent of the Pony Express route, banishing Jules (but only after rescuing him from a lynch mob).

This other version of the story, which includes Slade cutting off Jules's ears, also includes the details of Slade torturing Jules and slowly killing him. Slade's violent reputation only continued to grow (he was a strong practitioner of "shoot first, ask questions later"), and finally he was fired by the company (this after the Pony Express ceased to run, probably in the spring of 1863).

Slade drifted off to Virginia City, where most versions agree that his bad behavior, exacerbated by heavy drinking, led to his being lynched by miners in March 1864. Slade's widow, said to be a rather lively gal herself, cursed the citizens of Virginia City and had her husband's body shipped to Salt Lake City in a tin-lined coffin filled with whiskey. No two accounts agree on Mrs. Slade—whom one writer identifies as Maria Virginia, describing her as "a tall and striking woman who was herself proficient with guns and horses." Yet another popular historian of Slade's misadventures describes Mrs. Slade as "a sour-countenanced, heavy-haunched wife." She was reported by more than one historian to have assisted her husband in escaping the authorities or a lynch mob on at least one occasion.

Attempts to explain Jack Slade are curious and reflect when they were written. For a long time, western writers were content to paint him a badman straight out of a dime novel, but later popular historians blamed his problems on alcoholism and in one case speculated that "the absence of a strong father figure may have turned young 'Alf' Slade, as he was then known, into an uncontrollable youth."

———

En route to Nevada, Sam and Orion Clemens stopped, as many a traveler had before them, to have a look at the Mormons. (Mark Twain would make some use of this material later.) Orion paid an official call on Brigham Young. When the brothers finally reached Carson City, they were so filthy and rough-looking from three weeks on the overland stage that the reception planned to welcome Orion as the new secretary for former New York City police commissioner James Nye, the territorial governor, was canceled.

Twain's first biographer, Albert Bigelow Paine, recalled the disas-

trous arrival of the Clemens brothers in the Washoe. "The committee saw two wayworn individuals climb down from the stage, unkempt, unshorn—clothed in the roughest of frontier costume, the
same they had put on at St. Jo—dusty, grimy, slouchy, and weather-
beaten with longs days of sun and storm and alkali desert dust. It is
not likely there were two more unprepossessing officials on the Pacific coast at that moment than the newly arrived Territorial secretary and his brother. Somebody identified them, and the committee
melted away; the half-formed plan of a banquet faded out and was
not heard of again. Soap and water and fresh garments worked a
transformation; but that first impression had been fatal to festivities
of welcome."

The Clemens brothers quickly settled into this new life in Nevada
as part of the extended patronage family of Nye's camp followers
who had come west with promises of a bright future in the new territory. In a letter home to his mother, Sam Clemens reported: "The
country is fabulously rich in gold, silver, copper, lead, coal, iron,
quicksilver, marble, granite, chalk, plaster of Paris (gypsum), thieves,
murderers, desperados, ladies, children, lawyers, Christians, Indians,
Chinamen, Spaniards, gamblers, sharpers, coyotes (pronounced Ki-
yo-ties), poets, preachers, and jackass rabbits."

Despite Twain's enthusiastic memoirs of overland stage travel, his
anecdotes recall that the food offered to these travelers along the line,
like the fare that disgusted Burton and was eaten by the riders of the
Pony Express, was vile. ("Our breakfast was before us, but our teeth
were idle," Twain recalled.) He remembered a particularly unappe-
tizing breakfast in Nebraska:

> The station keeper unended a disk of last week's bread, of the shape
> and size of an old-time cheese, and carved some slabs from it which
> were as good as Nicholson pavement and tenderer.
>
> He sliced off a piece of bacon for each man, but only the expe-
> rienced old hands made out to eat it, for it was condemned Army
> bacon which the United States would not feed to its soldiers in the
> forts, and the stage company had bought it cheap for the suste-
> nance of their passengers and employees . . .
>
> Then he poured for us a beverage which he called "slumgul-
> lion," and it is hard to think he was not inspired when he named

it. It really pretended to be tea, but there was too much dishrag, and sand, and old bacon rind in it to deceive the intelligent traveler. He had no sugar and no milk—not even a spoon to stir the ingredients with.

Twain recalled that he neither ate nor drank anything at this stopover. Burton had loathed "discomfit," complaining all the way, but Twain would remember only a marvelous time, for this was the adventure that provided him with his earliest and most picaresque material. He also provides readers with some of the best description of overland stage travel ever recorded:

> The station buildings were long, low huts, made of sundried, mud-colored bricks, laid up without mortar (adobes, the Spaniards call these bricks, and Americans shorten it to "dobies"). The roofs, which had no slant to them worth speaking of, were thatched and then sodded or covered with a thick layer of earth, and from this sprang a pretty rank growth of weeds and grass. It was the first time we had ever see a man's front yard on top of his house. The buildings consisted of barns, stable room for twelve or fifteen horses, and a hut for an eating room for passengers. This latter had bunks in it for the station keeper and a hostler or two. You could rest your elbow on its eaves, and you had to bend in order to get in at the door. In place of a window there was a square hole about large enough for a man to crawl through, but this had no glass in it. There was no flooring, but the ground was packed hard. There was no stove, but the fireplace served all needful purposes. There were no shelves, no cupboards, no closets. In a corner stood an open sack of flour, and nestling against its base were a couple of venerable tin coffeepots, a tin teapot, a little bag of salt and a side of bacon.

Twain, writing from the comfort of his fine new home in Hartford, Connecticut, a decade later, recalled the occupants of these stations as a rough bunch of men. Washing was not a priority. The stations were sparsely outfitted, too. "The furniture of the hut was neither gorgeous nor much in the way. The rocking chairs and sofas were not present and never had been, but they were represented by three-legged stools, a pineboard bench four feet long, and two empty candle boxes. The table was a greasy board on stilts, and the tablecloth and napkins had not come—and they were not looking for them, either."

Burton had loathed this life, but Twain remembered it with great fondness and humor. Sam Clemens's chance encounter with the fast-mail service in western Nebraska especially thrilled him, and he wrote with undisguised affection and fascination of the Pony Express rider. The Pony Express was in its second year of operation—dead broke and famous—and had already in that time achieved tremendous fame across the country and even in Europe (the British foreign office had moved dispatches from its fleet in China across the Pacific and then by Pony Express to the East Coast and on to England). To Twain the riders were American "heroes on horseback."

Twain came down the path of the Pony Express—more or less following the route taken by Edward Creighton's crews stringing the transcontinental telegraph line—at the height of efforts to link the East and West via telegraph. But he makes no mention of this except to note that in remote central Nevada, unintentionally heralding the end of the Pony, it was possible to send a telegram to notify officials in Carson City that his brother, Orion, was en route. The telegraph line had reached Reese River Station (near what is today Austin, Nevada, in the center of the state) by early August.

Roughing It would help to immortalize the Central Overland California & Pike's Peak Express Company. An actual history of the Pony Express was still thirty-five years away when Twain published his personal narrative. But the fast-mail service of 1860–61 was already becoming something of an American legend.

Twain's eyewitness description, full of admiring detail, is the most often quoted account of someone who actually saw the Pony Express in operation. His description of the riders and their route, written entirely from memory, was vivid and precise:

The pony rider was usually a little bit of a man, brimful of spirit and endurance. No matter what time of day or night his watch came on, and no matter whether it was winter or summer, raining, snowing, hailing or sleeting, or whether his "beat" was a level straight road or a crazy trail over mountain crags and precipices, or whether it led through peaceful regions or regions that swarmed with hostile Indians, he must be always ready to leap into the saddle and be off like the wind! There was no idling time for a pony rider on duty. He rode fifty miles without stopping, by daylight, moonlight, starlight, or through the blackness of darkness—just as it happened. He rode a splendid horse that was born for a racer and fed and lodged like a gentleman: kept him at his utmost speed for ten miles, and then, as he came crashing up to the station where stood two men holding fast a fresh, impatient steed, the transfer of rider and mailbag was made in the twinkling of an eye, and away flew the eagle pair and were out of sight before the spectator could get hardly the ghost of a look.

Twain's detailed portrait of the Pony rider in the second year of the business reflects some changes in the operation. The riders, according to Twain, were unarmed and lightly outfitted—emphasizing speed:

Both rider and the horse went "flying light." The rider's dress was thin, and fitted close; he wore a "roundabout," and a skull cap, and tucked his pantaloons into his boot tops like a race rider. He carried no arms—he carried nothing that was not absolutely necessary, for even the postage on his literary freight was worth *five dollars a letter.* He got but little frivolous correspondence to carry—his bag had business letters in it, mostly. His horse was stripped of all unnecessary weight, too. He wore a little wafer of a racing saddle, and no visible blanket. He wore light shoes, or none at all. The little flat mail pockets strapped under the rider's thighs would each hold about the bulk of a child's primer. They held many and many an important business chapter and newspaper letter, but these were written on paper as airy and thin as gold leaf, nearly, and thus bulk and weight were economized.

Despite his penchant for hyperbole and a good yarn, a skill that he would polish in the Nevada mining towns as a young reporter before he wrote *Roughing It,* Twain here records quite vividly an accurate portrait of the cross-country mail relay riders. His details relating to costs, rider's weight and costume, and other such matters jibe with other accounts of the service.

"The stagecoach traveled about a hundred to a hundred and twenty-five miles a day (twenty-four hours), the pony rider about two hundred and fifty. There were about eighty pony riders in the saddle all the time, night and day, stretching in a long, scattering procession from Missouri to California, forty flying eastward, and forty toward the west, and among them making four hundred gallant horses earn a stirring livelihood and see a deal of scenery every single day in the year."

Sam Clemens and his brother had been hoping to see a Pony Express rider for themselves, but the couriers had "managed to streak by in the night, and so we heard only a whiz and a hail, and the swift phantom of the desert was gone before we could get our heads out of the windows."

After several disappointments, one day the driver on the overland stage shouted back to the passengers: "Here he comes!"

"Every neck is stretched further, and every eye strained wider. Away across the endless dead level of the prairie a black speck appears against the sky, and it is plain that it moves. Well, I should think so! In a second or two it becomes a horse and rider, rising and falling, rising and falling—sweeping toward us nearer and nearer—growing more and more distinct, more and more sharply defined—nearer and still nearer, and the flutter of the hoofs comes faintly to the ear—another instant a whoop and a hurrah from our upper deck, a wave of the rider's hand, but no reply, and man and horse burst past our excited faces, and go winging away like a belated fragment of a storm!

"So sudden is it all, and so like a flash of unreal fancy, that but for the flake of white foam left quivering and perishing on a mail sack after the vision had flashed by and disappeared, we might have doubted whether we had seen any actual horse and man at all, maybe."

This serendipitous encounter between Twain and one of the most powerful and enduring symbols of the Old West took place around August 1, 1861, somewhere in the flat, endless horizon of western Nebraska. No single American's account of the Pony Express has meant more in the near century and a half since the business operated. Despite Twain's usual and expected exaggeration, here is genuine information about the service. Twain tells readers of *Roughing It* that the travelers passed Scotts Bluff in western Nebraska and later Fort Laramie in eastern Wyoming not long after the encounter with the Pony Express rider. It is probable, given the number of cross-country runs the Pony was making, that Twain saw merely one express rider at close quarters. But he made the most of it.

And so the faint hoofbeats of the Pony Express rider pounded out of the pages of Twain's memoirs of his days on the frontier and into American popular lore.

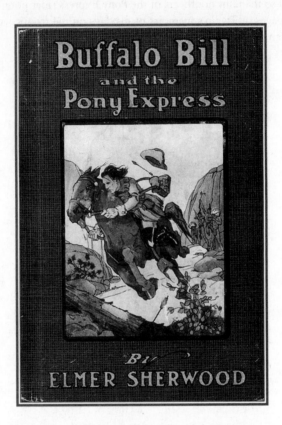

Cover of novel Buffalo Bill and the Pony Express *by Elmer Sherwood.*

Nine

BILLY CODY'S BIG

ADVENTURE

Our author would never consent to write anything except actual scenes from border life. As a sop to the Cerberus of sensationalism, he did occasionally condescend to heighten his effects by exaggeration. In sending one story to the publisher he wrote:

"I am sorry to have to lie so outrageously in this yarn. My hero has killed more Indians on one war-trail than I have killed in all my life. But I understand that this is what is expected in border tales. If you think the revolver and bowie-knife are used too freely, you may cut out a fatal shot or stand wherever you deem it wise."

—HELEN WETMORE CODY AND ZANE GREY
QUOTING BUFFALO BILL IN
LAST OF THE GREAT SCOUTS, 1899

The man often credited with discovering Buffalo Bill got off a Union Pacific Railroad train on a hot summer day in 1869 in North Platte, Nebraska, rented a horse or buckboard at a livery stable, and rode out to nearby Fort McPherson. That's one version of the story. He wasn't sure what he was looking for, but he *was* looking. The man who got off the Union Pacific train that morning was stout, barrel-chested, weather-beaten. He walked with a limp. Witnesses often said later that he had a military bearing. He was not yet fifty, but he looked older. He had lived a long and hard life. He'd spent years before the mast. He had been a soldier, too. His name was Edward Zane Carroll Judson, but countless barely literate Americans developing an insatiable appetite for pulp fiction knew him as one of the nation's most prolific authors. He was a dime-novel master who would leave a permanent mark on popular culture. He signed his work "Ned Buntline."

In the decade between the time that Richard Burton wrote his vivid account of traveling in the West of the Pony Express and Mark Twain finally set down his own lively recollections in *Roughing It,* the most significant event in the saga of the Pony Express took place in western Nebraska. Eight years after the Pony Express folded, a chance meeting on the dusty parade ground at Fort McPherson changed completely the legacy of the Central Overland California & Pike's Peak Express Company.

Though there had been stations nearby, no Pony Express rider ever stopped at Fort McPherson—the service was long gone when the fort was established near North Platte, Nebraska. The Gilman brothers from New Hampshire were not far off. Their red pump on the prairie was a short ride from the fort.

But Fort McPherson has a role to play in the annals of Pony Express lore. Here on a late summer morning in 1869, Ned Buntline, desperate for copy, or so the story goes, was turned away by a commanding officer who despised penny-dreadful newspapermen from the East. Buntline was said to be touring the West looking for material to be spun into dime novels. Another version of his travels is that he was returning from an unsuccessful temperance lecture tour in California (Buntline was a temperance lecturer who also drank). He might have been doing both. While not precisely the father of the dime novel, Buntline's paternal role in its robust development was critical. The founder of *Ned Buntline's Own,* a magazine started in the mid-1840s, Buntline was a fabulously prolific hack who is reported to have written four hundred novels—six in one week! Buntline (the name comes from a nautical term for a rope) was a larger-than-life character, a famed rascal who survived lynching on one occasion and had killed a man in a duel. He was a kind of prince of rogues, a P. T. Barnum with a pen, a promoter of himself and various ventures. He was the man who would invent Buffalo Bill.

Buntline is often referred to as "an adventurer"—an appropriate description. He'd run off to sea as a boy and served in the military in the Seminole Indian War in Florida and later in the Civil War. Buntline claimed he had been a colonel in the War Between the States and often referred to himself as "chief of scouts," but that appears to be nonsense. Don Russell, Buffalo Bill's best biographer (and no fan of Ned's), claimed that Buntline never saw any action in the war.

In a golden age of prevarication, Ned Buntline was one of the more stupendous liars who left in his wake assorted wives (seven by one count) and assorted debts and a legend at least as lively as anything he ever put to paper. His date of birth is disputed—either 1821 or 1823. He was said to be one of the wealthiest writers in America in his heyday, earning $20,000 a year, the equivalent of a freelance journalist earning more than $200,000 today. But debt always dogged him. He was in and out of jails on charges involving money owed to his various wives. He was involved with the bigoted Know-Nothing Party (a nativist and antiforeign organization), charged with inciting to riot against foreigners in St. Louis. He did a lot of bad things in his time. Buntline died in 1886, and although his works now are simply period curiosities purchased by collectors, his reputation as a rogue and promoter a la Barnum survives.

According to the hoary version of the meeting of Buntline and Buffalo Bill, the commanding officer at Fort McPherson, eager to find something or someone else to keep Buntline busy, pointed out a young man resting in the shade of a wagon. He was a scout and buffalo hunter named William Frederick Cody. He was not widely known as Buffalo Bill then, although he had shot 4,280 buffalo (by his own count) to feed railroad workers, and Buntline couldn't claim credit for the name later. Western historians like to point out that others were vying for the sobriquet Buffalo Bill.

But here on the Fort McPherson parade ground, something of the myth of Buffalo Bill was born, and here, too, is where some of the myth of the Pony Express began. It is difficult to dismiss the exposure of the young and unsophisticated Billy Cody of 1869 to a scamp of the pedigree of Ned Buntline. For if Buntline had some role in the begetting of Buffalo Bill, Buffalo Bill begat the story of the Pony Express.

Like any good folk hero, the man who would become Buffalo Bill, the first celebrity in the country's history, had humble roots. William Frederick Cody was born on February 26, 1846, in a four-room log cabin near Le Claire, Iowa, according to the family Bible and the U.S. Census of 1850. His biographers seem to agree on this; they don't always agree on everything. The family moved to "Bleeding Kansas," not yet a state, when Cody was eight. The territory of Kansas was rocked with violent disputes between pro- and antislavery forces. It was the world of the abolitionist vigilante John Brown and later the psychotic William Clarke Quantrill, a Confederate guerrilla who decimated Lawrence, Kansas, during the Civil War, killing 183 Union sympathizers. Cody's father, Isaac, though not political, was once stabbed by a mob of proslavery supporters. Isaac Cody later died of pneumonia when Will, as his family called him, was eleven. Thus began the adventure that would lead to Cody's lifelong association with the memory of the Pony Express.

In 1857, not long after his father's death, Will Cody was hired as a messenger for the freight-hauling firm of Majors and Russell (which would become Russell, Majors & Waddell). He was paid twenty-five dollars a month and outfitted with a gray mule. His mother is said to have implored Alexander Majors to hire the lad.

William Frederick Cody, who was first Billy Cody or Will Cody, gradually became Buffalo Bill, the most famous American of his time. He moved easily to the stage life of being Buffalo Bill the showman and purveyor of all things western and a true citizen of the West. People knew him everywhere. Kings and kaisers and presidents and even the pope honored him. He had name recognition, like a brand name, a trademark. In France, where the nation was mesmerized by Cody, a brightly colored postcard and poster showed the plainsman with the flowing hair. His name did not even appear. Merely the words *Je vien*. I'm coming. That was all France needed to know.

Buffalo Bill was a figure of myth, rooted in fact, a stage persona spun out of the real-life exploits of an actual scout and buffalo hunter. Cody's most thorough biographers and sympathetic critics admit that it is impossible to entirely sort out the real from the fantastic in his complex and controversial life. It was a life full of dime-novel heroics. Even Cody himself may not have been entirely sure in the end what was true and what was not. His most charitable apologists and defenders, and he is worthy of defense, admit that a lot of the legend was beyond sorting out. It had simply grown too big.

Despite the American appetite for debunking, Cody was not simply a fake. He was a genuine frontiersman with genuine credentials from years on the plains. He had scouted extensively for the army, fought Indians, seen plenty of action, been in the Civil War on the side of the Union, and hunted buffalo to feed hungry railroad workers. He was awarded the Medal of Honor by Congress for fighting Indians. (It was later revoked on a technicality and then reinstated.) He was elected to the Nebraska legislature but appears not to have served. He attempted to negotiate the surrender of his friend Sitting Bull (who had spent a season on the road with the Wild West show). He was said to have taken "the first scalp for Custer"—revenge for the Little Big Horn. Other of his exploits do not stand up to close examination. He had critics while he lived and more in death. He has been debunked a hundred times. Still, he remains Buffalo Bill.

Cody was a strapping, handsome, rugged man who appealed to women, really could shoot and ride with the best of them, and actually liked Indians and got along well with them. (He does not appear to have killed many Indians.) He drank heavily, alcoholically, but was said to have never missed a performance or shirked his duty. Old folks around North Platte, Nebraska, where he made one of his homes for much of his life, swore later that he was a falling-down drunk. But for every testament to his drinking there's another to counter it.

He was reckless and rash and sentimental and emotional. He wanted to name his firstborn boy after Ned Buntline (cooler heads prevailed and the child was named after Kit Carson). The child died young, breaking Cody's heart. He loved children. He was gallant. He was famously generous and kind. Get-rich-quick schemes entranced him. He made and squandered and made and squandered fortunes; so much so that he was forced to stay on the road, trouping his Wild West show even as an old man. He could not afford to quit. Like a kind of feudal chieftain, he had a vast retinue that depended upon him.

He appears to have loved animals, especially horses, although he shot a lot of animals in the line of work. Although he was married for fifty-one years, he liked women and was usually discreet. His divorce trial in Cheyenne, Wyoming, was the turn-of-the-century equivalent of a media circus. (The Codys were later reconciled.) He had a great sense of showmanship and a great sense of honor, too. He would perform before an audience no matter what the circumstances, even if he was ill, even if there was only a handful of patrons.

When Buffalo Bill went into a saloon, everyone drank—on him. He would scatter twenty-dollar gold pieces on the top of the bar. And the little boy who held his horse outside got a dollar, sometimes five if the Great Scout did not have change. There was never anyone quite like Buffalo Bill.

In popularizing the vanished Wild West at the end of the nineteenth century, Buffalo Bill would preserve and enshrine one of the most heroic chapters in the story of the frontier—the Pony Express. He had to take some liberties to do this, but Buffalo Bill was one of the first to understand that the story of the Pony Express was much, much bigger than the truth.

———

Ned Buntline's chance encounter and some brief time spent with Cody resulted in Buntline's *Buffalo Bill: The King of the Border Men—the Wildest and Truest Story I Ever Wrote,* a serial published in a New York newspaper. Buntline's yarn might not have been the truest story he ever wrote, but it was most certainly the wildest. The story of Buffalo Bill's adventures was nearly complete fabrication. Cody was embarrassed, but he would recover easily. The Buntline tale eventually resulted in a stage play based loosely on it, which begat Buffalo Bill the American folk hero. (Buntline had nothing to do with the play.)

When Cody visited New York in 1871, Buntline took him to see himself being portrayed onstage. The theater's manager, learning that the real Buffalo Bill was present, asked that he step onto the stage. A year later Buntline lured the still-wide-eyed Cody onto the stage again in Chicago in a dramatic presentation of his own devising.

Called *The Scouts of the Prairie,* the drama featured Cody, Ned Buntline, another plainsman-turned-showman named Texas Jack Omohundro, and an Italian actress, Giuseppina Morlacchi (she and Texas Jack were later married). One account claims that Buntline cranked out the play in four hours. It was not a masterpiece. The show was said to be a critical disaster, and Buffalo Bill was a poor actor by all accounts. But audiences loved him anyway. (Some re-

viewers of opening night reported that when the action flagged—
Buffalo Bill was afflicted with stage fright—Ned launched into a temperance lecture to kill time.)

Helen Wetmore Cody, recalling her brother's debut in Chicago,
claimed that he overcame onstage paralysis at the prompting of Buntline, who coached Cody through a bit of storytelling.

"One of the pleasures of frontier life consists in telling stories
around the camp-fire. A man who ranks as a good frontiersman is
pretty sure to be a good raconteur. Will was at ease immediately, and
proceeded to relate the story of Milligan's hunt in his own words.
That it was amusing was attested by the frequent rounds of applause.
The prompter, with a commendable desire to get things running
smoothly, tried again and again to give Will his cue, but even cues
had been forgotten.

"The dialogue of that performance must have been delightfully
absurd. Neither Texas Jack nor Wild Bill was able to utter a line of
his part during the entire evening. In the Indian scenes, however, they
scored a great success; here was work that did not need to be
painfully memorized, and the mock red men were slain at an astonishing rate."

Whatever its critical flaws, the play proved to be a financial success. Cody learned a valuable lesson, too, something that Buntline appeared to have known all along. Easterners would pay to see Buffalo
Bill. Cody was a better actor than he had realized, and a better showman. The season closed in Boston after a successful tour of major
American cities. The next season there was no need for Ned Buntline;
Buffalo Bill was his own showman.

Some of Cody's later biographers have sought to downplay Buntline's role in the invention of Buffalo Bill—fair enough—but Cody's
sister, writing in *Last of the Great Scouts,* credits Ned with a significant role in her brother's public career. It's hard to know how much
of it is true; historians have always cast a cold eye on her story. Helen
Cody Wetmore's coauthor was the pulp western master Zane Grey.

For the next decade, corny plays based on Buffalo Bill's adventures such as *The Knight of the Plains; or, Buffalo Bill's Best Trail*
were Cody's first efforts in show business. It was seasonal work. In
the summer months, Cody returned to the West, the less and less wild
West, to scout and guide for the military or for high-rolling sports.

He took out parties of wealthy dilettantes who wanted to shoot.

He took out the New York newspaper publisher James Gordon Bennett (a shrewd career move). He worked for General Philip Sheridan as a guide (ditto). One of his crowning achievements was taking the twenty-one-year-old Russian Grand Duke Alexis on a highly successful extended buffalo hunt at the request of the czar. And there was a near-endless procession of British noblemen as well. Buffalo Bill knew how to show folks a good time.

As America's first celebrity, Buffalo Bill served as an ambassador to the world, a role he would later perfect with his Wild West troupe. He did not call it a show. It was not a show for him. It was not a circus or a carnival act. This was his West and his world. A century or more later it seems silly or cheapjack, but for William Frederick Cody, Buffalo Bill's Wild West, which toured the world for four decades, was never merely entertainment.

Whether Buffalo Bill ever sat on the back of a Pony Express mount will never be resolved. He claimed to have been a rider, and his admirers believe so fiercely, picturing the fearless lad pounding across the plains with the red men in hot pursuit. But Cody's critics have raised serious questions about the fabulist's boyhood adventures on behalf of the Pony Express.

Alexander Majors, who always boasted of hiring Cody as a messenger boy, only briefly mentions Cody's service as a Pony Express rider in his autobiography, *Seventy Years on the Frontier.* He spends far more time recounting the exploits of Pony Bob Haslam. It bears noting that Majors dedicated the book to Cody, and Cody paid for its publication. Cody wrote the preface, too.

The history of the book is curious. A treasured piece of Pony Express lore, impossible to corroborate, is that Buffalo Bill found the elderly, poverty-stricken Majors living in a mining shack outside of Denver in the early 1890s. The old man was trying to write his memoirs in hopes of generating a little income. Some accounts of this reunion between the ancient Majors and little Billy Cody are touching (Cody was nearly fifty). Majors's memoirs, if that is what they are, enshrine Buffalo Bill's connection with the Pony Express. Majors was the last living owner of the firm and a kind of ancient patriarch of the vanishing American West when the book was published in 1893. His imprimatur solidified Cody's Pony Express bona fides.

Majors does include a brief anecdote about Cody, recounting that his route for the Pony lay between Red Buttes and Three Crossings in Nebraska, a distance of 116 miles, according to Majors. "It was a most dangerous, long and lonely trail, including the perilous crossing of the North Platte River, one-half mile wide . . ."

Majors wrote that once, on reaching Three Crossings, Cody found that his replacement rider had been killed, and he was called upon to make an extra trip until another courier could be found. "This round trip of 384 miles was made without a stop, except for meals and to change horses, and every station on the route was entered on time. This is one of the longest and best ridden pony express journeys ever made," recalled Majors.

Majors remembered Cody and his mother coming to him to seek a position with the freighters. "I gave him the place, though it was one of peril, carrying dispatches between our wagon-trains upon the march across the plains, and little did I then suspect that I was just starting out in life one who was destined to win fame and fortune," Majors recalled. Chapter 29 of Majors's memoirs is given entirely to Buffalo Bill's boyhood, with only slight mention of the Pony Express. These were stories Majors fondly retold on countless public occasions when he said a few words about his lifelong friendship with Buffalo Bill.

Colonel Prentiss Ingraham, a master craftsman of lively western prose, is said to have ghostwritten the book, but that seems improbable. It is not a very good book. Ingraham probably only edited the manuscript. Majors complained later that Ingraham had embellished his life. Ingraham always argued that he was merely trying to tell a good story.

Following, literally, in the footsteps of Ned Buntline, Ingraham played a significant hand in the popularizing of Buffalo Bill with a series of dime novels about the plainsman's exploits. Born in 1843 in Mississippi, Ingraham was a Confederate army veteran and soldier of fortune who saw action in Mexico, Austria, Crete, Egypt, and Cuba, and turned his swashbuckling adventures into pulp fiction.

Ingraham met Buffalo Bill in the West in the early 1880s and later became an advance man for the Wild West show. But his chief occupation was a literary one. For four decades, Ingraham was an extraordinarily prolific dime novelist who claimed to have authored, in longhand, six hundred potboilers (others claim one thousand). A precise tally is difficult, as Ingraham used countless pen names. Ingraham's speed as a hack writer includes the boast that he once wrote a 35,000-word novel in a day and a half and on another occasion a 70,000-word novel in five days. An uncountable number of these yarns (possibly as many as two hundred) featured the largely imagined exploits of Buffalo Bill. These entertainments were the advance publicity that brought Buffalo Bill and his Wild West show to the attention of a larger public.

Ingraham (who liked to call himself Colonel) was long associated with the publishing firm of Beadle & Adams, the popularizers of the dime and half-dime novels. Critics credit Ingraham with being one of the first pulp writers to turn the rough image of the American cowboy into a chivalrous hero a la Owen Wister's *The Virginian* (1902).

Cody's autobiography, *Buffalo Bill's Life Story,* is not the best place to look for facts about the Pony Express, but it does provide ample evidence that Billy Cody might have been telling a stretcher about his days in the saddle for Russell, Majors & Waddell.

"Excitement was plentiful during my two years' service as a Pony Express rider," recalled the Great Scout. He would be the only person who remembered riding for the Pony for two years—as the firm went out of business in about eighteen months. In *Buffalo Bill's Own Story of His Life and Deeds* (where we see the handiwork of his "boy-hood chum and life-long friend" William Lightfoot Visscher), Cody had a completely different memory of the Pony Express. His account of his days as a rider takes up a mere page with few details. Here Cody recalled: "I stuck to it for two months and then, upon receiving a letter informing me that my mother was very sick, I gave it up . . ." Later Cody would claim that he returned to the service of the Pony Express—hired to ride by the notorious Jack Slade in western Nebraska and eastern Wyoming. Here Cody modestly recalled being credited with "the longest pony express journey ever made."

Buffalo Bill's autobiography is so full of canards that it is difficult to hazard what is plausible or rooted in the truth. A particularly interesting howler takes place in the days before the Pony Express when Billy Cody met up with Jim Bridger, Kit Carson, and some of the other legends of the Old West. Cody recalls watching with fascination as these fabled explorers talked with the red men in sign language. "I used to sit for hours and watch him and the others talk to the Indians in the sign language. Without a sound they would carry on long and interesting conversations, tell stories, inquire about game and trails, and discuss pretty much everything that men find worth discussing."

Billy Cody found this fascinating, and he resolved to learn these skills, too. "I was naturally desirous of mastering this mysterious medium of speech, and began my education in it with far more interest than I had given to the 'three R's' back at Salt Creek."

Cody claimed that he picked up the sign language like a native and reported that it saved his life later on. However, General Hugh Lenox Scott, a veteran military man of the Old West who knew Cody well (and liked him, too), recalled in his memoirs that Cody could not talk to the Indians in sign language.

Cody's sister, Helen Cody Wetmore, filled in some of the details of Billy Cody's days in the saddle for the Pony Express. Hard to know what to make of these tales. She claimed that George Chrisman, who had been chief wagon master for Russell, Majors & Waddell, gave the young Cody the job and that he was working for the cross-country mail service from the first day of its operation. Cody's sister recalled that he had a short run of only forty-five miles in western Nebraska, based at Julesburg, Colorado. (He was only fourteen.)

Cody's sister's memory of her brother's riding is more than slightly flawed. She remembers him riding three times a day for three months. No one rode that kind of schedule. There were only weekly cross-country mails at first and then twice-weekly dispatches. So there would have never been any need for anyone to be in the saddle three times a day. Cody's sister recalled how young Billy wrote home with an exciting account of his days riding for the Pony, but Alexander Majors recalls that the boy was illiterate, and Cody makes a point of writing about this, too, in his life story. He had not yet even learned to sign his name.

The story of Buffalo Bill's longest ride on behalf of the Pony Express is conveniently four miles longer than the ride made by Pony Bob Haslam. (It was always important that Buffalo Bill shoot the most buffalo or ride the most miles.) It requires that we believe Buffalo Bill was riding for the Pony Express at fourteen, too.

Alexander Majors often spoke fondly of Cody (and he did make reference to Cody and the Pony Express), but the old man chiefly talked about the boy's days as a messenger. Whether Cody simply spun off from that widely documented experience to include adventures with the Pony Express is impossible to prove or disprove.

Don Russell, Cody's best biographer, believed that Cody had ridden for the Pony Express—or at least believed that no one had proved otherwise. Russell is among several historians who quote Edward E. Ayer, a wealthy contractor who founded the American Indian collection in the Newberry Library in Chicago. According to a private journal kept by Ayer, when he was crossing the plains in 1860 he saw Billy Cody riding past his wagon train once a month shouting out news to the pilgrims headed west. (Ayer must have been making slow progress for this to have happened more than once, but he let that stand.)

Russell also notes that Cody's autobiography has some confusing elements relating to the Pony Express. Cody gives the date of the start of the Pony Express as 1859.

Perhaps Russell, writing in 1960, was too quick to give Cody the benefit of the doubt. In the spring of 1985, *Kansas History,* the Kansas State Historical Society quarterly, published an article that remains little considered in the annals of Buffalo Bill's boyhood adventures with the Pony Express. *Fact Versus Fiction in the Kansas Boyhood of Buffalo Bill,* by John S. Gray, leaves no question about Cody ever riding for the Pony Express. Gray was a physician at Northwestern University Medical School in Chicago who had a strong interest in western history. He brought a scientist's standards to his examination of Buffalo Bill's Kansas boyhood. Dr. Gray pretty much deconstructed Cody's childhood, sorting out the real from the fanciful. His assessment was that Cody's autobiographical account of his boyhood "features such chronological confusion, absurd heroics, and sheer impossibilities as to defy anyone's credulity."

Dr. Gray found Ayer's recollection improbable. "Are we to believe that Ayer's train took a month to cover the forty-five or even seventy-six miles of Cody's run? Or that he recorded the names of the speeding riders? More likely, Ayer remembered what he had read in his Buffalo Bill books."

Dr. Gray also found that Ayer's trip across Nebraska did not coincide with Buffalo Bill's claims as to when he was in the saddle for the Pony Express.

"Not just every book about Cody but every one about the Pony

Express recites Cody's Pony Express exploits, even Alexander Majors' memoirs. All, however, are easily recognized as mere quotations, paraphrases, or embellishments of Bill's autobiography," noted Dr. Gray. "There is but one tiny ember beneath these billows of smoke: for two months in the summer of 1857, the eleven-year-old Cody rode as a messenger boy for Russell, Majors & Waddell within a three-mile radius of Leavenworth. There seems no point in resisting the inevitable; Bill's pony riding represents another spate of fiction."

Dr. Gray was not without admiration for his subject, noting at the end of his autopsy: "It is unfortunate that Cody so clouded the truth with fiction, for the reality is an impressive record of character and fortitude."

What seems probable is that Buffalo Bill invented this link with the Pony Express based on his brief experience as a messenger. The last of the great scouts found such an addition to his C.V. fortuitous; he later made the Pony Express a permanent and revered fixture in his Wild West show. What is even more fascinating is that none of the book-length works on Buffalo Bill published since Dr. Gray's painstaking analysis bother to mention this whopper. And so Billy Cody, boy Pony Express rider, gallops on.

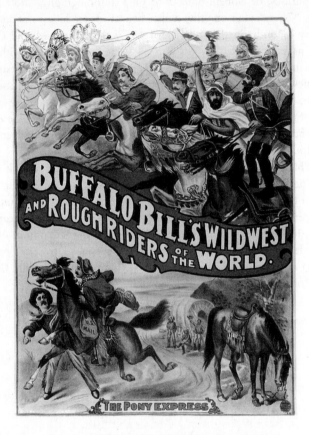

*Poster of Buffalo Bill's Wild West show with
Pony Express rider on the bill.*

Ten

BUFFALO BILL'S WILD WEST: "WHOLLY FREE FROM SHAM AND INSINCERITY"

> It is highly unlikely that the Pony Express would be so well remembered had not Buffalo Bill so glamorized it; in common opinion Buffalo Bill and the Pony Express are indissolubly linked.
>
> —DON RUSSELL, *THE LIVES AND LEGENDS OF BUFFALO BILL,* 1960

THE QUEEN WAS AMUSED
LONDON, 1887

The steamship *State of Nebraska* sailed from New York Harbor on March 31, 1887, with the Cowboy Band playing "The Girl I Left Behind Me," as the vessel carried Buffalo Bill's Wild West to England. The Great Scout was taking the Old West to the Old World. The idea of such a voyage appears to have come in part from Mark Twain, who greatly appreciated the Wild West and theatrics and knew a thing or two about showmanship. Twain, an enormous fan of Buffalo Bill's Wild West, had written to Cody after seeing the show during its sold-out New York engagement.

I have now seen your Wild West show two days in succession, and have enjoyed it thoroughly. It brought vividly back the breezy, wild life of the great plains and the Rocky Mountains, and stirred me like a war song. Down to its smallest details, the show is genuine— cowboys, vaqueros, Indians, stage coach, costumes and all; it is wholly free from sham and insincerity and the effects it produced upon me by its spectacles were identical with those wrought upon me a long time ago by the same spectacles on the frontier. Your pony expressman was as tremendous an interest to me yesterday as he was twenty-three years ago, when he used to come whizzing by from over the desert with his war news; and your bucking horses were even more painfully real to me as I rode one of those outrages once for nearly a quarter of a minute. It is often said on the other side of the waters that none of the exhibitions which we send to England are purely and distinctively American. If you will take the Wild West show over there you can remove that reproach.

If Twain's encouragement was not quite enough for Buffalo Bill and his longtime business associate Nate Salsbury, then the final endorsement for a road trip came from none other than the father of American showmen himself, P. T. Barnum. Then an old man laid up with gout, Barnum hobbled down from his home in Connecticut to see Buffalo Bill's Wild West, pronounced it marvelous, and told the press that it was headed for Europe. "It is the coming show," said Barnum, who knew a coming show when he saw one.

The company consisted of dozens of horsemen, cowboys, trick riders and ropers, and ninety-seven Indians of various tribes, some recently sprung from the Pine Ridge Reservation, preferring show business to life there. Their company included the Sioux chief Red Shirt, whose services were necessitated when Sitting Bull quit the show after a year. Miss Annie Oakley, perhaps the best known single performer, called Little Sure Shot, was on board, too. The Wild West menagerie, which gave British quarantine officers a fit, included 180 horses, eighteen buffalo, ten mules, five wild Texas steers, four donkeys, two deer, a trained elk, and a performing antelope. And because no Wild West show would be complete without these fixtures, Buffalo Bill also took along the Deadwood stagecoach and a rider of the Pony Express. After a wild passage (the Indians were seasick the entire voyage, as was Buffalo Bill), they arrived at Gravesend on April

16 and moved on to pitch camp in anticipation of the first performance, on May 9 at Earl's Court in London. But before the show even opened, Cody and his entourage were besieged by curious dignitaries. Former prime minister William Gladstone came to see them, as did the celebrated British actor Henry Irving, the actress Ellen Terry, and quite unexpectedly one afternoon as the troupe was still in rehearsal, Albert Edward, Prince of Wales, the son of Britain's long-reigning monarch, Queen Victoria.

Buffalo Bill's press agent, Arizona John Burke (who never set foot in Arizona), had made straight the way for the King of the Border Men by soliciting elaborate and enthusiastic testimonials from America's top generals. Burke, whom one of Buffalo Bill's biographers called "a master of the adjective to the exclusion of other parts of speech," spent thirty-four years promoting Buffalo Bill and had known Cody since the days of his stage show, *The Scouts of the Prairie*. Burke had the British primed for Buffalo Bill, who was sporting the newly obtained rank of colonel (a colonelcy from the Nebraska National Guard, but a colonelcy nonetheless). But nothing the wily Burke, a venerable pitchman who could manipulate even the Vatican on behalf of Buffalo Bill, could have conjured could compete with what happened serendipitously. Albert Edward had enjoyed Buffalo Bill's Wild West immensely. So about a week later, at precisely five o'clock on the afternoon of May 11, Queen Victoria, then celebrating her golden jubilee, the fiftieth anniversary of her reign over the British Empire, came to Earl's Court to see Buffalo Bill's Wild West for herself.

The ruler of the United Kingdom of Great Britain and Ireland and empress of India, who would reign the longest of any English monarch, was arguably then the most powerful person in the world. Her empire extended from the Canadian Rocky Mountains to the Khyber Pass, from Halifax, Nova Scotia, to Hong Kong. She had spent most of the previous twenty-five years since 1861 dressed in widow's weeds and in seclusion following the death from typhoid of her beloved husband, Prince Albert. The widow of Windsor was then, for the average British subject, a remote and mysterious specter, almost never seen.

Queen Victoria emerged from her shell almost without warning to view the spectacle at the insistence of her son, who would become King Edward VII. Her courtiers warned the American showmen that

Her Majesty could stay for one hour—no longer—and that she must see everything in that allotted time.

The queen did not travel light. She brought along a royal entourage that included the king of Denmark, the king and queen of Belgium, the king of Saxony, the king of Greece, the crown prince of Austria (whose assassination would start World War I), the crown prince and princess of Germany, Grand Duke Michael of Russia (in London looking for a bride), and Prince Louis of Baden.

As it turned out, the queen and her entourage were in no hurry to leave at the end of an hour. She stayed on. Buffalo Bill's Wild West had made another convert. No wide-eyed English schoolchild raised on tales of wild Red Indians and stampeding buffalo herds could have been more delighted than the sixty-eight-year-old dowager queen. Her Royal Highness clapped her hands like a six-year-old, enchanted with the spectacle of horsemanship, whooping Indians, the Deadwood stagecoach racing around the performing area, and the galloping rider of the Pony Express. The queen was amused. The queen was so amused that after the show she insisted on greeting Buffalo Bill, Chief Red Shirt (who had never heard of her), and Miss Annie Oakley, telling the twenty-six-year-old sharpshooter who looked half her age: "You are a very, very clever girl."

Old John Burke, barely able to contain himself, wired the American press that this was the first public appearance Queen Victoria had made in twenty-five years (which was not true, but it was not the first occasion in which Burke had taken liberties with the facts and it would not be the last). When Buffalo Bill rode into the performing ring at Earl's Court carrying the Star-Spangled Banner, Queen Victoria stunned the audience and even Cody by bowing from her seat to the American flag.

"For the first time since the Declaration of Independence, a sovereign of Great Britain saluted the Star-Spangled Banner—and that banner was carried by Buffalo Bill," John Burke cabled the American newspapers.

London went wild. Even Burke, who had followed in the footsteps of Ned Buntline, could not have cooked this up. "Buffalo Bill's Wild West stole the show while An Exhibition of the Arts, Industries, Manufactures, Products and Resources of the United States"—or American Exhibition, as it was more commonly called—failed abysmally. The American Exhibition (which Buffalo Bill's Wild West had been engaged as part of)—basically a cheesy trade show full of dull exhibits of inventions and industrial products—was an unqualified disaster, lampooned savagely by the British press as "an exhibition of dental surgery by distinguished Americans." One journalist noted that we "did not come to the exhibit to see the false teeth and the Christmas cards." Another added, "Nor are we likely to undertake a tour to West Brompton for the purpose of looking at such doubtless ingenious but decidedly ugly things such as coffee mills, stoves, Gatling guns, hand machines for executing embroidery presumed to be artistic, liquid fish-glue and an ironclad branduster."

Buffalo Bill's Wild West saved the day, mesmerizing the British public and bewitching the nation. Two and a half million English men, women, and children paid one to three shillings on average to see this wild spectacle of the Wild West that summer when it played Earl's Court before embarking on an equally successful tour of the British countryside. Thousands showed up merely to gawk at a real, live Indian.

The command performance for Queen Victoria was the high-water mark of Buffalo Bill's Wild West tour of England. At the end of the season, the venerable *Times* of London editorialized that Buffalo Bill's Wild West had brought England and America closer together, noting that the show was not merely a circus: "Those who went to be amused often stayed to be instructed. The Wild West was irresistible."

No one found it more irresistible than Her Royal Highness. The queen had been so enchanted with Buffalo Bill's Wild West that she demanded an encore, and on June 20 royalty from all over Europe attending her golden jubilee were entertained by the American cowboy and Indian troupe. Buffalo Bill got into the spirit of the occasion by personally taking the reins of the Deadwood stagecoach with young Prince Albert Edward riding shotgun and racing about the performing grounds with the kings of Denmark, Greece, Belgium, and Saxony in the back of the stage while Indians firing blanks and shouting bloodcurdling war whoops chased the royal caravan. "I've held four kings, but four kings and the Prince of Wales makes a royal flush, and that's unprecedented," Cody said later. As it turned out, someone pointed out that one of the royal personages was not, in fact, a king, but merely a prince—a detail that Buffalo Bill and Arizona John Burke would have easily overlooked.

Before Buffalo Bill and company left England a year later, to return triumphant to America, Miss Annie Oakley would shame the Grand Duke Michael of Russia by besting him in a public exhibition of marksmanship (it foiled his engagement strategy, too). Former Pony Express riders Broncho Charlie Miller and Marve Beardsley would win three hundred pounds in a six-day race against bicycles (they were on horseback). And the Sioux chief Red Shirt would go foxhunting with a party of English sporting gentlemen, displaying a style of horsemanship that amazed his hosts and wondering aloud what the big fuss was over chasing a tiny fox.

The King of the Border Men would troupe his show across the continent on and off for the next fifteen years. He would take it to see the kaiser in Berlin (Annie Oakley shot a cigarette out of the German monarch's mouth on a dare). He would take it to France and Spain and Italy. Buffalo Bill's Wild West show would even visit the Vatican, appearing before Pope Leo XIII.

The acts changed from year to year—Custer's Last Stand was replaced by the Rough Riders' charge up San Juan Hill, for example—but everywhere the show went it took certain permanent fixtures of the Wild West. From the first day the show had opened in Omaha, Nebraska, in 1883 until Buffalo Bill's final farewell in 1916 when it was no longer his show and he was so old and sick that he had to be hoisted onto the back of a horse, the Wild West always included the rider of the Pony Express. Wherever Buffalo Bill's Wild West went, in rain or in shine, triumphant or broke, the Pony Express went, too. Nothing ever did more to permanently brand the memory and the romantic image of the fast-mail relay rider on the mind of the public.

THE WHITE CITY
CHICAGO, 1893

The year after Buffalo Bill was tenderly reunited with his boyhood benefactor, Alexander Majors, in a Colorado mining shack, or so the story goes, the World's Columbian Exposition opened in Chicago, running from May 1 until October 26, 1893. More than 27.5 million people, nearly one-half of the population of the United States, turned out for the greatest public exhibition in the country's history. The American novelist Hamlin Garland, not long arrived in Chicago, put it best in a letter to his parents: "Sell the cookstove if necessary and come. You must see this fair."

The World's Columbian Exposition introduced the midway and the Ferris wheel to the American lexicon, and it featured, too, everything from Scott Joplin's ragtime to the compositions of Antonín Dvořák and the marches of John Philip Sousa. The dancer Little Egypt was on hand. Aunt Jemima, the pancake mix, made its debut there (like the Pony Express, born in St. Joseph). The largest demonstration of electricity in the nineteenth century took place in the fabulous White City, as the Chicago exhibition was called.

The fair celebrated not merely the four hundredth anniversary of Columbus's voyage of discovery (albeit one year late) but the beginning of the twentieth century (albeit a few years early), the age of technology and the end of the nineteenth century, a transitional time in America between rural and urban life. Chicago was the capital of the nation's heartland, and Americans were moving to the city. Nothing could keep them down on the farm. The West was disappearing in 1893, and the wild West of only yesterday was now Buffalo Bill's Wild West show.

The world's fair of 1893 was the greatest show on earth; and quite naturally, Buffalo Bill and his Wild West show were there, too, camped right outside the entrance to the White City. It did a roaring business. Buffalo Bill, befitting his standing as America's ambassador to the world, attended opening festivities with President Grover Cleveland. The Wild West might have been vanquished, but the American appetite for what Buffalo Bill represented had never been healthier.

Buffalo Bill's biographer, Don Russell, would write later that Buffalo Bill's Wild West hit its high point at the World's Columbian Exposition in Chicago in 1893. "It is said that there were those who mistook the entrance to Buffalo Bill's Wild West for the entrance to the Columbian Exposition and, after seeing the show, came away well satisfied," Russell noted in *The Lives and Legends of Buffalo Bill*.

"The success of the exposition contributed to the success of Buffalo Bill, for no one considered that he had seen the fair unless he had also seen the Wild West. It was a show worth seeing. A veteran

Chicago city editor, who from his vantage point in newspaper work had seen just about everything worth seeing once, told me that he considered Buffalo Bill's Wild West in 1893 the greatest show he had ever seen in his life," Russell recalled.

Buffalo Bill's old friend from the Indian wars Major General Hugh Lenox Scott paid it similar tribute in saying, "That was the most realistic show I have ever seen."

In Chicago, Russell noted that "crowds were turned away from the Wild West show on the opening day, a 130,000-attendance day for the Fair. Adam Forepaugh's Circus attempted to compete, but made not a dent in Buffalo Bill's business. It had been called the most successful year in outdoor show history, with profits estimated at from $700,000 to $1 million [the equivalent today of between $14 million and $20 million]. The Wild West cashed in on a long accumulation of public interest."

Buffalo Bill and the West he immortalized had been out of the country in Europe—playing only one year in the United States since 1888. Americans were hungry for the Old West. In Chicago, scene of Buffalo Bill's stage debut more than twenty years earlier, crowds turned out to see Annie Oakley, an attack on the Deadwood mail coach, and a reenactment of the Battle of Little Big Horn. They also witnessed, as every audience had since the first Wild West show, the Pony Express rider. The 1893 program noted the fourth act: "Pony Express. The Former Pony Post Rider will show how the Letters and Telegrams of the Republic were distributed across the immense Continent previous to the Railways and the Telegraph."

Cody's biographers would note, too, that such acts as a group of Mexicans demonstrating the use of the lasso and feats of horsemanship along with "cowboy fun, picking objects from the ground, lassoing wild horses and riding the buckers" were the stirrings of the commercial rodeo of the twentieth century.

Chicago provided the debut of Alexander Majors's much-edited and heavily rewritten life story, *Seventy Years on the Frontier*. Buffalo Bill had guaranteed its publication by Rand McNally. It sold poorly.

Chicago proved to be something of an unplanned family reunion for the best-known members of that extended clan associated with the Pony Express and its legacy. Not only was Buffalo Bill in town but also Alexander Majors, the inventive biographer and dime novelist Prentiss Ingraham, and Robert "Pony Bob" Haslam, perhaps the best-known rider of the Pony Express.

They were not the only Americans in Chicago that hot summer who were thinking about the vanishing American West. Frederick Jackson Turner was an unknown college professor from the Midwest staying in a dormitory at the University of Chicago. Turner, thirty-one, taught history at the University of Wisconsin (with a newly minted doctorate from Johns Hopkins University). The president of the University of Wisconsin had arranged for him to give a paper at the World's Congress of Historians, an event organized by the American Historical Association, one of a series of such presentations designed to bring a bit of erudition to the world's fair. A decidedly junior member of this conclave, Turner had published nothing of any consequence. He tried unsuccessfully to get out of the presentation, offering instead to send a promising graduate student in his place.

In the end, Turner read a short paper, which he had been working on right up until minutes before he took the podium. He was the last of five speakers that evening. It was brutally hot and listeners were tired. Many in the audience had left and others were dozing.

Turner's speech followed such illuminating talks as Dr. Reuben Gold Thwaites on "Early Lead Mining in Illinois and Wisconsin" and Dr. George Kriehn on "English Popular Uprisings in the Middle Ages." It had not been a lively evening. One of Turner's biographers noted that by the time the young historian rose to speak, it was before "an audience so deadened by this display of learning that he doubtless read only a portion of the lengthy essay he had prepared." Another Turner scholar noted that the four previous speakers had "tested the audience's mettle by presenting deadeningly old-fashioned scholarly exercises." Even Turner's parents, who had come to Chicago to see the world's fair, with young Fred as their guide, had not bothered attending.

Turner's paper was called "The Significance of the Frontier in American History." A century after the paper was presented, John Mack Faragher, distinguished professor of American history at Yale, called it "the single most influential piece of writing in the history of American history."

The impetus, in part, for Turner's paper was the U.S. Census Department announcement of 1890 that there was no longer a frontier in the American West. Taking this as his cue, Turner argued that the fundamental dominating factor in American history had been the frontier and the movement west. "The existence of an area of free land, its continuous recession, and the advance of American settlement westward explain American development." Turner's thesis was that America's national character and its institutions had their origins in the frontier movement west. Turner believed that the closing of the frontier marked a major change in the nation's history and development.

Turner's frontier theory—revised and expanded upon during his lifetime—has come in and out of favor for more than a century since it was first proposed. It has been denounced and defended, deconstructed and reconstructed, ridiculed and revived. Vast reams of critical response have been written about Turner's thesis. It has kept the schoolmasters busy for a century. But it remains somehow part of the canon, not to be ignored. Samuel Eliot Morison called Turner's short essay "the most influential ever written on American history."

Half the country was in Chicago that summer, and the White City was full of coincidences. On the evening that Fred Turner offered his momentous theory on the history of America and the significance of the American West, a young Harvard-educated Philadelphia lawyer was squiring his mother and a family friend around the wonders of Chicago. Turner's paper was not publicized, so the lawyer, Owen Wister, did not attend the talk. Wister had his own ideas about the West, too, and was heading to Wyoming after seeing the sights in Chicago, traveling to the still-remote Wind River region where he was doing the research that would become the first great popular American novel about the West—*The Virginian*, published in 1902. On Wister's Wyoming sojourn, he would stop for a hot meal at a remote inn in the Yellowstone country, and there he would meet a fellow easterner, a Yale-trained artist whose representations of the West became equally famous—Frederic Remington.

As it would happen, Turner's colleagues in Chicago paid no attention to him. There was no immediate response or even recognition of his presentation. On the hot afternoon of July 12, the rest of the notables attending the meeting of historians took up a generous offer for a few hours' free entertainment. They had left poor Fred Turner sweating in his dormitory room, fussing over the final draft of his theory of American history—a theory that one scholar later noted would roll like a tidal wave through the nation's universities. Turner's esteemed colleagues took the afternoon off and went to the shores of Lake Michigan next to the grounds of the fair to view a dramatic presentation that was based, coincidentally, on the vanishing American frontier, too—Buffalo Bill's Wild West.

Colonel William Lightfoot Visscher
in the 1890s.

Eleven

THE COLONEL AND HIS
THRILLING AND TRUTHFUL
HISTORY

. . . One of the most romantic and daring business ventures
this country, or any other country, ever knew. That was the
Pony Express.

—WILLIAM LIGHTFOOT VISSCHER

He called himself Colonel William Lightfoot Visscher. He was not a
colonel, and he was not a historian, either. The trail was long cold
and memories dimming when Colonel Visscher sat down to compose
the first history of the Central Overland California & Pike's Peak Express Company.

Visscher went to Chicago to cover the world's fair of 1893 for various newspapers back in the Pacific Northwest, his latest stop in a
lifetime of wandering the country. He would remain in Chicago after
the fair closed, serving later as librarian for the Chicago Press Club
(his legal address on occasion).

Visscher's *A Thrilling and Truthful History of the Pony Express*
would not be published until 1908—fifteen years after the informal
Pony Express reunion that brought Buffalo Bill, Pony Bob, Alexander Majors, and Prentiss Ingraham together at the world's fair. But
the events that would determine the fate of that slim volume began

that spring and summer when the memory of the Wild West mesmerized Chicago.

Visscher had been variously a peripatetic journalist of some renown, a prolific if not accomplished poet ("Black Mammy"), and a writer of serial novels for the newspapers *(Carlisle of Colorado: A Thrilling Story of Chicago and the Far West)*. He had a touch of the greasepaint in his background, too. He had been on the stage as an actor and comedian. He had been a temperance lecturer. He took a drink, too. He was a lifelong Mason and member of the veterans' organization of those who had served with the Grand Army of the Republic. He loved to speak and recite original verse at Fourth of July celebrations. Any occasion was for him a good one for a poem and a stirrup cup.

Chicago was a literary boomtown at the end of the nineteenth century with a lively if outrageous newspaper scene. There were some half dozen daily newspapers in the city at the time and dozens of book and magazine publishers. Many American newspapers, even relatively modest ones, maintained a correspondent in the city. Eager to escape the isolation of the Pacific Northwest, Visscher was tired of three decades of roaming that had seen him cross the American Midwest and West from Indianapolis to San Francisco and back again.

The world of Chicago journalism at that time was colorful. John J. McPhaul, writing in *Deadlines and Monkeyshines: The Fabled World of Chicago Journalism,* recalled: "One of the most interesting press spas was situated in 'Newspaper Alley' near the offices of the News and the Herald. It was called the Whitechapel Club in honor of the London district in which Jack the Ripper had performed informal autopsies on ladies of the evening."

The then-popular novelist Opie Read was a member, too. He recalled:

The bar was in the shape of a coffin. The walls were adorned with ropes donated by the county hangman, and blood-stained Indian blankets Charley Seymour of the Herald had brought back from the Sioux War in the Dakotas. Guests of honor were required to don a sword used by a West Side teamster in the decapitation of his unfaithful spouse. They were served ale in two silver-lined skulls. One was claimed to be the headpiece of the late Roxey Brooks, renowned as the world's champion woman heavyweight boxer. The other, it was said, had been used initially by Frances Warren, alias Waterford Jack, a "pug-nosed, ugly-looking little critter" but withal reputed to have earned $1,000,000 in a decade of streetwalking. The members of the club were once reputed to have convinced the lone remaining member of a suicide club to fulfill his obligation. They then sold the story to the Chicago Herald for $500.

Visscher delighted in this world. Chicago would remain his home for the remaining thirty-one years of his life, and it was here, far from the Wild West and the romance that he had sought across the wide Missouri as a younger man, that he would begin to help shape the legend of Buffalo Bill as one of a long list of the great showman's rewrite men. In addition to a hand in crafting *Buffalo Bill's Own Story of His Life and Deeds,* Visscher wrote "Buffalo Bill, a Knight of the West," a poem that appears in *Poems of the South and Other Verses*. But before he did that, Visscher warmed himself to the task by an invaluable contribution toward the construction of the myth of the Pony Express.

William Lightfoot Visscher belonged to that nineteenth-century tribe of wandering scribes that he called Bohemians in his 1873 memoirs, *Vissch*. These were the foot soldiers of the American newspaper business in Visscher's long working life—roughly from the mid-1860s until shortly before his death in 1924.

Bohemians are the people who make the modern newspaper . . . They are generally city editors and reporters . . . Sometimes on western dailies he occupies at the same time the position of city editor, local reporter, commercial reporter, river reporter, musical and dramatic critic, telegraph and news editor and proof-reader; perhaps attends a little to the general business of the establishment, carries a route in an emergency, and often when the chief is away for a few months, distributing visiting cards in New York, will condescend to perform the duties of that leisurely mortal. The Bohemian is in many cases more intimately acquainted with the people, the streets, the business and the 'ins and outs' of a dozen or twenty different cities than their mayors, policemen and oldest inhabitants collectively. It is not uncommon for him, within the space of an hour, to be called upon to visit the lowest hovels of the most degraded and poverty-stricken, there to see a poor wretch who is going to his last account, uncared for and unkempt, and to promenade the salons of the wealthiest and proudest and most exalted of the land, mayhap to witness a grand bridal ceremony which starts a fortune-kissed couple along the delightful pathway of a beautiful life. He may stand at a festal board at night, and witness the very waste of hundreds of dollars worth of champagne, which is even wasted when it is drank, (this opinion is not held for very stringently, however,) and before the noon of the same night, hear the last faint moan of a dying woman who had no bread. He may dine with a clergyman, and interview a murderer before the next refection."

Despite a lifelong fondness for late hours, liquor, and tobacco, Visscher lived a long and busy life. No better man was suited to compose the first history of the Pony Express, for he brought to this task a mad, romantic love of the American West and its heroes real and fancied. Visscher was the quintessential dude with an exaggerated sense of chivalry that seemed comic even in his time. Opie Read, a close friend of Visscher's, recalled: "He worshipped all heroes and his vanity often expressed itself in his willingness to fight. He said that he would not even borrow money off a coward. Toward woman his hat was ever ready to sweep the sidewalk."

According to Read, the only writer Visscher appears to have admired or even read much of was Sir Walter Scott. Visscher's poetry, and he wrote reams of bad poetry, mostly on deadline to fill newspaper space, reflects his feelings for the West of Manifest Destiny. The poems are full of references to "bands of hardy men" and "riders bold."

Then Ho! For the land of plenty, under the western sun!
And Ho! For the land of flowers, land of the vine and tree!
Ho! For the land of grit and gold, the land of heroes won!
Ho! For the land of Fortune's home, along the western sea!

Read recalled that "ambition inflamed Visscher to become a cowboy, and he went out far into the west but found no acceptance in this wild employment . . ." He did meet Buffalo Bill and the two became friends.

Read noted in 1930 in his memoirs, *I Remember:* "Visscher was truly a poet, but he was as far from personifying the part physically as any man that ever cursed a broken shoestring. He was short, pudgy and squat-gaited when he strode."

One of the few photographs existing shows him looking like a nineteenth-century comic actor playing Cyrano de Bergerac. There was quite a bit of Don Quixote in there, too, and some Falstaff. He resembled the American film comedian W. C. Fields, favoring hats with broad brims and handlebar mustaches, the ends of which were twirled and waxed to sharp points. During one of his sojourns into vaudeville, he appeared onstage dressed as a matador.

Looking Back, a history of the Pacific Northwest published almost a century after Visscher's era, recalled that he described himself when he described a character in one of his novels, *Way Out Yonder.* "The trousers were of a black and white, small-checked pattern, the vest and coat of black tricot—the latter a 'Prince Albert' cut—and his hat was a soft felt, as broad brimmed as a sombrero." A photograph of Visscher in just such garb exists. He looked preposterous.

The *Tacoma Daily News* once observed that Visscher had a "long and lurid" experience with liquor. He was by the accounts of even his friends and admirers a drunkard. A century after his antics scandalized the town, the *Fairhaven Gazette,* noting Visscher's "red potato nose," recalled that he despised children. "Visscher often threatened to sell bothersome children for a pint or less of stiff drink and in a fit of good humor prevailed upon the only surviving member of a suicide club to complete his obligations so that Visscher and his friends at the Chicago Press Club might partake of his cremation at their next outdoor 'bar-b-que.' "

Visscher was born on November 25, 1842, in Owingsville, Kentucky (he retained a lifelong affection for his native state and frequently visited). The minutes of the Washington State Press Association from 1887 to 1890 report that he spent much of his boyhood in Danville, Kentucky, "called in those days 'the Athens of the West.' " He claimed to have descended from Huguenot aristocrats. He was educated at the Bath seminary and the University of Louisville, where he graduated from the law school in 1867. There is no record of him ever practicing law. Visscher's education was interrupted by the Civil War. He helped to raise Company I of the 24th Kentucky Infantry and served with that regiment from the summer of

1861 until the surrender at Appomattox. Later versions of Visscher's life often claimed that he had been a colonel in the Union army (something he never bothered disputing). He had, in fact, served as a hospital steward during the war. His military title was an honorific bestowed by the Washington State National Guard.

Visscher loved words as much as he loved the sound of his own voice and "Kentucky's justly celebrated liquid staple." He began his career in 1865 with George Dennison Prentice, celebrated editor of the influential *Louisville Daily Journal*. Visscher was Prentice's stenographer, office boy, secretary, runner, and cub, a position he would describe as "amanuensis." Prentice was a Connecticut Yankee who was educated at Brown University, studied law, and founded the *New England Review*. He went to Kentucky originally to write the biography of Henry Clay.

At the time that Visscher showed up looking for a job, the sixty-one-year-old Prentice was one of the best-known journalists in the country and a spectacular eccentric, famous for his love of women and dueling. Prentice had been afflicted since about 1840 with "scrivener's cramp" (probably carpal tunnel syndrome or some other repetitive stress disorder of the hand) and spent the remainder of his life dictating his editorials and other works.

Prentice had played a significant role in the xenophobic Know-Nothing riots in Louisville, which resulted in a number of deaths. His editorials were fiercely anti–Roman Catholic and antiforeign (Irish and German in particular), and helped fuel the riots of August 6, 1855, in which Roman Catholic churches were burned and at least twenty-two died.

After the *Journal* and the *Courier* were consolidated, Visscher began publishing a daily newspaper on a Mississippi River steamboat, *Richmond*, which traveled the river between Louisville and New Orleans. From there he was on to newspapers from Indianapolis to Cheyenne. Eventually he turned up on the West Coast, working for various San Francisco papers for five years, worked as a comedian and actor, and returned to Grub Street in Chicago. From there Visscher moved to the Pacific Northwest for a stint as an editorial writer at the *Portland Oregonian*, followed by the *Tacoma Daily Globe* and the *Fairhaven Herald*.

Biographical material in the files of the *Tacoma News-Tribune* calls Visscher "a true peripatetic." The *Fairhaven Gazette* remembered him for his wild antics and "inebriated gait." "According to those who knew him, Visscher was never quite happy as a newspaperman unless he was in hot water with someone. This may have been his undoing."

Visscher kept unusual company. In January 1889, he turned up in Tacoma aboard the steamer *The State of Washington*. Tacoma was a wide-open and wild town where Harry Morgan acted as a kind of godfather to local crime. Morgan was variously a saloon operator, gambling house proprietor, variety theater impresario (Theatre Comique), and brothel keeper ("A town without saloons and gamblers ain't worth a damn"). He was also a celebrated opponent of women's suffrage. Reputed to be worth a million dollars (nearly $20 million by today's calculations), Morgan had no legitimate business interests save a modest cedar shingle mill, a front for his more lucrative enterprises.

Morgan started the *Globe,* largely to counter opposition in the local press to his activities. It was a lively broadsheet, celebrated for lurid headlines such as this one over an account of a hanging: "Jerked to Jesus."

Morgan hired Visscher to edit the *Globe* and to serve as a kind of public relations man. Visscher's instructions, according to accounts of the period, were "to make vice nice." Visscher was just the man for the job. The colonel and the *Globe* painted Morgan as a kind of good-hearted Robin Hood whose various enterprises were run solely to provide jobs for the citizens. Visscher was, in the parlance of the newspaper business, "a howler," a booster of causes and promoter of business, a kind of Rotarian-for-hire, a hail-fellow, a man who enjoyed his cocktails and the companionship of those who did likewise.

Journalism was also rough in Tacoma, typical of the West then. Newspapermen routinely shot at one another. Visitors to newspaper offices, rankled about a dispatch, came armed or bearing a horsewhip to settle things with the editors. No stranger to violence, Visscher could be a formidable pugilist when the situation required—a skill he cultivated under the tutelage of George Prentice. If Visscher was drinking, all the better.

Visscher once shot a policeman who attempted to arrest him for public drunkenness (the cop lived) and on another occasion knocked out a journalist with whom he was having an argument. The Washington State Press Association loved him nonetheless. "Col. Will L. Visscher holds a tender spot in the hearts of all who know him; he combines the wit and gentleness of the Kentuckian with the energy necessary to success in his profession, and those who have read, laughed and cried over his quaint poetry in Southern dialect, portraying characters of the South and of the Rebellion, will then only have realized his genius and power of thought."

According to Opie Read, Buffalo Bill told this story about the hard-drinking newspaperman:

> In a mining camp Visscher chanced to find himself and realized that as he was a poet he was broke. His Kentucky blood curdled at the thought of his asking for a drink but his tongue lolled for liquor. Not a penny had he, but the nymph of quick fortune smiled upon him. He heard that a bad man had just entered the favored saloon of the tented berg. Into the place the poet went, took off his bushel hat, wiped his brow and spoke:
>
> "I understand that a rude, wild fellow is going about this place compelling people to drink when they are in principle against that degrading vice. I am a Kentucky gentleman, never took a drink in my life: and I want to say right here that I'd like to see the fellow that could—" Up sprang a lithe and buck-skinned man, snatched out a gun and commanded: "Throw up your hands." Visscher was startled but obeyed. Then the bad man turned to the bartender. "Set out five drinks there, all in a row." The bartender was hasty to obey. "Now, sir," said the shooter to the poet, "you begin up there and drink your way down. Quick. No words." The poet made swift use of his hands, ah-hahed his way, and reaching the end of the liquid journey, turned to the bad man and said: "Say, have him fill 'em up again and I'll drink my way back."

There are several other versions of this story (the setting and number of drinks change). Visscher frequently passed himself off as a temperance lecturer to trick strangers into buying him free drinks. His misadventures with alcohol were innumerable.

Shortly before the Chicago world's fair opened, Visscher was on the hustings preaching the good news of sobriety to the citizens of Denver. The *Field and Farm* reported on April 8, 1893, that Visscher was giving personal testimony about the evils of drink to those who would listen in the Colorado capital. They were hearing an expert.

"Colonel Will L. Visscher who has been in Colorado the past fortnight lecturing under the auspices of the Keeley gold-cure league, was about as heavy a 'lusher' as was seen around Denver years ago and his reform is the eighth wonder of the world."

The *Field and Farm* printed a spirited and frightening account of Visscher's experiences with the "jim-jams"—delirium tremens.

Delirium tremens is produced by drinking too much whisky. I drank too much whisky and got the "jims." I didn't know I was getting them, but the bar-keeper did. I sat down in the bar room one day and began to pick imaginary bugs off my hands. The bar-keeper suggested I had better go home. I did so, and shortly after getting there I was a first-class lunatic, by means of a number one dose of jim-jams. Three gentlemanly neighbors came in and sat on me and smoked tobies and enjoyed themselves. I did not know exactly what was going on, but I had a faint idea that it was a sort of go-as-you-please picnic, in which I was left. I saw no snakes but I saw turkeys. They came in through the window and marched around my bed in single file. I asked some of them a few questions in a friendly way, but they never said a word, and at the same time I felt that there was no animosity between us. After a while they left but soon came in again; this time each turkey had a monkey on its back, and each monkey seemed to be in a hilarious condition and wanted to have fun. I laughed at that. The gentlemen who sat on my legs and scratched matches on the soles of my feet to light their cigars said I laughed. My wife cried, however, just to be contrary. Then the turkeys went out again, and every monkey was carrying a red, white and blue parasol when they reappeared. I never had so much fun in my life until about a hundred and fifty brass bands commenced to play, and each band was playing a different tune. I was trying to get them all to play the same air, but it was no good, and I got so exasperated that the three gentlemen had to sit on my legs worse than ever. However, I came through it, but feeling like a dishcloth and looking as though I had been through a threshing machine. I have had my turn at the wheel and if any healthy young buck wants "the snakes" he can have my share of them.

After his Pacific Northwest adventures, friends from those wild days recalled Visscher as capable of drinking up to two quarts of gin a day. Half a century after his arrival in Tacoma, the *Bellingham Herald* remembered that he entered the community "broke and thirsty" and went immediately to a notoriously rough bar to con the locals into letting him drink free.

When the proprietor of the Green River distillery in Owensborough presented Opie Read and Visscher, then on a reading tour, with a quart of whiskey, Read recalled that Visscher took a silk shirt and swaddled the bottle. "I am going to wrap this liquor up in it and nurture it as a mother would her child."

Even the dry *History of Whatcom County* in the state of Washington commented on what a wild character Visscher was. "Colonel Visscher was a genius. His literary ability, both as a newspaper man and a writer of verse, was known and recognized throughout the country . . . With his genius, however, there was a carefree attitude toward life, which had led him to many scenes of activity and many vicissitudes. He was a 'bon vivant' as well as a genius, and this, while it doubtless contributed to his lack of ultimate financial success, added greatly to the picturesqueness of his career."

Despite the demands of his extracurricular activities, Visscher was a prolific hack in the tradition of Ned Buntline and Colonel Prentiss Ingraham. He published *A Thrilling and Truthful History of the Pony Express with other sketches and incidents of those stirring times* forty-seven years after the last courier galloped in with the mail. Visscher's slim book was the first history of the fast-mail service. It contains no bibliography, no footnotes, no table of contents. There are no acknowledgments of sources, although Visscher knew the various members of the Pony Express fraternity—many as drinking companions.

Much of the book has nothing to do with the Pony Express. The "other sketches and incidents of those stirring times" account for a substantial piece of Visscher's volume. (The Battle of Wounded Knee, which took place thirty years after the Pony Express folded, gets a write-up.)

Visscher got the "thrilling" part right, but that was his forte. The book, a mere ninety-eight pages, was copiously illustrated. Although he knew Alexander Majors, Buffalo Bill, and Pony Bob Haslam, Visscher's thrilling and truthful history was a total rewrite job—borrowing heavily from the few published sources available. The first of those works was *The Great Salt Lake Trail*, by Colonel Henry Inman, the old cavalry veteran who looked like Mark Twain. It was published in 1898, a decade before Visscher's book. Inman was ably assisted in his literary efforts by none other than Colonel William F. Cody (Buffalo Bill loved to offer editorial advice to a struggling author). The only other book published at the time that made any attempt to chronicle the Pony Express was a serious work—*The Overland Stage to California*, by Frank A. Root and William E. Connelley, published in 1901. Visscher stole from that book, too.

There is actual information about the Pony Express in Visscher's book, but the writer gives no hint of where any of it came from (the most likely source was Alexander Majors). Visscher interviewed Charlie Cliff, a fixture around St. Joe as a spinner of Pony Express tales. Noting that Cliff was only seventeen when he rode, Visscher dubs him "one of the most daring" riders on the route. Poor Cliff, who rode in eastern Kansas, complained to any interviewer who would listen that nothing interesting ever happened to him while riding for the Pony.

Much of the confusion about the Pony Express's origins dates from Visscher's book, including the disputed date of the start of the express, the exact time, and who the first rider was. Visscher tells readers that the men were lightly armed and then notes that some riders were carrying Sharp's rifles.

Visscher's greatest service to the legend of the Pony Express was his enshrinement of Buffalo Bill as the king of the fast-mail couriers. Visscher claimed to be "a boy-hood chum" of Buffalo Bill's, which was a preposterous fiction. In addition to Buffalo Bill's legacy, Visscher greatly enriched the legend of Pony Bob Haslam in the saddle. These are cornerstones of the thrilling story.

Visscher's account has the badman Joseph Slade hiring young Billy Cody to carry the mail—replete with stirring dialogue. Visscher also includes pages of Ned Buntline–like adventures for young Cody with "Injuns" and road agents.

> "Hold! Hands up, Pony Express Bill, for we knew yer, my boy, and what yer carried."

> To which the bold lad replied:
> "I carry the express; and it's hanging for you two if you interfere with me," was the plucky response.

If the whoppers with young Billy Cody were not sufficient, Visscher also included additional "romantic stories" about the Pony Express including a heartwarming tale of an old trapper named Whipsaw and a two-year-old Pawnee child he adopted. The old trapper wound up as a station tender for the Pony Express, and the Indian boy saved the day.

When Visscher sat down to write, he was given a letter by Huston Wyeth, a prominent citizen in St. Joseph, Missouri. The letter, from J. H. (Jack) Keetley, a Pony Express veteran, then in the mining business in Utah, was full of errors. Keetley insisted that Alex Carlyle was the first rider out of St. Joe, a position favored by few others. Looking back over nearly half a century, Keetley took a tack favored by many a veteran of the saddle. He insisted that *he* had ridden the longest distance in the history of the Pony Express. "I made the longest ride without a stop, only to change horse. It was said to be 300 miles, and was done for a few minutes inside of twenty-four hours." Keetley claimed that he rode from Big Sandy in Nebraska to Elwood, Kansas (across the Missouri River from St. Joe), and back to Seneca (about eighty miles west of St. Joe) without relief.

In addition to making a wild claim about the first rider and boasting of his own prowess in the saddle, Keetley had the starting date of the Pony Express wrong—claiming it was April 16, 1860. He has the starting time wrong, too, saying it was 4:00 P.M. He has the location of the stables two blocks east of the Patee House, instead of two blocks west. He does describe the mochila (which he spelled "macheir") correctly. And he also claims (as did the young Chicagoan John D. Young, heading for the gold fields of Colorado) that the riders actually rode right into the Patee House to pick up the mail. (It is a description confirmed at the time by Secretary of State William Seward's secretary, too.) His description of the garb worn by Pony Express riders was elaborate and detailed. "We always rode out of town with silver mounted trappings decorating both man and horse and regular uniforms with plated horn, pistol, scabbard, and belt, etc., and gay flower-worked leggings and plated jingling spurs resembling, for all the world, a fantastic circus rider."

According to Keetley's memory, these trappings were decorative and merely for show.

Keetley's letter is so full of confusion and obvious mistakes that it would be easy to dismiss it completely. Colonel Visscher, as was his editorial practice, printed the entire letter without comment. He had come of age when journalists were paid by the column inch, and Keetley had written a nice long letter. Visscher tossed it into what the *National Geographic* later called "the buck-a-roo stew" that was to be the story of the Pony Express. It would be easy to ignore Keetley's letter but for this observation:

> The Pony Express was never started with a view to making it a pay-ing investment. It was a put-up job to change the then Overland mail route which was running through Arizona on the southern route, changed to run by way of Denver and Salt Lake City, where Ben Holladay had a stage line running tri-weekly to Denver and weekly to Salt Lake. The object of the Pony Express was to show the authorities in Washington that by way of Denver and Salt Lake to Sacramento was the shortest route, and the job worked success-fully, and Ben Holladay secured the mail contract from the Mis-souri River to Salt Lake, and the old southern route people took it from Salt Lake City to Sacramento. As soon as this was accom-plished and the contract awarded, the pony was taken off, it hav-ing fulfilled its mission. Perhaps the war also had much to do with changing the route at the time.

The colonel set the standard for exaggeration and embellishment that would chart the history of the Pony Express. Few writers would ever come down the trail after Visscher without paying homage to the master.

When he died, in 1924, at the considerable age of eighty-two (given his lifestyle), the *Tacoma Times* eulogized the jolly old hack. "Visscher was a brilliant man of parts, a picturesque soldier, writer, actor, newspaperman, and model of bonhomie." His books are long out of print, and only a short street in the north end of Tacoma bears his name—but his real legacy was his "thrilling and truthful history" of the Pony Express. When he finished, no one would ever be entirely sure what was true.

The gang's all here. Standing, left to right, Pony Bob Haslam and Colonel Prentiss Ingraham. Seated, left to right, J. B. Colton, Alexander Majors, and Buffalo Bill Cody.

Twelve

___

PONY BOB HASLAM: A TRUE RIDER OF THE PURPLE SAGE

Tales of hardships and perils stranger than fiction, could be written of this "Pony Express" enterprise.
—WILLIAM M. THAYER,
MARVELS OF THE NEW WEST, 1888

The citizens of Virginia City in Nevada celebrated the Fourth of July holiday early in 1868 with a horse race that pitted riders from two express mail lines—Wells, Fargo & Co. and the newly formed Pacific Union Express Company—against each other.

The correspondent for the *Territorial Enterprise,* whose dispatches were reprinted in the California newspapers, reported that the July 2 race had "stirred up an intense excitement in the city, not only in sporting circles, but among men not often in the habit of backing their opinions with coin. There were many heavy bets made, both as to the time which could be made and as to which company would first get into the city." About eighteen thousand citizens—mostly men—lived in and about Virginia City at the time of the race. It was a highly transient population, primarily miners and those who made their living off of miners: saloon keepers, whores, cardsharps, and dry goods merchants. Most were foreign-born or recent arrivals from "the states."

"All was excitement, avarice, lust, deviltry, and enterprise," one early witness of Virginia City recalled. "A strange city, indeed, truly abounding in strange exhibitions and startling combinations of the human passions."

Although gambling, wagering on anything, and drinking a stupefying concoction called Forty Rod—the distance one might walk after a few glasses—were the primary forms of relaxation in the fabled Comstock Lode, prizefighting, bare-knuckled brutal near-death matches between men, cockfighting, bearbaiting, and other forms of sport provided diversion for the citizenry.

Nearly a century after the boom days in Virginia City, Effie Mona Mack described something of this world in *Mark Twain in Nevada*. "Formal amusement in these early mining towns was not to be had. To make up for this lack of entertainment, every event, large or small, was played up as much as possible. Any kind of contest was the occasion for much betting, be it a horse race, a badger fight, hopping fleas, or a political contest."

The wandering Dublin-born journalist J. Ross Browne described this scene from in front of the International Hotel on C Street:

> . . . Store-keepers rolling their merchandise in and out along the wayside; fruit vendors are peddling their fruits; wagoners are tumbling out and piling in their freights of dry goods and ore; saloons are glittering with their gaudy bars and fancy glasses, and many-colored liquors, and thirsty men are swilling the burning poison; auctioneers, surrounded by eager and gaping crowds of speculators, are shouting off the stocks of delinquent stockholders; organ grinders are grinding their organs and torturing consumptive monkeys, hurdy-gurdy girls are singing bacchanalian songs in bacchanalian dens; Jew clothiers are selling off prodigious assortments of worthless garments at ruinous prices; bill stickers are sticking up bills of auctions, theatres, and new saloons; newsboys are crying the city papers with the latest telegraphic news; stages are dashing off with passengers for "Reese" [Austin, Nevada], "Frisco" . . .

On the literal edge of this Nevada mountainside, perched more than a mile above sea level, was a world that contained the mansions of millionaires made rich from lucky strikes, and joss houses and opium dens full of Chinese coolies who sweated sixteen-hour days as cooks and laundrymen and everything in between. Every member of this society would have been following the Fourth of July holiday race of 1868.

The race was run along a twenty-two-mile course—the road linking Reno, then a railhead, and Virginia City. The correspondent of the *Territorial Enterprise*—the newspaper on which Mark Twain had cut his teeth (and adopted his pen name) a few years earlier—reported that both Wells, Fargo and its competitor had been buying up fast horses for the contest.

Frank Henderson was in the saddle for the Pacific Union Express Company. He was a local, "a young man who has for some time been engaged as a driver on the omnibus line between this city and Gold Hill," noted the *Enterprise*. We do not know Henderson's age, but he weighed 139 pounds, an important factor for punters to consider—the route from Reno was a rough one and the last miles were up a steep mountainside to an elevation that eventually reached 7,200 feet.

In anticipation of the Reno–Virginia City race, both Wells, Fargo and Pacific Union had fast horses stationed at four-mile intervals along the route—five horses for each rider. The start of the race was to be the arrival of the train in Reno, bringing mail for Virginia City.

Three thousand people, hanging from the fronts of buildings and from roofs and balconies and windows and doors, lined C Street in Virginia City to watch the riders cross the finish line. The saloons, including the Bucket of Blood and the Sawdust Corner, were busy on this late summer afternoon.

Young Frank Henderson got off to a fine start—about ten rods ahead of his competition from Wells, Fargo. But this would be a brief illusion of victory for the Pacific Union Express rider, for he was almost immediately passed by his competitor, who gradually and easily increased his lead to some two miles before thundering down the main street of Virginia City about 5:00 P.M. to the wild cheers of miners and cardsharps and Chinese. (A practical joker had ridden down the street first "just for deviltry," the *Enterprise* reported, pretending to have won the race.)

The winning time from Reno was one hour and four minutes—about three minutes to the mile. Frank Henderson finished six minutes behind his competitor, who had allowed the young Pacific Union rider the lead out of Reno by pausing rather too dramatically to adjust his mailbag on his back. Six minutes behind was not bad time considering that Henderson had also fallen off his horse as he entered

Virginia City, badly cutting his head and knee. The driver of a light buckboard rig—the Wells, Fargo & Co. "lightning express wagon"—who was also making the run from Reno claimed he came close to beating both of the mounted riders, although he was twenty-five minutes behind the winner.

The *Territorial Enterprise* hardly needed to tell readers much about the horseman for Wells, Fargo, although the newspaper did. He was not merely one of the best-known riders in the American West in those years after the Civil War—he may have been one of the best riders in American history. The newspaper had described him as "an old rider for the company on the old Overland Pony Express route," and was well known in the state as "Pony Bob." The nickname alone would have been enough for all but the most tender greenhorn recently come over the Sierra Nevada from California to seek his fortune in the Silverado. Men came to see him ride.

The courier for Wells, Fargo & Co. was Robert Haslam—"as nervy and daring as possible for a man to be, and the most famous of the Pony Express riders," in the words of William Lightfoot Visscher. Haslam weighed 130 pounds, but the difference in weight was a minor factor in considering his ability. The smart money in the Comstock Lode was not on Henderson, whatever local appeal he might have had. Old hands in the territory knew who would win the race from Reno, and they were not disappointed.

It was not merely a horse race on a holiday—a common enough occurrence in 1868—that drew them away from their claims. They had come to town, left mining claims in the foothills at Sun Mountain and Silver City and Chinatown and walked or rode into Virginia City, to see Pony Bob Haslam, only twenty-eight years old on that Independence Day but already an almost mythic figure in Nevada and California. Men would tell their grandchildren fifty years later that they had seen him streak past.

The *Territorial Enterprise* dispatch reporting in detail the Wells, Fargo–Pacific Union race concluded: "The racing caused the greatest excitement we have seen in the city in a long time—even the ladies became excited, though we did not hear of them betting."

———

Pony Bob raced from Reno to Virginia City and on into the annals of Pony Express lore. No official mention of him predates those newspaper dispatches in the summer of 1868. He was like a character out of Owen Wister or a Hollywood horse opera. He *was* the Virginian. He *was* Shane. He rode in from nowhere and then vanished. He was a ghost even while he was alive.

The career of Robert H. Haslam in the saddle for the Central Overland California & Pike's Peak Express Company was the stuff of dime novels, although if anyone ever wrote a dime novel about Pony Bob, it does not survive. In a country where men rode from very early childhood, rode hard, and rode half-wild horses brought in off the plains, horses so wild that it took three men half a day to shoe one, Pony Bob was a rider's rider. The smart money in Virginia City on that long-ago Fourth of July holiday was all on Haslam. Even tinhorns from the East knew the name Pony Bob, knew that he had once crossed Nevada, a vast lifeless and waterless stretch of nearly four hundred miles, in less than two days (the distance between Boston and Baltimore) at the height of the Paiute Indian War. They knew that he rode without relief. That he rode when no one else would ride. And that he rode when no one else was alive to ride. Every corner boy and idler in the Washoe knew that Pony Bob could change horses in twenty seconds. He was an especially taciturn fellow in a world with many men of few words, but when he said something, his listeners tended to remember it and write it down. "I passed the bodies of 90 Chinamen who had been killed by Paiutes," he would tell a historian many years later, recalling one of his dangerous missions. "Only one escaping to tell the tale."

Here was a true rider of the purple sage. To see Pony Bob in the saddle was reason enough for most in the Washoe to leave their claims and come up to Virginia City on this July afternoon.

Colonel Visscher found him later in Chicago. He was a long, long way from the alkali flats of Nevada. The colonel was an inveterate hail-fellow and had heard all the stories at the Chicago Press Club bar while he was researching *A Thrilling and Truthful History of the Pony Express*. "The most famous of the Pony Express riders, except Col. W. F. Cody, 'Buffalo Bill,' was Robert Haslam, known throughout the West as Pony Bob . . . He was the hero of many fights with Indians and 'road agents,' and the principal actor in such a number of hair-breadth escapes and all manner of peril incident to the westward trail that they alone would make a great volume of intense and strenuous adventure."

Pony Bob's regular route for the Pony Express had been from Friday's Station on the California–Nevada line in the Sierra Nevada (where the resort of Lake Tahoe is today) down across the desert to Buckland's Station, near Fort Churchill—about seventy-five miles. (Fort Churchill was not established until after the Paiute Indian War.)

Colonel Visscher's account of Pony Bob and his famous ride across the Nevada desert is largely lifted from other works, as was so much of the colonel's best work. Visscher took substantial chunks of Colonel Henry Inman's account of the Pony Express verbatim from *The Great Salt Lake Trail* and plunked them down in his thrilling and truthful history.

Visscher most certainly knew Pony Bob from his Chicago days, but how much actual interviewing he did is impossible to gauge. Haslam was a quiet, modest fellow—in all probability justly credited with the exploits attributed to him. There are no accounts of Haslam exaggerating, nor are there accounts of Haslam attempting to profit from his relationship with the Pony Express.

His tale of adventure, repeated in varying forms by every narrator of the Pony Express for more than a century, begins about five weeks after the fast-mail service started when the Paiute Indian War broke out in Nevada.

Virginia City, about fifty miles from Buckland's Station, was a mining town in its infancy. The place was under siege—anticipating attack by the Paiutes, whose signal fires were visible on every mountain around the town, according to Haslam. The citizens of Virginia City had turned a stone hotel on C Street into a fort and housed women and children there. Haslam picks up his famous account of his ride: "When I reached Reed's Station [east of Buckland's Station] on the Carson River, I found no change of horses, as all those at the station had been seized by the whites to take part in the approaching battle. I fed the animal that I rode, and started for the next station, called Buckland's, afterward known as Fort Churchill, fifteen miles further down the river. It was to have been the termination of my journey, as I had changed my old route to this one, in which I had had many narrow escapes, and been twice wounded by Indians."

Haslam relates that on arriving at Buckland's Station, his relief rider, Johnson Richardson, refused to go on.

"The superintendent, W. C. Marley, was at the station, but all his persuasion could not prevail on the rider, Johnson Richardson, to take the road. Turning to me, Marley said: 'Bob, I will give you $50 if you make this ride.'

"I replied, I will go at once."

Haslam left minutes later, armed with a seven-shot Spencer rifle and a Colt revolver with two cylinders.

"From the station onward it was a lonely and dangerous ride of thirty-five miles, without a change, to the Sink of the Carson." Haslam made it there and rode on to Sand Springs "through an alkali bottom and sand hills, thirty miles farther, without a drop of water all along the route."

He changed horses at Sand Springs and continued to Cold Springs, about thirty miles farther down the trail. He changed horses again at Cold Springs and rode another thirty miles to Smith's Creek.

"Here I was relieved by J. G. Kelley. I had ridden 190 miles, stopping only to eat and change horses."

Colonel Visscher claimed this run was the fastest on record for the entire route of the Pony Express.

Haslam stayed at Smith's Creek for nine hours, presumably sleeping, then he started back down the line, heading west.

"When I arrived at Cold Springs to my horror I found that the station had been attacked by Indians, the keeper killed, and all the horses taken away. I decided in a moment what course to pursue—I would go on. I watered my horse, having ridden him thirty miles on time, he was pretty tired, and started for Sand Springs, thirty-seven miles away. It was growing dark, and my road lay through heavy sage brush, high enough in some places to conceal a horse. I kept a bright lookout, and closely watched every motion of my poor pony's ears, which is a signal for danger in Indian country."

It was a cold night, late spring, and Haslam recalled hearing the mournful howls of wolves and coyotes as he rode west in the dark (the British explorer Richard Burton made the same observation later that year). He reached Sand Springs safely and reported the Cold Springs attack. He warned the station keeper at Sand Springs to come with him, fearing imminent Indian attack. The station keeper took his advice. The next day, after they left, Indians attacked Smith's Creek. "The whites, however, were well protected in the shelter of a stone house, from which they fought the savages for four days. At the end of that time they were relieved by the appearance of about fifty volunteers from Cold Springs. These men reported that they had buried John Williams, the brave keeper of that station, but not before he had been nearly devoured by the wolves."

Pony Bob rode on west, arriving at the Sink of the Carson to find "the station men badly frightened, for they had seen some fifty warriors decked out in their war-paint and reconnoitering."

There were fifteen armed men at the Sink of the Carson Station in a fortified adobe building which also housed ten or fifteen horses, with a spring next to it. Haslam recalled that he rested for one hour and started for Buckland's Station after dark—he was only three and a half hours late. His adventure was not over.

"I found Mr. Marley at Buckland's, and when I related to him the story of the Cold Spring tragedy and my success, he raised his previous offer of $50 for my ride to $100. I was rather tired, but the excitement of the trip had braced me up to withstand the fatigue of the journey."

He rested for about ninety minutes and then headed west again toward Friday's Station, recrossing the Sierra Nevada.

"I had traveled 380 miles within a few hours of schedule time, and was surrounded by perils on every hand."

That was Pony Bob's story, as told to Colonel Visscher in 1907. That account appears in near-identical form in a number of other histories of the Pony Express. A couple of versions, including Alexander Major's autobiography, don't include the famous ride. (Majors mentions Haslam affectionately, though.) Several authors even embellish the story.

Hollywood-style dialogue between Pony Bob and other employees of the mail service was introduced by Samuel Hopkins Adams in 1950. And Ralph Moody, who wrote *Riders of the Pony Express* in 1958, added other details. "Haslam was known all about the desert country as 'The Ridin' Fool.' Pony Bob was one of the most daring horsemen who ever lived."

Moody describes Haslam as a smart judge of horseflesh. "Every mount in Bob Haslam's string was a half-wild bronco. A desert man, he had picked himself a string of mustangs that could match the desert's cruelty with speed and endurance." Moody reports that Pony Bob's favorite horse was named Old Buck, and said the rider talked at length to his horse. Moody recounted one of Bob's monologues: " 'Simmer down, old bird dog, simmer down,' Bob whispered to him.

'Keep that head up and them ears a-workin'. I'll need to know right plumb where those varmints is at.' "

Moody pulls out all the stops in recounting one of Pony Bob's adventures, calling it "possibly the greatest ride in American history." This was not the long ride of the Paiute Indian War, but the delivery of Lincoln's inaugural address to California. During his leg of the journey, Haslam was said to have set the speed record of 120 miles in eight hours and ten minutes using twelve horses. The cross-country delivery of Lincoln's address took seven days and seventeen hours—the record for the service.

Pony Bob appears to have been born in London and came to the United States as a youth (the Mormons did extensive missionary work in England at the time). He told the newspapers in Salt Lake City in 1897 that he had originally arrived there in 1856, when he was sixteen years old. He worked variously in Salt Lake City and on a ranch at Big Cottonwood.

"I was engaged by Capt. P. T. Turnley, who was assistant Quartermaster at Camp Floyd, as Government messenger in the spring of 1859."

In the late winter of 1860, Bolivar Roberts, division superintendent along the central part of the Pony Express route, was looking for some wiry, tough riders to fast-race the mail overland and recruited Haslam to ride for the Pony Express. He would have been twenty that year.

Although the telegraph had eliminated the cross-country Pony Express, there was still demand for express mail riders in remote areas unreached by the telegraph. After the Pony Express folded, Pony Bob rode for Wells, Fargo—first in Nevada, site of his Fourth of July holiday horse race. He rode from Virginia City to Friday's Station and back—about one hundred miles—or so he told Colonel Visscher. He made that run every twenty-four hours, and he made it in ten hours, leaving ample time for sleep. Then he became the fast-mail courier between Reno, site of the railhead, and Virginia City, making that twenty-two-mile run every day—in one hour. He used fifteen horses to do this. Technology kept pushing Pony Bob along. The telegraph line between Reno and Virginia City made the route obsolete. Wells,

Fargo sent him up to Idaho—still wild country—to ride a hundred-mile express route from Queen's River to the Owyhee River. There was nothing between those two points, so Haslam used one good horse to make the run. He told Colonel Visscher years later in Chicago that he had been at Owyhee River when Colonel Charles McDermit was killed at the start of the Modoc War (August 7, 1865). This was about the time that he saw the ninety dead Chinese, probably coolies brought in for the railroad. "Their bodies lay bleaching in the sun for a distance of more than ten miles from the mouth of Ives Canyon to Crooked Creek," he told Visscher. (He told Colonel Henry Inman a somewhat less lively version of these events, too, a decade earlier.) The ninety dead Chinese were enough for even Pony Bob—he resigned as an express mail rider. (His successor, Sye Macaulas, was killed by Indians on his first trip.) But Pony Bob was already headed back to Utah.

"I made up my mind that I have seen rougher countries than this, but not much," he recalled more than thirty years later. He told Visscher that he bought a Flathead Indian pony at Boise, Idaho, and rode to Salt Lake City—about 500 miles, alone, in two weeks. When he reached Salt Lake City, Wells, Fargo took him on again as a messenger. Then Joshua Hosmer, his brother-in-law, who was the United States marshal for Utah, appointed Haslam deputy marshal, but Pony Bob soon returned to the thing he knew best—riding for Wells, Fargo. His next run was 720 miles from Salt Lake City to Denver.

The name died before the man. He was like an old prizefighter, a washed-up college football hero, someone who had once upon a time, long, long ago, been famous.

Visitors to the Congress and Auditorium Hotels in Chicago at the turn of the last century often met a somber gentleman in the lobby who chatted pleasantly with travelers. He presented tourists with his business card which listed his name, Robert H. Haslam, and included a sketch of himself on horseback when he was known as Pony Bob, famed rider of the Pony Express.

Alexander Majors, writing in *Seventy Years on the Frontier*, reported: "At present [1893] 'Pony Bob' is living on 'the fat of the land in Chicago,'" Majors was being very generous. Pony Bob had become a kind of greeter then, an old retainer, a washed-up hero from long ago. He made his living as a steward, running errands. He was a minor celebrity.

Colonel Visscher knew him in those autumn days, knew him from the lobby of the Congress Hotel. But the colonel always had a good word for everyone.

"At this writing, the autumn of 1907, Mr. Haslam, who is still called 'Pony Bob' by his intimates, is a hale, happy, and prosperous citizen of Chicago, attending industriously every day to his business, which is associated with the management of the vast Congress Hotel organization that includes the Auditorium Hotel and its magnificent annexes."

Visscher added: "To see Mr. Haslam as he is in the conventional garb and quiet calling that are now of his life, one would find a test of credulity when informed that the bland, mild-mannered, and affable gentleman indicated had ever experienced the dangers, privations, and hazardous adventures that have marked the career of 'Pony Bob' in blazing the western way."

A photograph of Pony Bob included in Visscher's history of the Pony Express shows Haslam, then in his late sixties, looking for all the world like an elderly bank teller, formally attired with hat in hand and a blackthorn walking stick, his shoes buffed to a fine and glowing shine. He was balding and wore a full mustache. He'd put on a lot of weight. Other photographs from the same period, the Chicago days when Buffalo Bill, Alexander Majors, and Prentiss Ingraham were together, show a Pony Bob that bears no resemblance to the daredevil of 1860–61.

In 1932, writing when there was virtually no one left who remembered the days of saddles and spurs, as Raymond Settle called them, Arthur Chapman had this to say about the most famous rider of the Pony Express: "In later years 'Pony Bob' lived in Chicago, where he was connected with one of the big hotel companies. His business card was unique, bearing a sketch of himself when, as a youth of twenty, he made his famous ride on the 'Pony' trail through hostile Pah-Ute country in Nevada. Many persons, after conversing with a quiet, affable stranger, who seemed to be taking life easy in the lobby of the Congress Hotel, were amazed to find, once exchanging cards, that they had been talking to 'Pony Bob,' of Pony Express Fame."

We know that he did a stint with the Wild West show, but he might have been too old for daredeviltry at that point. The records of the company indicate that he worked for Buffalo Bill a few seasons in the mid-1880s, "a task to which he brought no experience and little capacity," according to Don Russell, author of *The Lives and Legends of Buffalo Bill.* Show business was not his calling. "At Cincinnati he hired a steamboat to convoy the show southward. The stops he arranged along the way proved bad guesses, and the steamboat tour ran in the red. Then came disaster."

In Mississippi, the steamboat collided with another steamboat and sank. Cody came to the rescue, reorganizing in a mere eight days to open on time in New Orleans.

Pony Bob drifted around to Texas in 1878 and New Orleans a few years later. Newspapers at the time reported that Haslam, who was then fifty, was with Buffalo Bill when the Great Scout went to help negotiate the unsuccessful surrender of Sitting Bull in December 1890. In the midsummer of 1897, when the Mormons were celebrating the fiftieth anniversary of the founding of Salt Lake City, Pony Bob showed up, and the Salt Lake City newspapers reported on his visit. In his fifties, Pony Bob still scouted for the army, too, and served in Cuba, the Philippines, and Puerto Rico, according to his obituary in the *Chicago Record Herald,* which called him "the last of the old scouts to serve in modern warfare."

Nearly fifty years after Visscher went down the trail looking for the Pony Express, Robert West Howard wrote *Hoofbeats of Destiny: The Story of the Pony Express.* He traced Pony Bob to Chicago.

"Pony Bob came back to Chicago in 1905 or 1906 and took a job as a clerk, or steward at the Hotel Auditorium. Cody kept track of him. Then, when he failed to find Haslam at the hotel in 1911, he trailed him down to a shabby rooming house on Wabash Avenue. The little horseman had suffered a stroke. Cody called a meeting, launched a fund-raising campaign with Will J. Davis, manager of the Illinois Theater, as treasurer, and led off with a substantial personal check. Newspapers in the West reported that Pony Bob was in dire straights. The *San Francisco Call* told its readers in the summer of 1911 that 'Robert H. Haslam, "Pony Bob" as he was known in the early days of the plains, where he earned a reputation as a daring pony express rider, is paralyzed at his home here, and it is thought he can never recover. "Pony Bob" carried the first news of the election of President Lincoln through a country beset with hostile Indians. He rode through the Piute country in Nevada in 1859 [wrong year] and brought help to the settlers at Cold Springs when they were threat-ened with annihilation.' " (There were no settlers at Cold Springs in 1859.)

When he died in a sixth floor walk-up on Chicago's South Side in the winter of 1912, he was seventy-two. A newspaper described him as "a hopeless paralytic and in dire want."

The people who remembered him were kind. They did not say that he was broke and crippled. They did not write that he was a drunk. When he died in obscurity, most newspapers—the California newspapers in particular—were especially flattering. The *Sacramento Bee* headlined: " 'Pony Bob' Haslam, Who Knew No Fear, Dies in Chicago."

The California magazine *Overland Monthly,* founded by Bret Harte, remembered him as "a man once famous throughout the United States for his courage, endurance and skill."

They buried the old express rider down at Mount Greenwood Cemetery at 111 Street and Sacramento on the far South Side of Chicago. The headstone reads:

FAMED PONY EXPRESS RIDER

ROBERT H. HASLAM

"PONY BOB" 1840–1912

Buffalo Bill paid for the headstone.

Buffalo Bill, Charlie Cliff, and
"Cyclone" Thompson in 1912 at Patee Park.

Thirteen

"MEMORY AT THE BEST IS TREACHEROUS": THE STORY OF THE STORY OF THE PONY EXPRESS AND HOW IT GREW

No representations are made as to the historical accuracy of
these anecdotes but they have been widely published and are
of interest. Most of them appeared in newspaper articles.
—MABEL LOVING, *THE PONY EXPRESS RIDES ON!*, 1961

Colonel William Lightfoot Visscher was not the only improbable
chronicler of the Pony Express, merely the first. The subject provided
a powerful lure to eccentrics throughout the twentieth century, and
the books they produced wildly complicated an already wildly complicated and confusing episode of western history. Each book piggy-
backed on the previous one, piling one bit of apocrypha upon another,
producing over a century a crazy quilt of folklore, legends, and out-
right lies. In the end, no one would be entirely certain what was true
or what was not true. It would become impossible to gauge much
of the story of the story of the Pony Express. In the end, it no longer
mattered.

The year after Pony Bob died in a cold-water flat in Chicago, a St. Joseph, Missouri, housewife with little formal education began one of the most enterprising efforts on behalf of the memory of the Pony Express. Her name was Mabel Loving and she was an amateur poet. She was an amateur historian, too, who in the end unearthed some of the most valuable information about the Pony Express. Mrs. Loving started tracking down the surviving riders. No one had actually thought to do this.

They were already old men when she began in 1913—old men with failing memories. Many of them would have been forever forgotten had it not been for the imaginative Mrs. Loving. She had written a poem about the mail service, "The Pony Express Riders," and she sent this along with her earnest inquiries to the old riders. It began:

> 'Twas a day of pride and glory
>   In the hist'ry of old Saint Joe,
> When the first brave pony rider
>   Started west so long ago.

Mrs. Loving found Patrick McEneany in Washington, D.C. He was an elderly Irish immigrant who had served long in the U.S. Army on the plains. McEneany, who was eighty-three the year Mrs. Loving wrote to him, was the first of the old Pony riders she contacted. McEneany wrote back. In a spidery hand, he recalled the dangers of the trail and "hail and hailstones the size of tea cups." And so began Mrs. Loving's lifelong work. For more than forty years until her death in 1957, Mabel Loving compiled her history of the Pony Express. One rider led to another.

Richard Cleve, who rode from Midway Station to near Fort Kearny in central Nebraska, told her that not much interesting ever happened. He then proceeded to recount a 160-mile ride in a blizzard under whiteout conditions in which he was forced to travel additional miles when no relief rider was available. It was forty below zero. Cleve apologized for not having a more interesting story.

Mrs. Loving found William F. Fisher, who was seventy-six years old. A native of Kent, England, Fisher came out to Utah with his father's family in 1854, his fifteenth year. He was twenty years old when he rode for the Pony Express and survived the Paiute Indian War. Like Cleve, Fisher was modest about his adventures.

Mrs. Loving found Thomas Owen King in June 1913 on a ranch in Almo, Idaho. King was another Mormon boy, a native of England who had immigrated to Utah with his parents in 1853. Shortly before his twentieth birthday, King, a seasoned horseman, heard of the plan to fast ride mail overland.

"So when I heard about February 1860 that a Pony Express mail was to be established between St. Joseph in the East to San Francisco in the West and the scheduled time was to be ten days I was fully prepared to offer myself as a Rider and was accepted. It was considered that it required the best of riders and physically able to stand the strain of endurance by day or night and in all kinds of weather and other dangers to be met in the mountains and plains between the East and the West. And of such were collected as brave and daring and true a band of riders as could be found anywhere."

King recalled opening the first route for the Pony Express and distributing horses along the line.

"For on us depended the accomplishment of something unheard of before, and the wonder of the American people and the civilized World, crossing what was considered a Desert of nearly two thousand miles on Horseback in ten days."

On April 7, 1860, to help carry the first mail, King blackened his face with gunpowder to reduce the chance of snow blindness and waited for Henry Worley to arrive with the mochila. King rode in a snowstorm from Echo Canyon to Hanging Rock Station, about twenty miles, in less time than scheduled and on other trips from Salt Lake City to Bear River, about eighty miles. He met fellow Englishman Richard Burton, whom he called Captain Robert Burton, during his days as a Pony rider.

King remembered that riders often rode while asleep. "Many a time Henry Worley and I passed each other on the road both of us fast asleep. This is not strange, our horses were so used to the road and the gait of going and we were so used to the riding that it was easy for us to frequently doze off and as if by instinct keep our horses going. One station keeper would say did you see King on the road, no, well he left here an hour ago, the same question would be asked me."

King also remembered that riders were killed but does not elaborate. And then it was all over—a mere year and a half after it began.

"My friend Henry Worley joined the Confederate army and was never heard from. I wish all of the Boys could tell of thrilling experiences, so that mine would appear very tame, though mine was full of excitement and much that has passed from my memory that would be exceedingly interesting if recalled."

King remembered that his route for the Pony Express was over one of the roughest stretches of the run.

"I was not in so much danger from Indians as those riding more in the center of the plains East and West of Salt Lake although you could never tell when they would turn loose and two years afterwards Mail Drivers were killed on the part I rode over. Once I had to take it 80 miles West of Salt Lake and once I rode to Hams Fork 145 miles east of Salt Lake and returned the next day. In those days I did not know what it was to be tired. I rode the 145 miles in 13 hours and can very well remember taking a young lady out to see some Friends that evening."

Mabel Loving's letter had found Thomas Owen King working on a ranch, and when he finally got around to replying to her, he apologized for taking so long, saying he'd been too busy. "We had Cattle to round up, grain to put in, cattle to mark and brand, and lots more to do." He was nearing seventy-five then and was still in the saddle from dawn to dusk.

William Campbell recalled that snow was the biggest problem along the route. The viability of the Central Route had hinged on whether it was passable during the long winter snows.

Campbell also had a memory of sleeping in the saddle, remembering that he once fell asleep on a mule and the animal turned around and walked back to the station. Campbell told Mrs. Loving that the Indians along his part of the route were not hostile at the time of the Pony Express.

Mrs. Loving found G. G. Sangiovanni in Utah. What an Italian immigrant was doing among the Latter-day Saints was not explained. Sangiovanni was one of the rare stock tenders along the line who left any account of his experiences. Joseph Bromley, division agent for the Pony Express in Utah, had hired him early in the spring of 1860 to go to East Canyon, about twenty-five miles outside of Salt Lake City, to open the second station east of the Utah capital.

"Mr. Bromley warned me to be on the alert on account of horse thieves, for they were more to be feared than Indians," Sangiovanni wrote to Mrs. Loving.

According to Sangiovanni's recollections, a stable was built at the site of the station, and there was "a good comfortable cabin for me to live in." But fearing attack by Indians or horse thieves, Sangiovanni pitched a tent next to the stable and slept there, where he could keep an eye on the horses.

"I was then handy when the 'Pony' would arrive. He would always come giving a War-Hoop."

Sangiovanni recalled that "the saddles used were of the old Mexican order, besides the saddle tree and stirrups, was a loose leather cover in two sections, two edges back to-gether and thrown over saddle, it fit over the pommel, pockets in the corner that held the dispatches." Sangiovanni recalled, too, that dispatches were written on thin paper and cost five dollars an ounce. The stations were from ten to fifteen miles apart, according to the lay of the country. Other than a brush with a horse thief, whom Sangiovanni thwarted, the station tender recalled nothing else exciting, noting that "my station was situated in one of the roughest portions of the Wahsatch [sic] mountains."

Sangiovanni remembered the pleasures of terrifying stage travelers with frightening stories of what awaited them. "I used to amuse myself telling the Overland passengers all kinds of thrilling stories, not only about road agents, indians and 'Mormons,' bears. We killed a large grizzly, I have bruins' all four paws tacked on my cabin door. Us boys used to keep those pilgrims in hot water all the time."

On April 7, 1913, Mrs. Loving got a letter from Buffalo Bill, then staying at the Continental Hotel in Philadelphia, thanking her for her poem and saying that he hoped to include it in his autobiography. Cody said nothing of his own days with the Pony Express. He missed the unveiling of a monument to commemorate the fast mail in St. Joe but stopped at the monument for photographs the next time he was in town.

Mabel Loving worked on her little history for more than forty years. She worked in complete obscurity. No one had any idea what she was doing. In her final years, she lived alone in the old Hotel Robidoux, where an enormous map of the route of the Pony Express hung over the bar. She never published a single word in her lifetime.

But death did not slow her dedication to the memory of the Pony Express. Her will stipulated that her life's work be published. Mary Reichert, the literary executrix of Mrs. Loving's estate, spent a year trying to interest a commercial publisher in the book. No luck. She then exercised her second option. Mrs. Loving had no illusions about her talents; she left $2,500 to pay for the publication of her book if all else failed. Miss Reichert, a local librarian, hired a St. Joseph job printer in 1961 to produce one hundred copies of *The Pony Express Rides On!* It was an unusual book to edit. Two of the chapters were missing, but that did not impede publication. The table of contents merely noted that they were missing. In the front of the book, the First Trust Company, trustee of Mrs. Loving's estate, added a personal note, uncharacteristic for bank officers. "Customarily a writer will dedicate his or her book to some other individual. It seems fitting and appropriate that in this instance we dedicate this book to Mabel Loving. It would appear unfair to do otherwise because it meant so much to her."

Today, hard-to-find copies of Mabel Loving's little book are very expensive collector's items. Much of the 163-page volume consists of bits of Pony Express arcana she picked up. She does not say where. She also quotes most of the other historians of the Pony Express. Mrs. Loving's invaluable contribution to the story, a contribution completely overlooked by every writer who has taken up the subject, was her firsthand reports of the fast-mail service by survivors.

Whatever faults her little book may have, Loving was not a completely wide-eyed enthusiast. She understood what a tall tale the story had become. "Almost as many locations are claimed for the express office from which the first Pony Express started at St. Joseph as there are purported 'first' riders," she observed. Historians, many of whom were depending on the recollections of citizens who were very old when they recorded their observations, or were not there at all, have placed the start of the Pony Express at numerous locations around the town of St. Joseph. Mabel Loving, who spent her life pondering this matter and knew St. Joe intimately, believed firmly that the Patee House was the site of the start. John D. Young of Chicago, the man who headed off to make his fortune in the Colorado goldfields, and who was there when the Pony started, agrees. The Patee House, mentioned widely in advertising for the Central Overland California &

Pike's Peak Express Company, was headquarters for the venture. The Pony appears to have started there. It may have made other stops in St. Joe before beginning its run.

Mrs. Loving's little book adds a great deal to the strange and thrilling legacy of the Pony Express. But in the tradition of the saga, the book contains no footnotes, no index, no bibliography. No source material is cited.

Many of Mrs. Loving's claims about the Pony Express appear irrefutable. She prefers Johnny Frey as the first rider out of St. Joe—which most agree with today. She insists that the name of the ferry that brought Frey across the Missouri to Elwood, Kansas, was not the *Denver* as many claimed, but the *Ebenezer,* with E. Blackiston, owner and captain at the wheel. She introduces to her chronicle many characters who either do not or rarely appear in any other account of the fast-mail service.

Old St. Joe never needed much reason to recall its history, real or imagined, and in 1923, the town celebrated its legacy with a grand historical pageant. The year was of no special significance. Naturally, a bit of research was deemed appropriate for this occasion, and so another odd chronicler joined the ranks of those who wrote about the Pony Express.

"After sixty-three years the Pony Express will ride again!" trilled Louise Platt Hauck in the July 1923 issue of the *Missouri Historical Review.* Mrs. Hauck was a Missouri author and one of a standing army of Pony Express "authorities" who contributed to a century and a half of confusion and error.

Mrs. Hauck may seem an unusual choice to research this subject. She was the author of countless romance novels such as *Marriage for Rosamond* ("Young, sheltered and indulged by an adoring family, Rosamond Bruce enters into marriage with Jim Daingerfield, bringing him all the innocence, trust and ecstasy of first love . . .") and *Anne Marries Again* ("Anne Lowell takes over her husband's business when he dies and discovers abilities she didn't know she had. Then she marries another man and tries to balance her relationship with her new found business interests"). Among other works were *Life, Love and Jeanette* and *Lance Falls in Love.*

Mrs. Hauck applied her skills to the story of the Pony Express. "One of the most picturesque chapters of Missouri history will be rewritten this summer when seven states will combine in a celebration commemorating this important event," she wrote.

For reasons unexplained by Mrs. Hauck, Nebraska—site of many of the most historic events associated with the Pony—was left out of the reride celebration. Colorado, with only the slimmest Pony Express connection, was included.

The high point of the gala, which ran from August 25 until September 1, was the nightly historical pageant, a Chautauqua-like tableau with a cast of several hundred. One of the episodes celebrated in the pageant was the arrival of the Hannibal & St. Joseph Railroad train from the East carrying the mail for the first Pony Express. The program lists an unnamed rider as one of the characters. Another highlight of the fete was a cross-country relay race with two teams competing. For some odd reason, this race made almost no attempt to follow the actual route. For "authenticity," William Frederick Cody Goodman, a nephew of Buffalo Bill, was rounded up for the race.

The program noted that the memory of the Pony Express was confusing. "The St. Joseph roll of Pony Express riders is faulty and incomplete; but in so far as we know it, we honor that gallant band. A touch of the charm of the unknown hangs about the names of those riders. It grips our imagination."

A Pony Express committee of prominent St. Joseph citizens had been empaneled to ponder the ticklish question of who the first rider might have been. The committee even offered a hundred-dollar reward if someone could sort this out once and for all. After much deliberation, the committee—Miss Ada Clare Darby, Miss Emily Stauber, and Mr. I. R. Bundy—declared in its report: "Your committee has met several times and has done its best to sift all available evidence. It became plain at once that the chief obstacle to a definite decision as to the first rider would be, not the lack of evidence, but the contradictory nature of much of it. Printed evidence of a sort was found for no less than ten contenders for the honor. Much of this is to be found in the numerous books on the subject and much more in the several scrap books of newspaper clippings and other material that has been collected through the years by the reference department of the Public Library."

By the time the committee began to deliberate, there was virtually no one alive with firsthand recollections of the days of the Pony. This did not impede citizens from coming forward with what they believed was irrefutable proof. There was no shortage of first riders, and the anecdotes the committee sifted through were many and lively. The material examined and the witnesses interviewed—there were at least sixteen—were contradictory and confusing. The conclusion, despite a strong tendency to favor Johnny Fry (they preferred this spelling), was that they could come to no conclusion.

Mrs. Hauck's account in the *Missouri Historical Review* was contradictory and confusing, too. She got the number of riders hired by the Pony Express wrong and the number of horses, too. She gave William Hepburn Russell's first name as Henry. She insisted that Johnson Richardson was the first rider out of St. Joe despite the Pony Express committee's finding. She made a point of noting that the reriders would be dressed in authentic garb, but no reliable account of the fast mail indicates that the riders had a standard uniform. In the historic reenactment, the riders looked like extras out of the musical *Oklahoma!*

Mrs. Hauck unearthed a letter supposedly written at the time of the Pony Express that confirmed Johnson Richardson's role along with a page torn from a diary and "sent anonymously." That was sufficient for Mrs. Hauck. "In my historical work I have never accepted reminiscence as authoritative, as memory at the best is treacherous," she wrote. The problem with her conclusion was that she appears to have mixed up two men named Richardson, both associated with the venture. The first was Billy or William Richardson, a stable boy sometimes thought to have been the first rider out of St. Joe. The second was Johnson William Richardson, the man for whom discretion was the better part of valor, who refused to relieve Pony Bob during the Paiute Indian War in Nevada. Even the redoubtable Raymond Settle made this mistake.

Mrs. Hauck acknowledged that the first mail did not leave on time and that the train did not arrive until after dark. She concluded with a heartfelt salute to the riders. "Then they vanished into the mists of the past and only the sound of their ponies' hoof beats comes echoing down to us through the years. Their brief career forms a theme more fitting for the romancer than the historian, so colorful, so dramatic is it."

Four years later she published *The Youngest Rider: A Story of the Pony Express*. Despite her insistence on the strictest accuracy, Mrs.

Hauck produced a historical novel for children which used real characters from the time of the Pony Express and introduced young Charlie Holt, a fictive rider for the fast mail. She would not be the last historian of the Pony Express to use this method.

In 1912, the year Pony Bob died in Chicago, Professor Glenn Danford Bradley published *The Story of the Pony Express: An Account of the Most Remarkable Mail Service Ever in Existence, and Its Place in History.* Unlike Colonel Visscher, Professor Bradley was a historian with a doctorate from the University of Michigan, but unlike Mrs. Loving, Professor Bradley did not bother to interview anyone associated with the Pony Express. Bradley fully mined the few existing sources: Majors's memoirs, Root and Connelley's *The Overland Stage to California,* Inman and Cody's *The Great Salt Lake Trail,* and "the file of Century Magazine," which includes W. F. Bailey's 1898 article on the Pony Express. Virtually all information about the Pony Express descends from these works.

Bailey was one of the first to extrapolate upon the adventures of two of the Pony's greatest horsemen—Buffalo Bill and Pony Bob Haslam. Bailey also added a good deal of fascinating information that made its way into the annals of Pony Express lore—for good or ill—including a collection of newspaper items from the time of the Pony Express reporting on the dangers of the ride and Indian attacks. Bradley used this material, too, without directly crediting Bailey.

Bradley's book added to the story, but—in the tradition of most Pony Express books—there was no index, table of contents, bibliography, or source notes. (These materials were probably deleted by a commercial publisher because an academic would have been inclined to include such information.)

Bradley managed to produce his book without mentioning Alexander Majors other than a passing reference to his firm. He ignored William Lightfoot Visscher, too, though Visscher was living in Chicago, where the Bradley book was published. Bradley knew of the considerable myth the Pony Express had accrued in the half a century since it had failed. He wrote: "While I have diverged occasionally from the thread of the narrative, my purpose has been merely to give where possible more background to the story, that the account as a whole might be more understandable in its relation to the general facts of history."

Like Visscher, Bradley went west as a young man and taught school in Kansas for several years. "In younger days he had mingled the romantic years with the final episodes of the Old West and, catching its spell, wove the Old West's passing into books that live," recalled a University of Toledo tribute published at the time of his death. Bradley's little book might have vanished, too, after his early death in 1930 at the age of forty-five. But it wound up having a surprising second life.

Americans love anniversaries, and as 1960 approached, the country rediscovered the legacy of the Pony Express. A century made it possible for a whole new level of enthusiasm. By the time the centennial was planned, there was no one alive who had been there, and the celebrants were relying on memories and a very odd collection of books. Previous celebrations to honor the memory of the Pony Express—1935 was the seventy-fifth birthday—had been odd affairs. In 1954, a group of riders at the behest of the National Junior Chamber of Commerce reenacted the days of the Pony Express by racing day and night from Ogden, Utah, to Colorado Springs, nowhere near the actual route.

As the centennial approached, Waddell F. Smith, grandson of William Bradford Waddell, and the greatest professional Pony Express promoter of modern times, made himself known. Smith operated the Russell, Majors & Waddell Pony Express Foundation and Pony Express History and Art Gallery out of his home in San Rafael, California. In 1960, he produced *The Story of the Pony Express: Official 1960 Centennial Edition*. He called himself the editor, but the book is none other than Glenn Danford Bradley's little tome reissued—and annotated—with an index by Smith.

Smith, who spent his golden years engaged in a baffling dispute with Wells, Fargo & Co. over claims whether the firm had operated the Pony Express, was an entrepreneur when it came to the Pony Express. As the centennial neared, he snapped up the Bradley book and began annotating what he felt was the definitive story. (It saved time and meant he did not have to write his own book.) He enlisted Raymond Settle, author of *Saddles & Spurs: The Pony Express Saga*, the best history of the Pony Express, to write an epilogue. With Settle's imprimatur, Smith rounded up endorsements. Smith even corraled President Dwight Eisenhower, honorary chairman of the board of governors of the National Pony Express Centennial Association, to bless the project. (Ike was a Kansan—Pony Express country.)

What Waddell Smith liked most about Bradley's book was the complete omission of Alexander Majors—the real hero of the Pony Express. Smith's familial connections with the saga were powerful, and it must have rankled him that his grandfather, the bookkeeper, was largely forgotten. Smith was not without success in recasting history. In 1954, the *New York Times* credited his grandfather with being the chief founder of the Pony Express—a spectacular bit of revisionism that has Waddell F. Smith's fingerprints on it.

The centennial was a great time for America to honor the Pony Express. Bronze markers—a blessing from the Eisenhower administration and private organizations—began sprouting across the countryside, and historical societies from St. Joe to Old Sac festooned the roadsides with commemorative plaques. Towns along its route from Genoa, Nevada—on the edge of the desert—to the plains of Nebraska in places like Gothenburg and Cozad, polished up their connections with the days of glory, real or imagined. (The Pony Express did not actually stop in either Gothenburg or Cozad, but both towns today maintain "authentic" Pony Express stations, the provenance of which is best left unquestioned.)

Robert West Howard, whose *Hoofbeats of Destiny: The Story of the Pony Express* reintroduced Americans to the Pony, writing in the *Christian Science Monitor,* observed "A centennial can be a telescope, offering full, clear, perspective." His perspective was anything but full and clear. Howard used imaginary citizens of Old St. Joe to tell the story. Newspaper editors, who'd been among the Pony's loyalist champions when it started, believed that they had an obligation in the centennial year to sort out the twisted history of the Pony Express.

The *Sacramento Union*—"The Oldest Daily West of the Rockies"—decreed in the winter of 1960 that experts were needed. San Francisco and Sacramento were battling over which city could be claimed as the western terminus of the Pony Express. The *Union* stood fiercely behind Sacramento.

The newspaper lined up Raymond Settle, then residing in California and the recognized authority on the Pony Express, as its star witness. Settle sided with Sacramento.

The *Union* believed that rascals in San Francisco hoping to profit from this enormous honor had been behind the dispute. The newspaper editorialized: "The plain fact is that in all the mass of material on the Pony Express there is not a single document or statement by any recognized historian which can be brought forward as proof that San Francisco was ever the western terminus. The claim is as false as the other canard that Wells Fargo had anything to do with the operation of the Pony, except to serve as agents."

The second dispute involved whether or not Wells, Fargo & Co. had operated the Pony Express. The firm had acted as agents for the Pony in the West during its last months.

Once again the *Union* turned to Settle, who demurred that experts must study this matter.

The actual observation of the centennial was as comic as the debate in California. One of the reriders staging the cross-country mail run accidentally shot another. The low point occurred when the reriders were unable to bring the mail overland on time and their tired horses had to be put on a truck. When they finally showed up in Old Sac, the mail pouch had been accidentally left behind.

In the end, the "battle of truth" that the *Union* called for—a crusade to find out the true story of the Pony Express—never happened. The year before the centennial, Roy S. Bloss, a California historian, published *Pony Express—the Great Gamble,* a 159-page book billed as "a fresh, unbiased approach to an emotion-packed historical episode."

The editors of the *Union* must not have read its preface. "Probably the final, complete and authentic word on the Pony Express will never be written. For all of the notable episodes in United States history, few have been so scantily annotated as the horseback mail, the trail of which has been indelibly—but only grossly—etched in the panorama of American pioneering. Even the parade of Caesars, or the Gallic Wars, or our own Revolution—all in the days when historical narration lacked the incentive of the common man's literacy— even these events have been better documented and more accurately interpreted than the relatively recent Pony Express."

Noting that there were few records of the mail service, Bloss added, "In several instances, the inexorable wear and tear of time caused buncombe to be offered as gospel."

Bloss argued that the Civil War eclipsed the memory of the Pony Express and noted that nearly half a century passed before the first history of the fast-mail service was written. "But by then most of the principals, the riders and station keepers had passed from the scene. That raised a problem for the early historians. Seemingly, few records of the nineteen-month mail service were then (or now) extant. The living participants, pressed for their recollections, occasionally resorted to colorful embellishment or a self-serving memory."

Bloss acknowledged that what he set out to do—sort out the story of the Pony Express—was not going to make him popular. "Whenever sympathetic legend or nostalgic romance has threatened to collide with objective deduction (a recurring hazard in this lore-laden subject) objectiveness deliberately has been given the right-of-way. Admittedly, such arbitrariness may find disfavor among some devoted followers of the Pony; if so, their displeasure is risked with apologies."

Bloss was not the first to make these observations. It had been a theme for half a century—although it had made not the slightest impression on the American public or Pony Express devotees.

Writing in 1932, Arthur Chapman, journalist-turned-historian, offered his assessment in *The Pony Express: The Record of a Romantic Adventure in Business*. "The records of the Pony Express, as kept by the Central Overland California & Pike's Peak Express Company were long ago either lost or destroyed. The fact that the Pony Express was not a Government institution, but was privately owned and controlled, absolved postmasters from the duty of making official records of arrivals and departures. Old letters and diaries, which have been submitted, have only tended to make the confusion greater, as they too have been conflicting in the names of riders."

Even Raymond Settle and his wife, Mary, in whom the *Union* placed such faith, had doubts, noting in *Empire on Wheels*, their history of Russell, Majors, and Waddell's freighting empire:

> The Pony Express was a romantic, glorious yet brief incident, which although it proved nothing except that it could be done, is eminently worthy of remembrance. Even though the amount of mail it carried was relatively insignificant and out of proportion to the fame it achieved, nobody begrudges it the spotlight. The tattoo

of the flying hoofbeats, awakening the echoes by day and night along the two-thousand-mile stretch of boundless prairie, lonely canyon, and mountain slope, wrote into the body of strictly American folklore such a romantic tale of youthful grit as is given few peoples to possess. It has been the source of a thousand tales of daredevil courage and will continue to make its contribution to that thrilling body of literature which concerns itself with stark courage and dauntless enterprise.

In 1958, William H. Floyd, yet another amateur historian in St. Joe, produced *Phantom Riders of the Pony Express* to sort out this "web of fancy," as he called it. Floyd pronounced the whole Pony Express story part of "a dim bob-tailed era in which fact and fiction can be hopelessly scrambled." He deemed the saga "fragmentary and often conflicting." Floyd's exasperated conclusion: "This was the Pony Express. Fact and fiction. Truth, half-truth, and no truth at all. These have become so thoroughly blended that, after nearly a century . . . legend has largely replaced and superseded a clear and unclouded record, if indeed such a chronicle ever existed."

Curiously, genuine documents from the earliest days provide no greater detail about the Pony Express. One of the oldest records, dating from September 6, 1879, was written in San Francisco by Joseph Samuel Roberson, an employee of Russell, Majors & Waddell. It is a nine-page, handwritten account on onionskin paper. Roberson, who spent many years in the freighting and transportation business and was in St. Joe the day the first rider headed west, claimed to have made up the first mail pouch headed west. But his eyewitness account wildly muddles the story. He does not mention who that first rider was. He gets the time of the ride's departure wrong. He places the action at the United States Express Company office in downtown St. Joe. He never mentions the Patee House. He does mention the excited crowd of well-wishers plucking hairs from the tail of the first horse. He credits the transcontinental telegraph with putting the Pony out of business, but he gets the start and finish of the telegraph wrong. He also has the Pony Express operating until 1862.

Emily Jo Roberson, his daughter, felt so strongly about her father's memoir that she swore out an affidavit in San Francisco in 1923 attesting to its authenticity. Why that was necessary is another question. Its authenticity is not at issue; its accuracy is suspect. The Roberson account, of which there are mysteriously two not quite identical versions, housed at the prestigious Henry E. Huntington Library in suburban Los Angeles, merely adds to the confusion. Floyd was right about truth, half-truth, and no truth at all.

Ricardo Cortez as a Pony Express rider,
from the 1925 Paramount picture.

Fourteen

THE BORDERLAND
OF FABLE

No country is marked between the Western landscape and a country of fable. Sawtooth and desert, the land is habituated to mirage: fantasy has been a native amusement to its inhabitants.

Such events happened on the borderland of fable, the unmarked frontier between Washoe and fantasy . . .

—BERNARD DeVOTO

Colonel William Lightfoot Visscher was still doing research at the Chicago Press Club's bar when the first film about the Pony Express was made in 1907. A second short, silent film followed in 1909 and two others in 1911 and 1912. The first film to capture this romantic bit of western history had preceded even the first book on the subject. Hollywood had discovered the Pony Express.

If historians, professional or otherwise, were perplexed and daunted by the saga, filmmakers had no such concerns. Hollywood knew well the borderland of fable, that far country where the true riders of the purple sage galloped. An absence of facts here was an asset, not a liability. From the earliest days of film, Hollywood was at home where the buffalo roamed and filmmakers were always especially generous to the memory of the Pony Express. Here was a true

American story that celebrated the classic virtues. Here was a story that could have been concocted for the movies and in many ways was; a tale where no one was entirely certain what was true and what was not. Here was a benign and beloved yarn of the vanished Wild West, never controversial, fond and familiar to Americans (and Europeans, too) who knew the West only as romance and illusion.

Hollywood relied on the Pony Express at the very birth of the western. The story had everything a good western needed: fearless young men on galloping horses, a two-thousand-mile race against time across a vast wilderness, heroics, danger, Indians, desperadoes, blizzards, swollen rivers, and even some genuine celebrities from the days of "saddles and spurs" like Buffalo Bill Cody and Wild Bill Hickok.

The western was essentially a morality tale, largely formulaic, that celebrated simple virtues. Helped along by Buffalo Bill and his Wild West and shelves of dime novels, the Pony Express was a powerful symbol in the mind of the average American, representing the Old West at its best, heroic and honorable, a place where chivalry survived.

Taciturn horsemen like the mysterious Pony Bob Haslam could have easily ridden straight out of Owen Wister's western novel *The Virginian,* which became one of the earliest Hollywood westerns. It takes little effort to imagine Pony Bob, the man who rode without relief nearly four hundred miles through an Indian war, warning, as Wister's hero the Virginian does: "When you call me that, smile!" It is one of the most famous lines in western literature.

And so in the place of Pony Bob and the largely forgotten true riders of the Pony Express came the new riders of the Pony Express. They rode from the dime novel and the Wild West show straight onto the silver screen of the Saturday matinee. They would eventually include Roy Rogers, "the king of the cowboys," in the 1938 western classic *Frontier Pony Express,* and Gene Autry, "the singing cowboy," who made *Last of the Pony Riders* for Columbia in 1953 (a Pony Express rider loses his job when he buys a stagecoach and finds out that crooks are working to sabotage the express operations in order to get its mail contract). Other stars cast as Pony riders were Johnny Mack Brown and Fuzzy Knight in Universal's 1940 release *Pony Post.* And their ranks included Slim Pickens, Tom Mix, Harry Carey, Hoot Gibson, and still others.

The British Film Institute, which studies such things, once noted: "In the cinema, the short life of the Pony Express has not prevented the myth of the venture from being exploited to the full . . . the subject was one of the most popular in the early Western . . ."

The first full-length feature (well received, too) was *The Pony Express (A Romance)* made in 1925 with Ricardo Cortez (a Rudolph Valentino look-alike) as a Pony Express courier. Based on a book by Henry James Forman, the silent film uses what was pretty much the accepted saga of the saddle for that time—a story somewhat long on imagined intrigue and short on fact.

The Pony Express makes cameo appearances in other films. Even John Ford, the great master of the western, fell for the Pony, and fell hard. In his 1949 feature *She Wore a Yellow Ribbon,* one of Ford's celebrated cavalry trilogy with John Wayne and many of Ford's repertory company of regulars, the Pony Express makes a lively guest appearance. Typical of most references to the Pony Express in film, it's wrong. The Ford movie opens with a Pony Express rider thundering across the Arizona desert (Monument Valley) to bring the news of Custer's Last Stand to settlers and soldiers on the frontier. But Custer's Last Stand took place on June 25, 1876, fifteen years after the Pony had folded. And the route taken by the Central Overland California & Pike's Peak Express Company was hundreds of miles to the north—far from Arizona, where the film was set.

Ford understood, nevertheless, the power of the Pony Express as an indelible image of the vanished West. It was an acknowledgment he made at the end of his classic *The Man Who Shot Liberty Valance* in 1962. The story is a western morality tale. Eastern lawyer Ransom Stoddard, played by Jimmy Stewart, comes west toting his lawbooks, bringing law to the lawless. He is bullied and beaten by the outlaw Liberty Valance (Lee Marvin at his most malevolent). But Stewart is ultimately willing to die facing the outlaw gunman. As it turns out, Valance dies in the gunfight and Stewart goes on to glory, including a seat in the United States Senate. But it is really the hard-bitten westerner Tom Doniphan (played by John Wayne) who shot Liberty Valance, making it appear that Stewart had won the gunfight. Stewart, the mythic hero, prospers (he even gets John Wayne's girl) and Wayne dies a pauper, forgotten. But faced with the facts, that the story long cherished is just not true, the local newspaper editor pronounces firmly at the end of the film a line famous in the annals of westerns: "This is the West, sir. When the legend becomes fact, print the legend!"

That is the fate of the Pony Express, too, particularly in film and on television, where references to it are more myth than reality. *The Young Riders,* a popular television series aired from 1989 to 1992, featured a cast of Pony Express riders that even Colonel William Lightfoot Visscher could not have dreamed up on his best day at the Chicago Press Club. The television show is set in a mythical place called Sweetwater (there is a Sweetwater River in Wyoming along the route of the Pony Express). There are also confusing references to Rock Creek (the Nebraska site of Wild Bill Hickok's debut as a bad-man—hundreds of miles from the Sweetwater). Here in this fantasy world (the scenery is very southwestern and high desert), Buffalo Bill Cody and Wild Bill Hickok (a decade apart in age in reality) play teenage Pony Express riders. Madcap scenarios include an episode when the Pony Express riders help runaway slaves. There's even a young woman riding for the Pony in disguise. The company features a youthful Jesse James, a famous badman but no Pony Express rider, and a character called "The Kid," a mysterious reference to William Bonney, the sociopathic Billy the Kid, who was in fact an infant prob-ably living in New York City in 1860–61. The buckskin-clad Buffalo Bill Cody, who appears in *The Young Riders* as a plainsman, rides for the fast mail with a powerful Hawken rifle by his side, a formidable weapon completely improbable for a Pony Express rider and nearly impossible (and dangerous) to fire from a moving horse. *The Young Riders* was a farrago of nonsense.

The best bad movie about the fast-mail service is *The Pony Express,* made in 1953 by Paramount. (This film went head-to-head with Gene Autry's *Last of the Pony Riders* at the box office.) Featur-ing Charlton Heston as Buffalo Bill, Forrest *(F Troop)* Tucker as Wild Bill Hickok, and Rhonda Fleming and Jan Sterling as the love inter-ests, *The Pony Express* is a spectacular fraud. If the American public was not confused enough about the dim legacy of the Pony Express, this film would create a permanent fiction. It was neither a critical success nor a box-office bonanza, although it was made at a time when Americans were besotted by westerns. *High Noon* was released the year before and *Shane* the year after.

The Pony Express was based on a story by Frank "One of the Most Prolific of the Great Pulpsters" Gruber, a pulp master who wrote dozens of westerns *(Fort Starvation)*, detective stories *(The Corpse Moved Upstairs)*, murder mysteries *(Swing Low, Swing Dead: An Original Johnny Fletcher Mystery)*, and historical fiction. Gruber was also the creative genius behind *Tales of Wells Fargo*, a western TV dramatic series that ran from 1957 to 1961. He sometimes worked under the names Charles Boston and Stephen Acre, to cite but two of his noms de plume. He was also a biographer of Zane Grey, the king of the cowboy scribes. Gruber was what was known in the trade as a speed guy—he worked fast. Facts were not his specialty.

The odd thing about the 1953 film *The Pony Express* is that there is almost no actual Pony Express in it. Other than a brief bit of horsemanship with a voiceover and a finale in which Buffalo Bill brings the first mochila into Old Sac, the actual operations of the Central Overland California & Pike's Peak Express Company are of no interest to the makers of the film.

The film opens with Charlton Heston, as Buffalo Bill, narrowly escaping death at the hands of Yellow Hand and his savage Indian braves—hinting at some long-standing animosity between Buffalo Bill and Yellow Hand. The official synopsis of the film explains:

> *The role the Pony Express played in welding California to the rest of the United States and preventing it from becoming a separate republic is the basic plot of this Western. Buffalo Bill Cody breaks up an incident that was intended to incite a separatist movement in California masterminded by a brother and sister who are manipulated by foreign agents and greedy businessmen.*
>
> *They arm the Indians to prevent Cody and Wild Bill Hickok from forming the Pony Express, forcing Cody to defeat the Indian chief in single combat to save the line. A young girl who loves Cody dies saving his life.*

One of the most enduring bits of the Buffalo Bill Cody legacy is the story that Cody killed Yellow Hand (sometimes called Yellow Hair) in hand-to-hand combat to avenge the massacre at the Little Big Horn. Period lithographs depicting the death struggle, showing Buffalo Bill with Yellow Hand's scalp raised, were entitled *First Scalp for Custer*. Like a lot of Cody lore, the story worked itself into dime novels and the Wild West show. Buffalo Bill often dramatized his purported killing of Yellow Hand for audiences.

Although the actual fight, *if* it took place at all, occurred some fifteen years after the Pony Express went broke, the filmmakers thought it a good idea to toss this into what was already a merry mix of fantasy. It plays a major role in the dramatic development of the story, as Buffalo Bill eventually kills Yellow Hand about two-thirds of the way through the film. This has nothing to do with the Pony Express, by the way.

The Pony Express contains virtually no facts in its entire 101 minutes. Unlike modern westerns that anguish over historical accuracy and detail, the film is absolute nonsense. The action jumps all over the route of the Pony Express, and there are some very odd details (such as buffalo herds in the Nevada desert). The gist of the film involves Buffalo Bill (who was not known as Buffalo Bill in 1860) and Wild Bill Hickok (who had also not picked up his sobriquet) teaming up to start the Pony Express. There's plenty of intrigue with hints of efforts to scuttle the Pony Express by Californians who oppose the Union—recalling the old yarn that the fast-mail service *alone* saved California for the Union.

Purists may note that Billy Cody was fourteen years old when the Pony Express started, and even his greatest admirers never credited him with the establishment of the Central Overland California & Pike's Peak Express Company. William Hepburn Russell—there is no Alexander Majors or William Waddell in this film—is played as an uncouth windbag. The historical errors are numerous. Jim Bridger, the fabled mountain man, makes a cameo appearance, although he probably never met either Cody or Hickok. Despite Alexander Majors's famous dictum, Buffalo Bill and Wild Bill drink constantly throughout the film, even while riding.

But Hollywood cannot take all of the blame or credit for the enrichment of the story of the Pony Express. Those stories started along the borderland of fable long before the first filmmaker or dime novelist considered the saga.

The most spectacular, which in a real sense inspired many that followed, involved Wild Bill Hickok, a gunslinger and gambler who never sat on the back of a Pony Express mount, although he is routinely cited as a veteran of the service. It began on the afternoon of July 12, 1861, at Rock Creek Station in the territory of Nebraska. In the annals of western whoppers, this is a milestone.

Hickok was not Wild Bill when the McCanles gang rode up to

Rock Creek Station near the Nebraska-Kansas border. He was merely twenty-four-year-old James Butler Hickok. He was recuperating from fighting (hand-to-hand, in some stories) a grizzly bear in Colorado while guiding a wagon train. At least that was the story.

Descended from Vermont Yankees who migrated to Illinois shortly before his birth, Hickok was born in Troy Grove, Illinois, on May 27, 1837. His parents were abolitionists.

Biographers claim that Hickok displayed what was described as "an uncommon interest" in firearms from an early age. When he was twelve, he was already a crack shot who bested adults in marksmanship competitions. When he was eighteen, Hickok fled Illinois under the mistaken impression that he had killed a man. The man survived the shooting. Hickok went to "Bleeding Kansas," then the site of some of the bitterest fighting between pro- and antislavery factions. He joined the Red Legs, a violent antislavery militia. By 1861, he was working as a stock tender at Rock Creek.

The first thing to consider about the McCanles gang was that it was not much of a gang. Dime novels and popular accounts of the incident put the membership as high as fourteen. In reality, it consisted of David McCanles, his twelve-year-old son, William Monroe McCanles, and two hired hands—James Woods, a cousin, and James Gordon.

McCanles was from North Carolina and had headed west in 1859 with high hopes for the Pike's Peak gold rush in Colorado. After encountering failed gold seekers returning from the Rocky Mountains, McCanles decided to settle in Nebraska, where there was money to be made off struggling pilgrims headed west or defeated dreamers retreating east. McCanles, whom all writers agree was industrious, settled at Rock Creek, where a station on the Overland Trail existed, and built a toll bridge.

When Russell, Majors & Waddell began operations for the Pony Express, McCanles leased them property. Horace Wellman and his common-law wife, Jane Holmes, were hired as station keepers, and James W. Brink, who is referred to as Doc or Dock in most accounts, was stock tender. He also rode for the Pony Express.

According to various descriptions of the incident, McCanles, who appears a bit of a wise guy and bully, began calling Hickok "Duck Bill" because Hickok had a prominent nose and upper lip. Hickok's admirers and dime novelists always paint the gunman as a fine figure of a man, handsome, appealing to women. But a tintype made two years after the shootings at Rock Creek does not support those claims. Hickok was a homely man. Better clothing and a mustache improved his appearance over the years.

The Pony Express owed McCanles money, and that brings us to the late afternoon of July 12, 1861. McCanles, Woods, Gordon, and twelve-year-old William Monroe were at Rock Creek to collect the money owed.

McCanles, most writers agree, confronted Wellman, as representative of the Pony Express. Wellman balked. Some versions claim Wellman went into the house and his wife, Jane, continued to argue with McCanles. Then the shooting started. McCanles was shot dead—probably from ambush by Hickok or possibly by Wellman, who might have shot McCanles from inside the house. In either case, Hickok got the credit.

Hickok, Brink, and Wellman and his wife then killed Gordon and Woods, using a garden hoe to dispatch the latter. William Monroe McCanles escaped. The precise events remain much disputed. Either Hickok was badly wounded in the affray or he wasn't even scratched.

An analysis of the incident published in 1927 by *Nebraska History Magazine,* when there were still actual survivors alive, claimed that the McCanles party was unarmed. (Other narratives claim they were armed.)

George W. Hansen, a banker and early pioneer from nearby Fairbury, Nebraska, who compiled the *Nebraska History Magazine* article, disputed the popular versions. Hansen's investigation was prompted largely by the wild stories that had been told over the decades since the shootings at Rock Creek. Exaggerated tales about the incident became popular because they involved Hickok. (Hickok eventually even fell into the hands of the great dime novelist Colonel Prentiss Ingraham, who produced the dime novels *Wild Bill, the Pistol Dead Shot: Or, Dagger Don's Double* and *Wild Bill, the Pistol Prince.* Ingraham was still a master craftsman of western prose when he took up Alexander Majors's autobiography at the behest of Buffalo Bill nearly a quarter of a century later.)

The mother of all Wild Bill yarns—by Colonel George Ward Nichols, claiming to be an interview with Hickok—appeared in the February 1867 issue of *Harper's* magazine. This tale set the standard for embellishment. Hickok told Nichols that McCanles was the leader of "a gang of desperadoes, horse thieves, murderers and regular cut-throats who were the terror of everybody on the border." Hickok also claimed that these "border ruffians" were Confederate sympathizers (a strong card to play, with the memory of the Civil War still fresh). The *Harper's* story also claimed that the "McCanles gang" was ten strong. A tale of bloodletting that would have delighted Hollywood, it gave Wild Bill his first national publicity.

A stagecoach heading we are not sure where stopped at Rock Creek Station about an hour after the killings, but even the addition of more witnesses closer to the actual incident does not clarify the events of this hot afternoon. Were there ten dead? Or was it fourteen? Or only three? The bodies of the dead were buried immediately at the site. Coincidentally, Samuel and Orion Clemens, en route to the Comstock, came down this line two weeks after the events of July 12. But Twain makes no mention of the shootings or the station in *Roughing It*.

Hansen's reexamination of the incident points out that McCanles had been a peace officer in North Carolina with no criminal record and arrived in Nebraska after the border troubles in nearby Kansas. Hansen also quotes numerous local residents, by name, who were familiar with what happened on July 12, and none of these individuals corroborated the Hickok version of the story. Hansen's assessment of the *Harper's* story—some sixty years later—finds it "impossible and absurd." Popular novelists took the tale, impossible and absurd as it was, and ran with it.

In 1905, Emerson Hough published *The Story of the Outlaw,* basing his account on Nichols's yarn. Hansen claimed that Hough's novel "gave this story greater publicity than any other modern story of crime has ever received." Hough went with the theory that the McCanles gang consisted of a large party of desperadoes and has Hickok dispatching them.

In 1912, Charles Dawson published *Pioneer Tales of the Oregon Trail and of Jefferson County.* Dawson refers to the events of July 12, 1861, as the Wild Bill–McCanles Tragedy.

He paints a more critical picture of McCanles, noting that he could be moody and even violent. But he found McCanles a hard worker, generally well regarded in Nebraska. A popular local orator, McCanles spoke publicly on the Fourth of July, only eight days before he was shot. Dawson also introduces the element of intrigue by alleging that McCanles had a mistress, one Kate Schell, a twenty-year-old who had followed him west from North Carolina. She was living on the west side of Rock Creek at the time of the shooting. Dawson claims Schell had also attracted the attention of Hickok and that there was long-standing animosity between him and McCanles.

Painting a less flattering portrait of McCanles than Hansen does, Dawson adds several violent incidents involving McCanles during which he tortured men with whom he had disagreements. He also claims McCanles and his hired men were armed the day of the confrontation. But he does not make him a villain. According to Dawson, Wild Bill emerged unscathed from this encounter. Dawson felt confident about his account and included in it a letter written on January 8, 1912, from W. M. McCanles of Kansas City, Missouri, the surviving member of the "McCanles gang." William Monroe McCanles dismissed Emerson Hough's version as "the worst misrepresentation" of the July 12 events. He was, however, pleased with Charles Dawson's account. "I want to compliment you upon your effort. You certainly have done well with the material you had to start with. I believe with a few corrections you will have the only true story ever written of this affair."

In the end, no one was convicted in connection with the killings at Rock Creek. Hickok left to scout with the Union army out of Fort Leavenworth, Kansas. He was later marshal of Abilene. He had a reputation. Some historians of western gunplay credit Wild Bill with an innovation that any Hollywood film viewer would be familiar with—the walk-and-draw gunfight.

At six o'clock in the evening of July 21, 1865, Wild Bill and one Davis K. Tutt, a gambling man and Confederate army deserter, walked out into the square in front of the courthouse in Springfield, Missouri. They were settling a gambling score. Tutt claimed Wild Bill owed him money. It wasn't much money. Maybe twenty-five dollars. Maybe a little more. Tutt missed. Wild Bill did not. A Union army colonel, who was an eyewitness to the gunfight and recorded his impression within hours of the shooting, said the gunfighters were about a hundred paces apart. As near as such things can be established, the duel between Tutt and Wild Bill was the first such gunfight of its kind, and its image remains fixed in the popular imagination. Well, that's the story.

Wild Bill was acquitted of the shooting of Tutt. Self-defense.

How the Pony Express became part of Hickok's résumé we do not know. When precisely he became Wild Bill is uncertain, too.

In 1872, Hickok began appearing on the stage with Buffalo Bill, Texas Jack, and such additional players as "Snakeroot Sam" and "Fire Water Tom," whom the program described as "a drunken Red man." He was not an Indian.

Newspaper reviewers found Wild Bill a "bad actor," but crowds turned out to see the badman. A badman will win over a bad actor any day. Hollywood understood that, too.

In *Buffalo Bill's Life Story,* Cody recalled some wild exploits with his "old pard" Wild Bill Hickok. Cody even claimed Wild Bill was a rider for the fast-mail service (not even Wild Bill made that claim). Cody was nearly ten years younger than Hickok, although he claims they met in 1857 while they were freighting (he would have been eleven). Cody also has a dime-novel-like account of Hickok wiping out the McCandless (his spelling) gang that is nearly as wild as the *Harper's* yarn.

Buffalo Bill Cody and Wild Bill Hickok had a complex relationship. Buffalo Bill was often said to be jealous of Wild Bill and described him later as "difficult to deal with."

Four years after Cody and Hickok's stage debut, Wild Bill was shot dead playing poker in Nuttall & Mann's No. 10 saloon in Deadwood, South Dakota. He was shot from behind by Jack McCall, a disgruntled poker player who had lost to him. Wild Bill was holding aces and eights, the dead man's hand.

Wild Bill is often said to have been a Pony Express rider, but "the West's greatest gunfighter" came no closer to the fast mail than feeding the horses at Rock Creek.

Broncho Charlie Miller, Christmas, 1937.

Fifteen

BRONCHO CHARLIE MILLER, "THE LAST OF THE PONY EXPRESS RIDERS"

> In an undertaking such as the Pony Express it is difficult to draw a sharp line between fact and legend ... That accounts do not agree in every detail is not surprising, since many are based on bubbling hearsay.
>
> —WILLIAM H. FLOYD III,
> *PHANTOM RIDERS OF THE PONY EXPRESS*, 1958

On his last birthday, the New York newspapers declared Broncho Charlie Miller as "spry and chipper as ever." He was in a wheelchair then, but the nurses at Bellevue Hospital wheeled him out for an interview. He was still telling the old stories. Broncho Charlie Miller said he'd known Buffalo Bill and Wild Bill Hickok. He'd seen Annie Oakley shoot. He claimed that he had shaken Abraham Lincoln's hand, and met Jesse James and Sitting Bull.

At the end of his long life, well-wishers were sending up to fifty letters a day to the old man, many simply addressed to Broncho Charlie, many others to "The Last of the Pony Express Riders." It was 1955. The post office in New York City somehow got the letters to Bellevue. The old man was 105 that winter, or so he said.

Newspapers across the West had been reporting the death of "the last of the Pony Express riders" for decades. On April 3, 1913, the *Tonopah Bonanza* in Nevada said of seventy-six-year-old Louis Dean: "Last of the Pony Express Riders Dead." A year later, on May 15, 1914, the same paper reported that Jack Lynch, "last of the pony express riders," was dead, too. Billy Pridham, said to be "the last of the Pony Express riders of the picturesque days of Nevada," died in June 1921, according to the *Reno Evening Gazette*. On August 23, 1929, the *Review Miner* in Lovelock, Nevada, noted that Thomas J. Reynolds, eighty-one, "one of the last of the riders of the old-time pony express across the western states," had died in a Sacramento hospital. The *Reno Evening Gazette* reported that seventy-six-year-old James Cummings was dead on March 3, 1930. He would have been six or seven when he was supposedly riding for the Pony Express in Kansas.

But on January 15, 1955, when Broncho (he preferred that spelling) Charlie Miller died in his sleep of pneumonia, the *Post-Star* in Glens Falls, New York, declared: "The brotherhood of the Pony Express Riders wound up its affairs." In his obituary, the *New York Times* called him "the incarnation of the Old West for thousands of delighted youngsters—and some folks not so young."

America loved Broncho Charlie Miller. He had not been on the back of a horse in a while, but when he was 102—just to show his critics and some smart-aleck reporters—he snapped a cigarette out of a volunteer's mouth at thirty paces with a cattle whip. The New York reporters liked that trick a lot.

Broncho Charlie Miller had no hometown, but he was at home everywhere he went, and so he went and he went. He was a rambling man. In Glens Falls, where he spent many years in the Adirondacks, far from the West of his youth, the newspaper understood him perfectly. If he was not what he claimed he was, the editors of the *Post-Star* shrewdly concluded, no one else was still alive to prove otherwise.

With his ten-gallon hat and flowing white hair, Broncho Charlie certainly looked like an old westerner. He wore feathers in his hair and Indian jewelry and a necklace made out of bear claws.

When he was eighty-five, the *Post-Star* explained: "Broncho Charlie is a picturesque figure, wearing his hair long in the custom of long ago days in the west. It is his distinctive feature, as horsemanship and cowboy tricks with whip and lasso are his accomplishments. Having known Buffalo Bill and other famed characters who made western history, Broncho Charlie appeals to the popular imagination as a romantic and glamorous personage and is particularly fascinating to young boys."

The New York newspapers featured countless photographs of him entertaining wide-eyed kids who believed they were in the presence of history. His story played best away from westerners, who asked too many pesky questions. He was on *The Jack Parr Show* when he was 104. He was on *What's My Line?* too. He rode in the Macy's parade at Thanksgiving a number of times.

Once, according to family lore, a steer escaped from an abattoir in New York City and ran through midtown. Tenderfoot Manhattanites were terrified. The old man roped the critter somewhere along Forty-sixth Street. Passersby were astonished to see him dressed in buckskins.

He was an especially big hit in Greenwich Village in the 1920s and '30s. He carved wood a great deal as he got older. In Montauk, on Long Island, he built a log cabin that later was made into a restaurant. The place mat showed the route of the Pony Express.

Broncho Charlie Miller could mesmerize an audience without raising his voice. His presence was hypnotic. Half a century after he died, his relatives were still getting letters from aging Boy Scouts who had met "the last of the Pony Express riders."

"Some 60 years ago I attended a Boy Scout Camporee at Camp Warren Cutler east of Rochester, New York, where I grew up," L. I. "Rusty" Haak recalled in a letter to Broncho Charlie's great-niece Lois Miller Ellsworth, nearly fifty years after the old cowboy's death. "The featured entertainer for some 15,000 scouts was Broncho Charlie Miller. I don't remember his exact age at that time, but young as I was, he seemed older than God. One of his exhibitions was a bull whip more than 20 feet long. It was said that he was the only man still alive who could handle one of that length. I was sitting in the first row on the ground with carrot-colored hair and freckles and he was drawn to me like a magnet. Though petrified, I was too shy to say no when he lifted me to my feet. I became even more petrified when he explained what he was about to do. There was no way out and I stood there with a wooden kitchen match in my teeth while he lit it with that bull whip. I was so glad to feel that flame under my nose that I almost forgot to spit out the match. I asked him if he would hold a match for me so I could light it with my .22 caliber rifle, which I had done, though not under someone's nose. He declined, saying he had lived so long by not being stupid, and that I didn't look like Annie Oakley to him."

He was one of the greatest trick whip stuntmen ever. Too many people saw him perform to dispute that. Nearly fifty years after he died, eyewitnesses still swore they had seen him take the top off a milk bottle at thirty paces with a whip. He could light a match with a whip, too. A match held in the mouth of a volunteer. He never missed.

Seventeen years after he lit the match in the mouth of the Boy Scout in upstate New York, Broncho Charlie was still quick with the whip. He did it for *Parade* magazine. Describing a publicity appearance in New York City, the magazine noted: "Not long ago he appeared at a benefit here and brought down the house. He sang a chorus of 'Oh, Give Me A Home Where The Buffalo Roam' ["Home on the Range"], then did his whip trick."

With his nine-foot cattle whip, he neatly cut in half a cigarette that a young woman held between her lips. He took to using a shorter whip as he got older, fearing that he might take off the end of a volunteer's nose. Bowing to the applause, Charlie said: "Some folks say you can't do nuthin' when you're 102."

Broncho Charlie Miller was the epitome of all things western and nowhere more so than in the East, where he spent most of his life. When he died, the *Post-Star* observed: "When Bronco Charlie rode his horse in holiday parades the shades of Buffalo Bill Cody, Wild Bill Hickok and just about every other famous western hero rode with him.

Bronco Charlie was at his best with youngsters. He took them all the way from St. Joe to Sacramento over the Pony Express trail. With them he dodged bandits and escaped from Indians . . . The last of the Pony Express riders never lost the mail or an audience."

He didn't always say he was an orphan—that came later. "Folks killed by injuns," he said. He claimed that he'd been born on a buffalo robe in the back of a Conestoga wagon going west with the forty-niners. He said he was born up in Hat Creek in Modoc County in the high California sierra.

Broncho Charlie Miller's claim that he was the last of the Pony Express riders was based on his story that at the age of eleven, in

1861, he carried the mail for the Pony Express from Sacramento to Placerville, California—about forty-five miles—and back. It was a story that he had a lot of practice telling, and he told it well.

The California State Library's archivists, who have more experience in dealing with "last riders for the Pony Express" than New York tabloids, list him as "an adventurer" and accept his date of birth as January 1, 1850, in Hat Creek, Modoc County.

The facts are that he had been a wrangler and ranch hand and a performer in Buffalo Bill's Wild West. He broke horses for the U.S. Cavalry. He was, according to folklore in upstate New York and elsewhere, proficient in the theft of horses, too. By his own admission, he narrowly escaped hanging in New Mexico. He unashamedly admitted to stretching the truth at times. When he was sixty-seven or sixty-eight, he really did talk his way into the British army to fight in World War I. Like that early historian of the Pony Express, Colonel William Lightfoot Visscher, he was not a stranger to the cup that cheers.

Long after his death, his relatives claimed that he had really been born in New York City and his name was Julius Mortimer Miller. His father, a tailor, came from Germany. Young Charlie was a juvenile delinquent whose parents shipped him and his younger brother, Walter, off to sea as cabin boys. He jumped ship in San Francisco and never looked back (that part appears to be true). He reinvented himself from scratch. It was not mere coincidence that he would latch on to the saga of the Pony Express.

In 1889, he turned up in Glens Falls, New York, an Adirondack boomtown, with a bunch of stolen horses and married Carrie Potter, a homely twenty-one-year-old gal from a good family. Her family hated him and always would. It was not a good marriage. He left her often for the road, the call of the shows, and God knows what else. Three of their children died of diphtheria on the same day. Their graves went unmarked for more than a century.

Saved from drink by the Salvation Army when he was in his fifties, Broncho Charlie became a professional reformer (or at least he enjoyed a period of professional reform). He called himself the Converted Cowboy and in yet another incarnation toured on behalf of the Salvation Army, riding a horse onstage at Carnegie Hall during a revival. He was riding and roping for Jesus at this point, but he was still telling the New York reporters who turned out regularly to interview him that he drank his whiskey neat every day of his long life.

He smoked heavily until the day he died. His motto: "Live Right, Be Friendly."

He claimed to have the scars of two Indian arrows on his body. He'd show those to you if you asked to see them.

He claimed that he had known Chief Joseph, Sitting Bull, Jesse James, Buffalo Bill, Wild Bill Hickok, Bat Masterson, and Teddy Roosevelt. He also claimed that he had known Russell and Majors and Waddell. He said he was with Majors when they drove the golden spike in Utah. He said he had known Zebulon Pike and Joseph Robidoux. And Jim Bridger. And Joseph Slade. And the Englishman Burton. And he had once on a long-ago morning in Placerville, California, met a traveling newspaperman out of Virginia City come over the mountains into Californy. They called the place Hangtown then. The traveler was Mark Twain. He had also shaken Abraham Lincoln's hand at the St. Joe railroad station. He variously claimed to have been a friend of Wyatt Earp, Luke Short, Doc Holliday, Mysterious Dave, "and all the other boys." But that was all a very, very long time ago. He claimed he was the oldest member of the American Legion, too. He never shied away from staking a claim, and when he staked one, it was a big claim. He could jump a claim, too.

On his one hundredth birthday, he told the *New York Herald Tribune* that he had been a Texas Ranger, introducing the Lone Star State into his saga for the first time. He also told the *Herald Tribune* that he had known Sam Houston and Davy Crockett. He was thirteen the year Sam Houston died. Crockett was killed at the siege of the Alamo on March 6, 1836, roughly fourteen years before Broncho Charlie's birth on the aforementioned buffalo robe.

When he was eighty-two, he rode an old horse named Polestar from New York City to San Francisco to bring the mail across the country and celebrate the Pony Express. He carried a message from New York mayor Jimmy Walker to San Francisco mayor Angelo Rossi. It was the sort of man-bites-dog stunt that the American press never tires of, and Broncho Charlie got a lot of ink. Americans stood in the streets and cheered to see this funny old man sprung right out of the nineteenth century loping along on an old horse. Polestar had to be reshod a dozen times. Oddly, Broncho Charlie did not follow the route of the Pony Express—the Central Route—but took a version of the Southern Route, the Oxbow, a much longer trip.

The *San Francisco Chronicle* of May 14, 1932—the same edition that reported in banner headlines the finding of the Lindbergh baby's body—noted Broncho Charlie's arrival in town. "San Franciscans were startled yesterday at the sight of an 82-year-old man jogging up Van Ness avenue on a pinto pony. Surveying the passing automobiles and street cars with distaste, he drew up in front of City Hall, and set out in search of Mayor Rossi. The stranger was Broncho Charlie Miller, last of the Pony Express riders, who was completing the last lap of his 4,200-mile jaunt across the continent on horseback. Broncho Charlie has spent eight months traversing the country, and in his knapsack he carried a letter from Mayor Walker of New York to Mayor Rossi of San Francisco."

The *Chronicle* reported that he was heading back to New York after visiting Greene Majors, a police judge in Piedmont and former mayor of Alameda. Majors, whose father founded the Pony Express, hailed Broncho Charlie as the last of the riders. That was all the old cowboy needed. Greene Majors's imprimatur clinched the deal for him and drove skeptics wild.

Broncho Charlie Miller was old and tired and broke when he hit San Francisco. He sold Polestar for seventy-five dollars and came home on the train, too old for horses.

He was always available for publicity stunts, though. On April 3, 1935—the seventy-fifth anniversary of the start of the Pony Express—the *New York Times* (which good-naturedly accepted his claim to be the last surviving Pony Express rider) reported that Broncho Charlie rode from the rear of a United Airlines hangar in Newark, New Jersey, to a nearby airplane and handed two parcels to the pilot for delivery in Chicago. The following year he was asked to lead the parade in Brooklyn, New York, marking the Long Island tercentenary celebration

His wife, who was twenty years younger, died in 1936, and he moved to Tompkins Square House in New York City, a residential facility for old people. The *New York Post* found him there in May of 1944, and he was still in rare form, convincing the reporter that he had in his possession a scalp taken off a Mrs. Slocum by an Indian. He told the reporter not to worry, he'd killed the Indian.

Broncho Charlie Miller was still a handsome man when the *New York Herald Tribune* interviewed him a week before his hundredth birthday, describing him as "a striking figure with iron-gray hair down to his shoulders." He was a showman's showman. When there were no Wild West shows, he worked the trade shows. Shortly after his cross-country ride on Polestar, he appeared at the International Vacation Exposition at Grand Central Palace in New York on behalf of a Flagstaff, Arizona, promoter. Broncho Charlie brought along his scalp collection to delight the curious and teamed up with an old Indian who told reporters that he was Sitting Bull's nephew. Like Buffalo Bill, Broncho Charlie always knew where to find an Indian who was related to Sitting Bull.

The Associated Press, which closely chronicled his last years, believed that he last sat on the back of a horse on Labor Day 1949, four months before his hundredth birthday. But he was making public appearances and giving interviews right up until the week he died of pneumonia. On his 101st birthday, the AP tracked him down again in New York City (he told the wire service some real whoppers over the years). "I can still ride a horse, you know. And I can still use a bull whip. Can snap a cigarette in half from 28 feet out."

The AP reported that Miller spent his days whittling and playing "Old Black Joe" and "Nearer My God to Thee" on his musical saw. He played a few tunes for his visitor. One of his favorites was "Goodbye, Old Paint," which is sometimes sung as "Leaving Cheyenne." He'd been there, too, and left.

He enjoyed a robust afterlife. In December 1972, *Golden West* magazine, which specialized in "The West As It Really Was," rediscovered him. Its account had all the makings of a real Broncho Charlie tale. It begins by claiming that an old U.S. Cavalry scout found him in 1859, the lone survivor of a Shoshone Indian massacre, and brought the boy, then about nine, to Fort Bidwell in California, where crusty old Mike Cunyan was Pony Express station master. Crusty old Mike sounds a bit like Long John Silver in some versions of the story. He had a peg leg, too. This was the sort of yarn that enraged Pony Express purists. The Pony Express had not begun in 1859. It never stopped at Fort Bidwell, either. *Golden West* even had the date of Broncho's death wrong. But it was a good story. Broncho Charlie would have approved.

The *Pony Express,* a long-defunct magazine of Old West lore, branded the old man an imposter and fumed against his antics. "Broadway Hoodwinks Sacramento" was one headline. Easterners were too damn gullible. In 1950 the magazine theorized that Miller had taken on the persona of a real Pony Express rider with the same name:

> In the early days of 1860–61 there was a "Bronco Charlie" Miller who rode the Pony Express. He died many years ago, as did all the old time riders of that period including Buffalo Bill, youngest of the group, who passed away in 1917. Many have doubted the present "Charlie," who gets many glowing write-ups in newspapers after combing his long flowing locks in true western style. One of these major doubters is Dr. Ray H. Fisher of Oakland, Calif., son of Utah's Billy Fisher, who was one of the real riders and not a modern faker in long hair. Dr. Fisher's hair is not long, but it's still long enough so that "Bronco Charlie" gets into it. And one can hardly blame him for it. When impostors run around claiming to be 100 years old and riders of the Pony Express it's high time to say something about it, as Dr. Fisher has on sundry occasions. This is the first time "Bronco Charlie" has given his real name which is not Charlie, but Julius Mortimer Miller, which helps somewhat to disprove his claim to being the original "Bronco Charlie" Miller. Another and more important item which disproves it is the fact that he claims to be 100 years old. Let's allow that he is 100. If so, he would have been only 10 years old in 1860, and 11 years old in 1861 when the Pony Express operated. And this youthful age is absolutely ridiculous, as they didn't hire young kids to carry mail, firearms and fight the Indians. Evidently Julius Mortimer doesn't know when the mail route ran, or else he is not far along in arithmetical calculations to figure out a story that would carry water. If he were about 108 years old then he could have been a rider, providing he could still prove it. So enough about "Bronco Charlie" Miller and the gullible New York papers that fall for such fantastic tales.

Dr. Ray H. Fisher spent years debunking Broncho Charlie. He wrote in the magazine later:

> Now as for "Bronco" Charlie Miller. He was a colossal faker. I met him when I spoke before the American Legion here [in Oakland] in 1933. [This may have been at the time of Broncho Charlie's cross-country ride.] I found he was born in 1850. I said to him:

"You are an old man, Mr. Miller, and I would not like to offend you, but I have promised in all my lectures (I gave about 20 from 1932 to 1936) I would stick absolutely to the facts of history.

"You could not be more than 12 yrs. old in Oct. 1861. I know that government dispatches, money transfers, business of the big firms, state business of California, etc. were not interested in any 12 year old boy."

To buttress his case, Fisher included a copy of a *San Francisco News* article from May 19, 1932, which reported on Broncho Charlie's arrival in San Francisco at the end of his ride aboard Polestar. The newspaper article was full of Broncho Charlie's usual tales—his friendships with Wyatt Earp, Doc Holliday, Bat Masterson, etc.— proof positive, as far as Fisher was concerned, that the old man was a phony.

Though Broncho Charlie had his supporters in the West, Greene Majors and the *Sacramento Union* among them, others cast doubts, too.

In June 1949, Clarence Breuner, one of Sacramento's leading merchants, challenged the Broncho Charlie story, questioning Miller's age and the facts of his tale. "It's all right to fool the people of Broadway. They like to be fooled, and 'Broncho Charlie' has made a good job of it. But when Broadway tries to penetrate the western domain with 'smoke up' stuff that belongs in Hollywood and not Sacramento, the western land end of the Pony Express, it's high time some one took issue, or let out a boisterous guffaw. A big laugh is all it amounts to."

Breuner recalled Broncho Charlie Miller's visits to Sacramento in which he had met him. "In 1939 and 1940 I met this so-called 'Broncho Charlie Miller.' Old Jack Powers, caretaker of the Pony Express Station at Sacramento, said he was an imposter and looked to be about 65 years old. Jack had his number and wanted me to meet him, and arranged the time. All I can say it was a waste of time. His stories were of no value to the Pony Express, but he went East and did well. Even gullible women have listened to his fantastic tales that don't tally with dates, and places, and have written books about him. Nuf Sed. Nuf said."

The New York papers reported the story of Broncho Charlie Miller with considerable gusto for years, and no challenge of his tales was ever seriously considered. And Broncho Charlie never rebutted any critic. He did not even acknowledge that he had critics. He just kept talking.

His autobiography, *Broncho Charlie: A Saga of the Saddle,* as told to Gladys Shaw Erskine, complicates his tale. Written in a kind of "howdy, pardner" dialect, the book sounds dictated. By the time Miss Erskine discovered him, he was a seasoned celebrity who needed little coaching. The book was published in the United States and England in the mid-1930s. Most of the information about the Pony Express contained in it is accurate.

His account of how he was hired by the Pony Express at the age of eleven never changed. According to Broncho Charlie, he was working as an eleven-year-old ranch hand in central California when he first heard about the Pony Express. "And the thing that fired my mind was that all the riders seemed to be young boys, not much older than me—anywheres from twelve to eighteen."

Broncho Charlie vividly recalled the news spreading across the West about the Pony Express (recollections that are not inconsistent with accounts reported by any of the California newspapers at the time). "Then one night an old-timer drifted into the ranch, a friend of Mr. Thompson's, he was, and knew all about the Pony Express. He'd been in St. Jo. when it all started, and I sat late into the night and just drank in his words. I little thought then that I would soon be one of the youngest riders for that same famous Pony Express!"

His recollection of mail delivery in the California of the mid-nineteenth century is also accurate.

"You see, there wasn't no definite mail route then, and a letter had to go through a lot of adventures before it arrived at its destination . . . If it ever did! For instance, from St. Jo., if a letter was sent to some one on the Pacific coast, it would have to go by coach to a port, then by ship to Panama, then across the isthmus by a jerkwater railroad to the other side, and then by ship again to San Diego or San Francisco. And it took anywheres from thirty-six to one hundred and ten days, 'cause sometimes they had to go around by Cape Horn. Sometimes a letter would start out to try and get through overland. Then it had to wait in some little wayside place, making, maybe, jumps of two-three hundred miles at a time, to catch a wagon-train goin' in the direction its address showed it was headed for. Why, sometimes the sender of a letter would arrive and tell the folks the news before the letter they had sent months before was more than half-way through its journey!"

According to his saga of the saddle, tales of Pony Express adventures prompted him to quit wrangling and head up to Sacramento, where he was reunited with his family. (This is before he began telling the story about how they were massacred by Shoshone Indians.) Sacramento was a wide-open town full of saloons, dance halls, and plenty of shootin' and noise, Miller remembered.

One day, walking along E Street with his father, Miller saw a riderless Pony Express horse gallop past. Miller and his father raced to the Pony Express station to find that the rider had apparently been shot. There was no relief rider.

" 'Can't anyone else ride?' asked my father.

" 'Hell, yes!' said the wrangler. 'But he's got to be a real rider, and he got to know the trail from here to Placerville. The next rider will take it from there to Carson City.'

"My father's eyes met mine. Not a word was said. He lifted me up and put me astride the fresh horse that stood waitin' for his rider. 'He knows the trail,' he said to the watching men. And to me, 'Ride like hell, son!'

"And I was away, carrying the pouch of the Pony Express."

Broncho Charlie Miller had a boy's adventure on the trail for the Pony Express. ("That night was just about the longest I'd ever spent, and it seemed some way as though every sound was louder than it ought to be.")

His account includes a fairly detailed and accurate description of the mochila, and he also claimed how a day or two later he was sworn in as a regular Pony Express rider, repeating the famous oath. He was also given a Bible and a six-shooter. "I was told to use the Bible all the time and the gun only in case of necessity—to defend your body and the mail or your horse."

By most reckonings, Broncho Charlie did not come to anyone's attention until the mid-1880s when he joined Buffalo Bill's Wild West. The archives at the Buffalo Bill Historical Center in Cody, Wyoming, accept him as a rider with the Wild West. Records do not indicate a long stay with Buffalo Bill, probably three seasons. (He spent some time in Cody in the 1930s at the historical center, carving a totem pole that was later devoured by termites.)

After he married in late 1889, following his arrival in the Adirondacks, he more or less settled down for a number of years. He ran a riding school for a while.

It requires little effort to find holes in Broncho Charlie's story. On May 11, 1944, he moved his date of birth to 1849 when the *New York Post* ran a full-page Sunday feature on him titled "Those Were the Days When Men Were Men."

"He can see, hear and remember better than a lot of people half a century his junior. He eats what he likes in the T.S. House cafeteria, smokes cigars and drinks a moderate amount of whiskey—'but I don't put water behind it because it don't taste right that way.' "

The *Post* interview was vintage Broncho Charlie. "See that gun? That's killed white men and Indians." Miller then proceeded to tell the story of how he had made "a bad hombre named Reilly . . . bite the dust."

Reilly, so Miller's story went, was the drunken foreman of an "Idyho" cattle ranch who got too drunk "to take 20,000 head of cattle on a little 800-mile trek to another valley." Broncho Charlie was the man for the job in this cow-punching emergency. Charlie was never prosecuted for shooting Reilly; it was self-defense and the man needed killing. The *New York Post* loved this stuff.

In his nineties, Miller often increased the length of his imagined ride for Russell, Majors & Waddell. He told the *Post* he rode from Sacramento to Carson City with eighteen changes of horses, then slept twenty-four hours and rode back. "Two highlights from his Pony Express days were being wounded in his side, head and wrist by Indian arrows shot from a bluff above him and meeting Mark Twain."

In this version of his life story, pretty much straight out of the autobiography that Gladys Shaw Erskine had produced, Miller recalled meeting Buffalo Bill in Denver in 1885. "I was in Denver on a horse I'd never rode before and I wanted to see how he'd act to the rope. So I roped a Chinaman who was carrying a basketful of women's clothes down the street. I dragged the basket quite a ways, and the white clothes was balloonin' out—oh, it was funny! Then the sheriff come along and run me out of town. He chased me right past the Silver Dollar saloon. Buffalo Bill was on the steps and they told me afterwards that he said 'Who's that wild devil? I want him for my show.' " So Broncho Charlie, who had never been east of the Mississippi, rode Dynamite, a killer horse, for two seasons at Madison

Square Garden and then sailed for England, where the Wild West show helped to celebrate Queen Victoria's golden jubilee.

One of Miller's fondest memories, one that can be documented, is his six-day race inside a London circus ring against a cyclist. Miller rode a string of horses and chalked up 407 miles to his competitor's 422. The *London Illustrated News* reported this event replete with a drawing of the racers, Broncho Charlie in the saddle.

In 1987, Walter Miller, Broncho Charlie's great-nephew, taped a long family history, attempting to sort out some of his uncle's tales. According to Miller, Broncho Charlie and his brother were juvenile delinquents in mid-nineteenth-century New York City who were shipped off on a school ship, a kind of floating reform school. Two years later the boys jumped ship in California. Broncho Charlie escaped, but his brother was caught. His great-nephew believed that Broncho Charlie was about twelve when this happened. His nephew believed that Broncho Charlie had in fact ridden for the Pony Express.

Family lore also had Broncho Charlie working as a professional buffalo hunter feeding railroad workers and scouting for the army. He was also associated with the James gang. Another time, according to the younger Miller, his wandering great-uncle showed up with an Indian who helped him train horses. Miller estimated the old man was in his mid-seventies then.

Walter Miller remembered his great-uncle's tales when he was a child, recalling how Broncho Charlie once woke up with a six-foot rattlesnake sleeping on his chest. "The snake grew every time he told the story . . . But anyway it was very impressive."

As his 105th birthday approached, Broncho Charlie gave a last, long interview to the *Post-Star* in Glens Falls. It was a kind of "greatest hits" of his adventures. The old man was still smoking a pack of cigarettes a day.

The newspaper had banished any hint of doubt about the wild old man who'd come to the Adirondacks with a string of stolen horses and an even longer string of stories. In recounting Broncho Charlie's life, the *Post-Star* insisted: "His exploits in his very early youth, to many, may sound fantastic, however, all items mentioned have been thoroughly checked for truth."

He left no will (no one could ever find his birth certificate, and the facts on his marriage license were dubious), and he owned virtually nothing at the time of his death. He had just celebrated his 105th birthday, and his mind was clear and sharp right up until the very end.

Glens Falls buried him with a hero's send-off, complete with riderless horse. The American Legion later held ceremonies at his grave site, but a lot of townsfolk, nervous easterners and tinhorns, thought he was a fraud and a liar.

Pony Express station at Hollenberg, Kansas (near Marysville, home of the girl who remembered Johnny Frey), ca. 1930.

THE GIRL WHO REMEMBERED
JOHNNY FREY

We know this much is true. There once was a girl who remembered Johnny Frey. During all of the years when no one could say with certainty who the first rider of the Pony Express was, there remained in the extensive files of the Kansas State Historical Society in Topeka a ten-page, handwritten document from an eyewitness of the comings and goings of the Pony Express.

In the 1930s, an amateur historian, Florence Miller-Strauss, painstakingly took down the recollections of Mrs. A. J. Travelute, then in her nineties and at that time probably the last American to have seen a Pony Express courier cross the plains.

"Few persons are living now who saw the Pony Express and the Overland Stage in operation. Mrs. Travelute is one of them," Florence Miller-Strauss recorded.

Seventy-six years after the last pony rider galloped through Marysville, Kansas, Mrs. Travelute's recollections were clear and unadorned.

Her maiden name was Elizabeth Mohrbacher, and like most residents of Marshall County, she was the daughter of Bavarian immigrants. She remembered when there were still wolves and wild Indians on the plains of Kansas. She remembered when there were buffalo. She remembered when plagues of grasshoppers swarmed over Marshall County.

"It was dark like midnight when they came. We could not see across the road and they sounded like the ocean roaring."

The Mohrbachers, who had eight sons and four daughters, arrived in Marysville, then part of the territory of Kansas, on May 1, 1860, shortly before Lizzie's fourteenth birthday. They settled in Elm Creek Township, three miles south of Marysville, and built a solid, still-standing, limestone house. Nearly a century and a half after they built the house, the road leading to it remains unpaved.

Mrs. Travelute recalled the Mohrbacher party as consisting of "a small caravan of two prairie schooners, a few teams of horses, half a dozen cows." Most pioneers walked.

"As the caravan moved slowly along nearing Marysville, several of the boys and girls stepped from the prairie schooners to gather the Kansas wild flowers. The flowers were then placed on the harness of the teams. Every one was happy and full of hope," she recalled.

Elizabeth Mohrbacher became the first rural schoolteacher in Marshall County in 1863. She was seventeen that year. At the start of each week, she rode her pony overland, alone, nearly twenty miles, to Barrett. She carried a long barrel pistol in her waistband. There were fifteen pupils, the children of German pioneers. Classes were held from 9:00 A.M. to 4:00 P.M., leaving plenty of time on either end of the day for chores. Elizabeth boarded with a local family during the school week and then rode back to her father's farm at week's end.

She married her father's hired man when she was twenty, and they had six children. She lived to be the institutional memory of Marshall County. At the end of her long life, she was a last link with the pioneer past, living until the spring of 1939.

"Let it be understood there was not a log cabin or a dugout between this city and the Vermillion creek. It was all a vast plain, no laid-out roads, no cattle grazing in green pastures, and the only human beings who might cross your path was a squad of Otoe Indians, who were out on a hunt for a living. A pack of prairie wolves would frequently be seen and their desperate howling would fill the lonesome traveler with fright."

Lizzie Mohrbacher lived in a world out of Willa Cather's novel *My Ántonia,* the setting of which is two hours' drive west. The plains of Kansas were a place of husking bees with pumpkin pies for dessert. Boys wore trousers made from grain sacks that read "Amoskeag Seamless, Patent Applied For." Life was hard and simple and often unforgiving.

When Florence Miller-Strauss sat down to record Mrs. Travelute's memories of a vanished pioneer Kansas, a frontier barely imaginable in the 1930s, the old lady sat back in her rocking chair and slowly recited her favorite poem, "Whistling in Heaven." She had made a quilt that year from scraps of velvet, and a picture of her appeared in the *Marysville Advocate* with her quilt.

Elizabeth Travelute remembered the first flag raising when Kansas was admitted to the Union, January 29, 1861. She remembered the first Fourth of July celebration in Marysville in 1861. She was living in Marysville when Captain Sir Richard Burton rolled through town, and she was living there a year later when Mark Twain came down the line. She remembered seeing wagons with signs on them: "To Pike's Peak or Bust" and "Bound for Kansas, the Lighthouse of the World." And she remembered the Pony Express. "I saw Johnny Frey many times. He was the first rider to ride west out of St. Joseph on the express." She remembered him galloping the mail into or out of town. "He was a nice young man. He wore a tight jacket, leggings and dark trousers. During the summer he wore a straw hat and in the winter a cap," she told Miller-Strauss.

"I can still remember hearing and seeing the riders come galloping down from Schmidt's pasture at the east edge of what was then the town. Just before they came in sight at the top of the hill they blew a horn. It was a shiny tin horn and the rider carried it in the back of his saddle bag. When he blew the horn it was a signal to Jacob Weisbach, my brother-in-law, who was the postmaster, to have the mail ready. He had to be out of the post office with the mail in his hands so he could give it to the riders."

As near as Mrs. Travelute could recall, reaching back across three-quarters of a century—the entire history of Kansas—the riders rode on to the barn, which is still standing, just south of Broadway on Eighth Street, changed horses, and galloped on to Robert Shibley's ferryboat about half a mile north of the bridge over the Big Blue River. The next stop west was Hollenberg Station, which still stands, little changed from the days of the Pony.

"I'll tell you the pioneers were glad to see the Pony Express come through here from St. Joseph, Mo. We had no mail unless we went to St. Joseph after it, or got it once a week by stage coach. Sometimes father walked to St. Joseph and it took three days."

Miller-Strauss could think of no higher compliment for Mrs. Travelute than to note in her report: "This woman was the champion sock knitter of Marshall County at the time of the World War. She knitted 175 pairs of socks in 1917 for the soldiers. Oftentimes she slipped a note in the socks and occasionally a soldier answered with a letter of thanks."

The soldiers in the trenches in France did not know that they were writing to an old lady on the plains who remembered the lone riders of the Pony Express when there were still wolves in Kansas and wild Indians and buffalo roamed the plains.

THE BET

When Raymond and Mary Settle began composing *Saddles & Spurs* in the 1950s, one of their goals was to dispel myths about the Pony Express. One story that riled the Settles was that of a huge wager made by backers of the Pony Express—William H. Russell, in particular—that mail could be moved across the continent in ten days or less. It was an exciting story and a popular one. (In 1960, on the occasion of the centennial, even the *New York Times* repeated it.) But the Settles thought it apocryphal.

"There is an oft-told story that William H. Russell bet a large sum of money, the amount varying from $10,000 to $200,000 according to the ideas of the teller, that he could put the mail through from St. Joseph to Sacramento in ten days or less," the Settles noted. "Perhaps bets were made by others, but Russell certainly never made one, for the simple reason that he was too near bankruptcy to risk the money in that fashion. And more, had he done so, Majors and Waddell, being the kind of men they were, would have been mortally offended by such an act. To make it more certain that such a bet was never made, there is not the slightest evidence anywhere that Russell possessed 'sporting' tendencies even in the smallest degree."

It takes a special innocence to describe William Hepburn Russell as a sober fellow, opposed to risk, who would never consider a sporting proposition. A contemporary of the Settles', Ray Allen Billington, a prominent historian of the American West at Northwestern University, had a different view of William H. Russell. Writing at the same time, Billington noted: "Profits from freighting encouraged the exuberant William H. Russell, the irrepressible plunger of the combination, to involve his partners in two fantastic ventures that vastly benefitted the West but led inevitably to the company's downfall." An exuberant and irrepressible plunger sounds like a sporting man, a man who might make a little wager.

Billington's assessment of the end of the Pony Express also considers an aspect of Russell's character that many of his admirers and other historians of the venture avoid or neglect. It spoils the story. Russell was dishonest.

"Driven to desperation, Russell stooped to appropriating government securities with the co-operation of a good-hearted clerk in the Interior Department who was not above embezzlement to help a friend. This venture into low finance soon came to light; Russell vanished into a federal lockup and the firm of Russell, Majors and Waddell slid into bankruptcy."

Twenty years after the Pony Express folded, the *History of Buchanan County Missouri 1881* included "an interesting twist in the story of the Pony Express." Quoting a contemporary newspaper account in the *St. Joseph Morning Herald,* the editors claimed that Russell bet $200,000 that he could establish a fast-mail line between St. Joe and San Francisco in ten days. (It gets the starting date of the Pony Express wrong, but it's an exciting yarn.) The newspaper picks up the final miles of the ride as the eastbound horse comes pounding toward St. Joe. Johnny Frey (the newspaper preferred "Fry") was in the saddle.

"He had sixty miles to ride with six horses to do it. When the last courier arrived at the sixty-mile post, out from St. Joseph, he was one hour behind time. A heavy rain had set in and the roads were slippery. Two hundred thousand dollars might turn upon a single minute. Fry had just three hours and thirty minutes in which to win. This was the finish of the longest race and stake ever run in America. When the time for his arrival was nearly up, at least 5,000 people stood upon the river bank, with eyes turned toward the woods from which the horse and its rider should emerge into the open country in the rear of Elwood—one mile from the finish. Tick, tick, went thousands of watches! The time was nearly up! But nearly seven minutes remained! Hark? A shout goes up from the assembled multitude! He comes! He comes! The noble little mare 'Sylph,' the daughter of little 'Arthur,' darts like an arrow from the bow and makes the run of the last mile in one minute and fifty seconds, landing upon the ferry boat with five minutes and a fraction to spare."

Raymond Settle solidly pronounced the whole thing preposterous even though William H. Russell's launching of the Pony Express seems like a bit of a gamble. Settle was a deeply religious man, an ordained Baptist minister, who left his papers to a tiny Baptist school in rural Missouri, William Jewell College, his alma mater. The idea of wagering offended him. He even clung doggedly to Alexander Majors's oath story—the notion that all of the employees were devout Bible-study enthusiasts whose off-hours were spent with the Scriptures.

Should we trust the compilers of the *History of Buchanan County Missouri 1881* who apparently believed the bet story? Or should we look to a letter written to the amateur historian and correspondent with the last riders of the Pony Express, Mabel Loving, on Valentine's Day in 1916; written by an old man on a ranch in Almo, Idaho. He was Thomas Owen King and he had ridden for Russell, Majors & Waddell. He remembered the bet.

"About 1884–5–6 or 7 there was a splendid article in the San Francisco Bulletin on the first Express going through and a bet of $50,000.00 made that it would and would not arrive on time. I had it but an Editor lost it for me. I have written to the Bulletin and told them I would take the paper again and pay them besides if they would look it up and rewrite or publish it again. If I get it I will send it to you, and I am sure you would prize it highly to incert in your Book . . . With kind regards I am yours truly Thos. O King."

ORPHANS PREFERRED

Writing with her customary certainty and lack of source references, Mabel Loving reports in her little book that as the firm was being organized, Bolivar Roberts, superintendent of the Central Overland California & Pike's Peak Express Company, began placing the following notice in western newspapers:

WANTED

Young, skinny, wiry fellows, not over eighteen.

Must be expert riders, willing to risk death daily.

Orphans preferred. Wages—$25 per week.

Apply—Central Overland Pony Express
Alta Building Montgomery Street

———

Would that we knew where Mrs. Loving found that little bit of information. After the Russell bet story, no claim about the Pony Express is more disputed than this ad and its mysterious origins. Its veracity remains unproved, although publications ranging from *National Geographic* to the *Christian Science Monitor* to the *New York Times* have reproduced it. It is part, too, of the official account of the Pony Express published by the U.S. Postal Service. Early histories of the Pony Express do not mention it. But it has become one of the most thrilling and romantic images associated with the legacy of the Pony Express, and there is hardly a gift shop peddling Pony Express memorabilia from St. Joe to Old Sac that does not sell a quaint reproduction of this notice suitable for framing.

Mabel Loving believed in the authenticity of the "Orphans preferred" notice, but other writers about the Pony Express were skeptical or ignored it entirely. The size and age of the typical rider has been one of the most debated bits of Pony Express arcana. Mark Twain described him as "usually a little bit of a man, brimful of spirit and endurance." Richard Burton described the riders as boys. Burton and Twain saw them. The size of the riders was important because, like jockeys, their weight mattered to the overall performance of the service. Mabel Loving cites this factor in ruling out Billy Richardson as the first rider out of St. Joe, recalling that he was "a big, overgrown, good natured fellow."

"William H. Russell and Alexander Majors were both present when the start was made and they would not have permitted 'a big, overgrown' rider to start right under their noses."

So where do these orphans come from?

Mary Pack, writing in the August 1923 edition of the *Union Pacific Magazine,* in a cover story titled "The Romance of the Pony Express," makes no mention of any orphans. "Bolivar Roberts, local superintendent of the Western Division, hired upwards of 60 coolheaded, nervy men, hardened by years of experience in the open." No orphans there. One of those men was Robert "Pony Bob" Haslam. He was twenty years old, which in 1860 was well into manhood.

W. F. Bailey, one of the earliest writers about the Pony Express, writing in *Century* magazine in October 1898, does not mention any orphans or the advertising campaign to recruit daredevils. Bailey says the company consisted of "sixty agile young riders."

Bailey noted that these were the best men available in the West. "The riders were looked up to, and regarded as being 'at the top of the heap.' No matter what time of the day or of the night they were called upon, whether winter or summer, over mountains or across plains, raining or snowing, with rivers to swim or pleasant prairies to cross, through forests or over the burning desert, they must be ready to respond, and, though in the face of hostiles, ride their beat and make their time. To be last was their only fear, and to get in ahead of schedule their pride . . . 'Make your schedule,' was the standing rule."

Bailey's account is one of the earliest known attempts to write down some historical version of the Pony Express. Alas, he gets the starting time from St. Joe wrong as well as the name of the first rider. Bailey names Henry Wallace.

Five years before W. F. Bailey, Alexander Majors recalled in *Seventy Years on the Frontier*:

> Light-weights were deemed the most eligible for the purpose; the lighter the man the better for the horse, as some portions of the route had to be traversed at a speed of twenty miles an hour . . . The Pony Express, therefore, was not only an important, but a daring and romantic enterprise. At each station a sufficient number of horses were kept, and at every third station the thin, wiry, and hardy pony riders held themselves in readiness to press forward with the mails . . . The men were faithful, daring fellows . . .
>
> Not only were they remarkable for their lightness of weight and energy, but their service required continual vigilance, bravery and agility. Among their number were skillful guides, scouts and couriers, accustomed to adventures and hardships on the plains—men of strong wills and wonderful powers of endurance.

Fourteen years later Colonel William Lightfoot Visscher echoed Majors's description of the riders, adding: "They possessed strong wills and a determination that nothing in the ordinary could balk."

In 1913, Glenn D. Bradley offered this description: "The riders were young men, seldom exceeding one hundred and twenty-five pounds in weight. Youthfulness, nerve, a wide experience on the frontier and general adaptability were the chief requisites for the Pony Express business. Some of the great frontiersmen of the latter 'sixties and the 'seventies were trained in this service, either as pony riders or station men."

Then in 1945, the Burlington Lines railroad company published a small souvenir booklet, "Westward the Course of Empire," subtitled "The Story of the Pony Express, Forerunner of the Burlington Zephyrs." This booklet mentions a preference for orphans. It reproduces the fabled newspaper notice. An expensively produced monograph of only fifty-seven pages, the booklet was illustrated with elaborate linecut drawings. It was written by Gene Morgan, about whom nothing is known. Where he got the orphans information is a mystery. The publisher in Chicago—Lakeside Press, a division of the printing giant J. R. R. Donnelley—has no record of the book. It may possibly date from what is the oldest known and perhaps the first mention of a preference for orphans by the organizers of the Pony Express. That mention appears in the October 1923 issue of *Sunset* magazine, a popular western periodical founded in 1898 by the Southern Pacific Railroad, which variously published works by Mark Twain, Jack London, Bret Harte, Zane Grey, Dashiell Hammett, and Sinclair Lewis. In an article written by John L. Considine titled "Eleven Days to Saint Joe!" Considine attributes (as did Mabel Loving) the origin of the Pony Express ad to Bolivar Roberts.

According to Considine's account of the recruiting effort, Roberts at first placed the ads in San Francisco newspapers. Shortly after this (apparently still needing riders), Roberts went to Carson City. "Perhaps it was not easy to find desperate young orphan riders in a seaport," noted Considine. In Carson City, "within four days, he recruited sixty of the most daring riders in the world." We can be reasonably certain that they were young, skinny, wiry fellows. We can be reasonably certain that they were daring, expert riders, willing to risk death daily. But they were probably not orphans. *We know that much to be true.*

Bibliography

Adams, Samuel Hopkins. *The Pony Express*. New York: Random House, 1950.

Ault, Phil. *Wires West: The Story of the Talking Wires*. New York: Dodd, Mead, 1974.

Ayer, Edward E. Edward E. Ayer Collection. Newberry Library, Chicago.

Badger, Reid. *The Great American Fair: The World's Columbian Exposition & American Culture*. Chicago: Nelson Hall, 1979.

Bailey, W. F. "The Pony Express." *Century* 56, no. 6 (October 1898).

Baird, Mabel. " 'Pony Bob' and His Comrades of the Pony Express 1860–1861." *Overland Monthly* 66 (July–December 1914).

Banning, Captain William, and George Hugh. *Six Horses*. New York: Century Company, 1928.

Bennett, James. *Frederick Jackson Turner*. Boston: Twayne Publishers (G. H. Hall), 1975.

Benson, Joe. *The Traveler's Guide to the Pony Express Trail*. Helena, Mont.: Falcon Press Publishing, 1995.

Berthold, Victor M. "William H. Russell: Originator and Developer of the Famous Pony Express." *Philatelist Quarterly*, 1929.

Biggs, Donald C. *The Pony Express: Creation of a Legend*. San Francisco, privately printed, 1956.

Billington, Ray Allen. *Frederick Jackson Turner: Historian, Scholar, Teacher*. New York: Oxford University Press, 1973.

Billington, Ray Allen, in collaboration with James Blaine Hedges. *Westward Expansion: A History of the American Frontier*. New York: Macmillan, 1960.

Bloss, Roy S. *Pony Express—The Great Gamble*. Berkeley, Calif.: Howell-North, 1959.

Bogue, Allan G. *Frederick Jackson Turner: Strange Roads Going Down*. Norman: University of Oklahoma Press, 1998.

Bradley, Glenn D. *The Story of the Pony Express: An Account of the Most Remarkable Mail Service Ever in Existence, and Its Place in History*. Chicago: A. C. McClurg, 1913 (reprinted Gale Research Company, Detroit, 1946).

Brodie, Fawn M. *The Devil Drives: A Life of Sir Richard Burton*. New York: W. W. Norton, 1967.

Bromley, George Tisdale. *The Long Ago and the Later On; or, Recollections of Eighty Years.* San Francisco: A. M. Robertson, 1904.

Brown, Charles. "Diary." *Western Union Telegraph Company Records, 1820–1995.* Washington, D.C.: Archives Center, National Museum of American History, Smithsonian Institution.

Burg, David F. *Chicago's White City of 1893.* Lexington: University Press of Kentucky, 1976.

Burke, John. *Buffalo Bill: The Noblest Whiteskin.* New York: G. P. Putnam's Sons, 1973.

Burton, Richard Francis. Edited and with an introduction and notes by Fawn M. Brodie. *The City of the Saints and Across the Rocky Mountains to California.* New York: Alfred A. Knopf, 1963.

Burton, Sir Richard. *The Look of the West, 1860: Across the Plains to California.* Lincoln, London: University of Nebraska Press, 1963.

Carter, Kate B. *Riders of the Pony Express.* Salt Lake City: Daughters of the Utah Pioneers, 1947.

Carter, Robert A. *Buffalo Bill Cody: The Man Behind the Legend.* New York: John Wiley & Sons, 2000.

Chapman, Arthur C. *The Pony Express: The Record of a Romantic Adventure in Business.* New York/Chicago: A. L. Burt Company, 1932.

Clark, C. M., *A Trip to Pike's Peak and Notes by the Way.* San Jose, Calif.: Talisman Press, 1958.

Cody, Colonel W. F. *Buffalo Bill's Life Story: An Autobiography of Buffalo Bill.* Illustrated by N. C. Wyeth. New York: Rinehart & Company, 1920.

Cody, William F. *The Life of Hon. William F. Cody, Known as Buffalo Bill.* New York: Indian Head Books, 1991.

Coleman, Dabney Otis. *Great Western Rides.* Denver, Colo.: Sage Books, 1961.

Considine, John L. "Eleven Days to Saint Jo!—The Story of the Pony Express." *Sunset,* October 1923.

Covered Wagon Women: Diaries and Letters from the Western Trails, 1854–1860. Edited and compiled by Kenneth L. Holmes. Lincoln, London: University of Nebraska Press, 1987.

Davies, Henry M. *Ten Days on the Plains.* Dallas: Southern Methodist University Press, 1985.

Davis, Sam P., ed. *History of Nevada.* Nevada Publications, 1913.

Dawson, Charles. *Pioneer Tales of the Oregon Trail and of Jefferson County.* Topeka, Kans.: Crane & Co., 1912.

Delano, Alonzo, *Old Block's Sketch Book.* Santa Ana, Calif.: Fine Arts Press, 1947.

De Quille, Dan. *The Big Bonanza: An Authentic Account of the Discovery, History, and Working of the World-Renowned Comstock Lode of Nevada.* New York: Alfred A. Knopf, 1947.

DeVoto, Bernard. *Mark Twain's America.* Lincoln, London: University of Nebraska Press, 1997.

Driggs, Howard R. *The Pony Express Goes Through: An American Saga Told by Its Heroes.* New York: Frederick A. Stokes Company, 1935.

Egan, Ferol. *Sand in a Whirlwind: The Paiute Indian War of 1860.* New York: Doubleday, 1972.

Ellenbecker, John G. *The Pony Express.* Marysville, Kans.: privately published, 1937.

Elliott, Russell R. *History of Nevada.* Lincoln: University of Nebraska Press, 1973.

Ellis, John M, and Robert E. Stowers, "The Nevada Indian Uprising of 1860 as Seen by Private Charles A. Scott." *Arizona and the West* 3, no. 4 (Winter 1961).

Farwell, Byron. *Burton: A Biography of Sir Richard Francis Burton.* New York: Holt, Rinehart & Winston, 1963.

Findley, Rowe. "The Pony Express: A Buckaroo Stew of Fact and Legend." *National Geographic* 158, no. 1 (July 1980).

Floyd, William H., III. *Phantom Riders of the Pony Express.* Philadelphia: Dorrance & Co., 1958.

Forman, Henry James. *The Pony Express: A Romance.* New York: Grosset & Dunlap, 1925

French, Peter A. *Cowboy Metaphysics: Ethics and Death in Westerns.* Lanham, Md.; Boulder, Colo.; New York: Rowan & Littlefield, 1997.

Geismar, Maxwell. *Mark Twain: An American Prophet.* Boston: Houghton Mifflin, 1970.

Gianella, Vincent P. "Site of Williams Station." *Nevada Historical Society Quarterly* 3, no. 4 (1960).

Gilman, Musetta. *Pump on the Prairie.* Detroit: Harlo Press, 1975.

Greeley, Horace. *An Overland Journey, from New York to San Francisco, in the Summer of 1859.* New York: 1860.

Griffin, Charles Eldridge. *Four Years in Europe with Buffalo Bill.* Albia, Iowa: Stage Publishing Co., 1908.

Hafen, LeRoy R. *The Overland Mail.* Spokane, Wash: Arthur H. Clark Company, 1926 (reprinted in 1976 by Quaterman Publications, Lawrence, Mass.).

Hagen, Olaf T. *The Pony Express Starts from St. Joseph.* Kirksville: *Missouri Historical Review* 54, no. 3 (April 1960).

Hansen, George W. "The Wild Bill–McCanless Tragedy: A Much Misrepresented Event in Nebraska History." *Nebraska History Magazine,* April–June 1927.

Harlow, Alvin F. *Old Post Bags: The Story of the Sending of a Letter in Ancient and Modern Times.* New York, London: D. Appleton & Co., 1928.

Harner, Nellie Shaw. *Indians of Coo-yu-ee Pah (Pyramid Lake): The History of the Pyramid Lake Indians.* Sparks, Nev.: Western Printing & Publishing Co., 1978.

Harvey, Paul W., "Tacoma Headlines: An Account of Tacoma News and Newspapers from 1873 to 1962." *Tacoma News Tribune,* 1962.

Hauck, Louise Platt. "The Pony Express Celebration." *Missouri Historical Review* 17, no. 4 (July 1923).

Hewitt, J. N. B., ed., and Myrtis Jarrell, trans. *Journal of Rudoph Friederich Kurz: An Account of His Experiences Among Fur Traders and American Indians on the Mississippi and the Upper Missouri Rivers During the Years 1846 to 1852.* Lincoln: University of Nebraska Press, 1970.

History of Buchanan County, Missouri. 1881. Cassville, Mo.: Litho Printers & Binders, 1973 (reprint).

Holliday, J. S. *The World Rushed In: The California Gold Rush Experience.* New York: Simon & Schuster, 1981.

Howard, Robert West, et al. *Hoofbeats of Destiny: The Story of the Pony Express.* New York: Signet Books/New American Library, 1960.

Jabusch, David M., and Susan C. *Pathway to Glory: The Pony Express and Stage Stations in Utah.* Salt Lake City: Treasure Press, 1996.

Jensen, Lee. *The Pony Express.* New York: Grosset & Dunlap, 1965.

Johannsen, Albert. *The House of Beadle and Adams and Its Dime and Nickel Novels: The Story of a Vanished Literature.* Norman: University of Oklahoma, 1950.

Kasson, Joy S. *Buffalo Bill's Wild West: Celebrity, Memory, and Popular History.* New York: Hill & Wang, 2000.

Lately, Thomas. *Between Two Empires: The Life Story of California's First Senator, William McKendree Gwin.* Boston: Houghton Mifflin, 1969.

Lauber, John. *The Making of Mark Twain.* New York: American Heritage, 1985.

Lindberg, Richard. *Chicago Ragtime: Another Look at Chicago, 1880–1920.* South Bend, Ind.: Icarus Press, 1985.

Lovell, Mary S. *A Rage to Live.* New York: W. W. Norton, 1998.

Lyman, George D. *The Saga of the Comstock Lode: Boom Days in Virginia City.* New York: Charles Scribner's Sons, 1934.

Mack, Effie Mona. *Mark Twain in Nevada.* New York: Charles Scribner's Sons, 1947.

Majors, Alexander. *Seventy Years on the Frontier: Alexander Majors' Memoirs of a Lifetime on the Border.* Chicago: Rand McNally, 1893.

Mattes, Merrill, and Paul Henderson. "The Pony Express: Across Nebraska from St. Joseph to Fort Laramie." *Nebraska History* 41, no. 2 (June 1960).

M'Collum, M. D. *California as I Saw It.* Edited by Dale L. Morgan. Los Gatos, Calif.: Talisman Press, 1960.

McMurtry, Larry. "Inventing the West." *The New York Review of Books,* August 10, 2000.

Miller, William C. "The Pyramid Lake Indian War of 1860, Parts I and II." *Nevada Historical Society Quarterly,* September and November 1957.

Mitchell, Lee Clark. *Western: Making the Man in Fiction and Film.* Chicago, London: University of Chicago Press, 1996.

Monaghan, Jay. *The Great Rascal: The Life and Adventures of Ned Buntline.* Boston: Little, Brown, 1952.

Moody, Ralph. *Riders of the Pony Express.* Boston: Houghton Mifflin, 1958.

Morgan, Gene. *"Westward the Course of Empire . . .": The Story of the Pony Express, Forerunner of the Burlington Zephyrs.* Chicago: Lakeside Press, 1945.

Mullens, P. A. *Creighton: Biographical Sketches of Edward Creighton, John A. Creighton, Mary Lucretia Creighton, Sarah Emily Creighton.* Omaha, Neb.: Creighton University, 1901.

Mumey, Nolie. *Hoofs to Wings: The Pony Express, Dramatic Story of a Mail Service from East to West Which Existed One Hundred Years Ago.* Boulder, Colo.: Johnson Publishing Co., 1960.

Nathan, M. C., and W. S. Boggs. *The Pony Express.* New York, Collectors Club (Handbook No. 15), 1962.

Nugent, Walter. *Into the West: The Story of Its People.* New York: Alfred A. Knopf, 1999.

O'Connor, Richard. *Wild Bill Hickok.* Garden City and New York: Doubleday, 1959.

O'Dell, Roy Paul, and Kenneth C. Jessen. *An Ear in His Pocket.* Loveland, Colo.: JV Publications, 1996.

The Official Guide to the World's Columbian Exposition, 1492–1892. Compiled by John Flynn. Chicago: Columbian Guide Co., 1893.

Pack, Mary. "The Romance of the Pony Express." *Union Pacific Magazine,* August 1923.

Paine, Albert Bigelow. *Mark Twain: A Biography.* New York: Harper & Brothers, 1912.

———. *The Adventures of Mark Twain.* New York: Grosset & Dunlap, 1915.

Parks, Rita. *The Western Hero in Film and Television: Mass Media Mythology.* Ann Arbor, Mich.: UMI Research Press, 1982.

Pierson, James R. *The Pony Express Trail 1860–1861.* St. Joseph, Mo.: Pony Express Productions, 1960

"The Pony Express Riders." *Outing,* April 1904.

Quinn, Arthur. *The Rivals: William Gwin, David Broderick and the Birth of California.* New York: Library of the American West/Crown, 1994.

Reddin, Paul. *Wild West Shows.* Urbana, Chicago: University of Illinois Press, 1999.

Reinfeld, Fred. *Pony Express.* Reprinted Lincoln, London: University of Nebraska Press, 1973.

Rice, Edward. *Captain Sir Richard Francis Burton: The Secret Agent Who Made the Pilgrimage to Mecca, Discovered the "Kama Sutra," and Brought the "Arabian Nights" to the West.* New York: Charles Scribner's Sons, 1990.

Ridge, Martin. "Reflections on the Pony Express." *Montana,* Autumn 1996.

Root, Frank A., and William E. Connelley. *The Overland Stage to California.* Topeka, Kans., 1901 (reprinted by Long's College Book Company, Columbus, Ohio, 1950).

Rosa, Joseph G. *Wild Bill Hickok: The Man and His Myth.* Lawrence: University Press of Kansas, 1996.

Rosa, Joseph G., and Robin May. *Buffalo Bill and His Wild West: A Pictorial Biography.* Lawrence: University Press of Kansas, 1989.

Sarf, Wayne Michael. *God Bless You, Buffalo Bill: A Layman's Guide to History and the Western Film.* East Brunswick, N.J.: Associated University Presses and Cornwall Books, 1983.

Saum, Lewis O. *The Popular Mood of America, 1860–1890.* Lincoln, London: University of Nebraska Press, 1990.

Seabright, J. M. "The Pony Express Will Ride Again." *Outlook,* August 22, 1923.

Sell, Henry Blackman, and Victor Weybright. *Buffalo Bill and the Wild West.* New York: Oxford University Press, 1955.

Settle, Raymond W. and Mary Lund. *Empire on Wheels,* Stanford, Calif.: Stanford University Press, 1949.

———. *Saddles & Spurs: The Pony Express Saga.* Harrisburg, Pa.: Stackpole Company, 1955 (reprinted University of Nebraska Press, Lincoln, London, 1972).

Skelton, Charles L. *Riding West on the Pony Express.* New York: Macmillan, 1937.

Sorensen, Barbara. *A King and a Prince Among Pioneers: Edward and John A. Creighton.* Omaha, unpublished thesis at Creighton University, 1961.

Sorg, Eric. *Buffalo Bill, Myth & Reality.* Santa Fe, N. Mex.: Ancient City Press, 1998.

Stegner, Wallace. *Marking the Sparrow's Fall: The Making of the American West.* New York: Henry Holt, 1998.

———. *The Sound of Mountain Water: The Changing American West.* New York: Penguin Books, 1997.

———. *Where the Bluebird Sings to the Lemonade Springs: Living and Writing in the West.* New York: Penguin, 1992.

Talmadge, Marian, and Iris Gilmore. *Six Great Horse Rides.* New York: G. P. Putnam's Sons, 1967.

Thompson, Robert Luther. *Wiring a Continent: The History of the Telegraph Industry in the United States, 1832–1866.* New York: Arno Press, 1972.

Tompkins, Jane. *West of Everything: The Inner Life of Westerns.* New York, Oxford: Oxford University Press, 1992.

Townley, John M. *The Pyramid Lake Indian War.* Reno, Nev.: Jamison Station Press (Desert Rat Guidebook Series), 1982.

Tuska, Jon. *The American West in Film: Critical Approaches to the Western.* Westport, Conn., London: Greenwood Press, 1985.

Twain, Mark. *Roughing It.* New York: New American Library, 1962.

Visscher, William Lightfoot. *A Thrilling and Truthful History of the Pony Express with Other Sketches and Incidents of Those Stirring Times.* Chicago, 1908 (reprinted Charles T. Powner Co., Chicago, Ill., 1946).

———. *Ten Wise Men and Some More.* Chicago: Atwell Printing and Binding Co., 1909.

———. *Vissch: A Book of Sketches, Rhymes and Other Matters Credited to Matthew Mattox.* St. Joseph, Mo.: J. B. Johnson Publishers, 1873.

Walker, Franklin. *San Francisco's Literary Frontier.* Seattle, London: University of Washington Press, 1969.

Walsh, Richard J., in collaboration with Milton S. Salsbury. *The Making of Buffalo Bill.* Indianapolis, Ind.: Bobbs-Merrill, 1928.

Welsh, Donald H. "The Pony Express in Retrospect." *Missouri Historical Review* 54, no. 3 (April 1960).

West, Tom. *Heroes on Horseback.* New York: Four Winds Press, 1969.

Wetmore, Helen Cody (with Zane Grey). *Last of the Great Scouts "Buffalo Bill."* New York: Grosset & Dunlap, 1899 (1918).

Williams, George, III. *Mark Twain: His Life in Virginia City, Nevada.* Dayton, Nev.: Tree by the River Publishing Co., 1990.

Wilson, R. L. (with Greg Martin). *Buffalo Bill's Wild West: An American Legend.* New York: Random House, 1998.

Winget, Dan. *Anecdotes of Buffalo Bill: That Have Never Appeared in Print.* Chicago: Historical Publishing Co., 1927.

The WPA Guide to 1930s Nevada (Nevada Writers' Project of the Work Projects Administration). Reno, Las Vegas: University of Nevada Press, 1991.

Yost, Nellie Snyder. *Buffalo Bill: His Family, Friends, Fame, Failures and Fortunes.* Chicago: Sage Books, 1979.

Young, John D. Manuscript. Chicago: Newberry Library, Special Collections. Wren, Thomas, ed. *History of Nevada.* Cherry Hill, N.J.: Lewis Publishing Company, 1904.

Acknowledgments

I found the story of the Pony Express by accident, stumbling upon the remains of Fort Churchill, a lonely reminder of the lost days of Russell, Majors and Waddell in the Nevada desert. I had never heard of Russell, Majors and Waddell. The saga has proved to be a curious one. I am indebted to many people who helped me understand that.

In St. Joseph, Missouri, my work would have been impossible without the help and kindness of Gary Chilcote of the Patee House Museum and Pony Express Historical Association and his family. I also thank McAndrew Burns, formerly with the Pony Express Stables and Museum, and Travis Boley, its current director; Sheridan Logan; the staff of the River Bluffs Regional Library; Jackie Lewin, curator of history at the St. Joseph Museum, and Sarah Elder, photography archivist, and the staff there; the late Roy Coy and his wife, Ada; Marci Bennett of the St. Joseph Convention and Visitors Bureau; and the Northwest Missouri Genealogical Society.

At William Jewell College in Liberty, Missouri, I thank Bonnie Knauss, Special Collections librarian, for help with the Settle Collection, the papers of the Pony Express historians Raymond and Mary Lund Settle.

In Kansas, I thank Vergil Dean, Bob Knecht, and Christie Stanley at the Center for Historical Research, Kansas State Historical Society, in Topeka. I owe special thanks to Geraldine Holle and her daughter, Linda Schmidt, for their tireless research in Marysville on the trail of Lizzie Mohrbacher, the girl who remembered Johnny Frey.

In Nebraska, I am grateful to Wilmer and Doris Ruhnke and Wayne Brandt, superintendent at the Rock Creek Station State Historical Park.

In Colorado, thanks to Philip J. Panum, Special Collections librarian, Western History Collection, Denver Public Library.

In Wyoming, I appreciate the assistance of Nathan E. Bender, Housel Curator, McCracken Research Library, Buffalo Bill Historical Center in Cody, and his staff, as well as the staff at the American Heritage Center at the University of Wyoming in Laramie.

In Utah, I thank Doug Misner, Janell Brimhall Tuttle, and Linda Thatcher and the staff of the Utah State Historical Society at the Utah History Information Center in Salt Lake City; Daughters of Utah Pioneers, J. Willard Marriott Library at the University of Utah; and the Utah State Library.

In Nevada, thanks to Donald Hardesty of the University of Nevada, Reno, for sharing his research about the Pony Express stations at Cold Springs and Sand Springs; and to Mike Bunker of Ely for his observations and for providing me with a copy of the recollections of Private Scott. At the Nevada Historical Society in Reno, I thank former librarian Sue Bradley and current librarian Michael Maher for fielding many questions.

In California, Larry Carpenter, a veteran of many years with the National Pony Express Association, provided me with tremendous assistance and shared his vast knowledge. I could not have completed this project without his help. I also thank the California State Archives and its staff in Sacramento and the staff of the Huntington Library in Pasadena.

I also thank Lewis Saum for his essay on William Lightfoot Visscher's misadventures in the Pacific Northwest; Linda Denton in Kentucky for curious information about the "Colonel's" days in the Union Army; Leland R. Johnson for his assistance with Visscher's days as a journalist, and Joy Werlink, manuscript specialist at the Washington State Historical Society Research Center in Tacoma, for finding the photographs of Visscher.

In Chicago, I am indebted to John Brady of the Newberry Library; the Chicago Public Library; the Chicago Historical Society; Roosevelt University; Karima Robinson; Dr. Paul Edwards of Northwestern University, who helped me find the grave of Pony Bob Haslam; and my old friend Jerry Bloom, who took me to see Rico.

I appreciate the help of Susan Strange, reference specialist, Archives Center, National Museum of American History at the Smithsonian Institution in Washington, D.C.; Creighton University in Omaha; and the staff of the Library of Congress.

Special thanks to the very gracious Lois Miller Ellsworth and her husband, Larry, for sharing family yarns of Lois's great-uncle, Broncho Charlie Miller, and for keeping the memory of that lively old gentleman alive. In Glens Falls, New York, I thank Polly Wiswall, who remembered as a thirteen-year-old girl having Broncho Charlie knock a cigarette out of her mouth with a bullwhip, and for taking me to see his grave; and David Wordell in Connecticut for sharing boyhood recollections of Broncho Charlie.

I owe a special debt to Dale and Bonnie Ryan of Carson City, Nevada, who let me tag along when they followed the National Pony Express Association's annual re-ride in 2000 and 2001, when Dale was NPEA president. We had a lot of laughs and got to see the territory ahead. And thanks to Mash Alexander; the National Pony Express Association; the estate of the late Kate Wolf for permission to quote briefly from her song "Across the Great Divide"; and Bill Staines.

I am indebted to the Albin O. Kuhn Library at the University of Maryland, Baltimore County, and to Michael Romary, whom I was never able to stump. I also thank Tom Beck, chief curator of Special Collections, and Drew Alfgren, reference librarian. I thank Dr. Kenneth Baldwin for allowing me to complete this project and Dr. Jay Freyman of the Department of Ancient Studies for trying to figure out what William Lightfoot Visscher's Latin motto meant. We never reached a conclusion. In Baltimore, I was encouraged by Scott Shane, who looked at an early draft of this tale.

I am indebted to my friend and former editor Patricia Mulcahy, who referred me to Eric Simonoff at Janklow & Nesbit. He found Charlie Conrad at Broadway Books. I am grateful to both of them for their patience and generosity. Special thanks to Alison Presley, also of Broadway Books, and her predecessors, Claire Johnson and Becky Cole.

My greatest debt is to Don Reynolds, long associated with the St. Joseph Museum, and his wife, Maude, who advised on the odd history of the Pony Express, reminding: "It was written about something that never happened by people who weren't there." Don Reynolds also cautioned me "not to kill Santy Claus." Good advice.

I am in the debt of my old friends Paul and Christine Lundberg for their encouragement and to Stephen Desiderio, M.D., for his unerring editorial advice and friendship.

Last, I must thank August E. Bjorklun of Haxtun, Colorado, collector of antique spurs and bridle bits, for wisely telling me one morning near Mud Springs, Nebraska, "We don't lie out here. We just remember big."

Illustration Credits

TITLE PAGE: Courtesy of Archives of the American Illustrators Gallery, NYC; copyright © 2000 National Museum of American Illustration, Newport, RI (www.americanillustration.org)

PROLOGUE: Commerce Bank, St. Joseph, MO

ONE: Patee House Museum, St. Joseph, MO

TWO: Library of Congress, Prints and Photographs Division (LC-USZ62-13121)

THREE: St. Joseph Museum, St. Joseph, MO

FOUR: Library of Congress, Prints and Photographs Division (LC-USZC4-2458)

FIVE: Gilcrease Museum, Tulsa, OK (0127.2333 CT)

SIX: Amon Carter Museum, Fort Worth, TX (1961.232, oil on canvas)

SEVEN: Library of Congress, Prints and Photographs Division (LC-USZ62-127508)

EIGHT: Library of Congress, Prints and Photographs Division (LC-USZ62-112728)

NINE: From collection of the author

TEN: Buffalo Bill Historical Center, Cody, WY (Image 1.69.5644)

ELEVEN: Washington State Historical Society, Tacoma, WA

TWELVE: Henry Huntington Museum, Pasadena, CA

THIRTEEN: St. Joseph Museum, St. Joseph, MO

FOURTEEN: From collection of the author

FIFTEEN: Polly Wiswall

EPILOGUE: Historic American Building Survey, Library of Congress (HABS, KANS, 101-HAN.V,1-)

© JIM BURGER

About the Author

CHRISTOPHER CORBETT has been a working journalist for more than twenty-five years. A former news editor and reporter with the Associated Press, Corbett has also written for the *New York Times, Washington Post, Philadelphia Inquirer,* and *Boston Globe.* The author of the novel *Vacationland,* he lives in Baltimore and teaches journalism at the University of Maryland–Baltimore County.